A Study of As

Insai

Grace Helen Kent and A. J. Rosanoff

Alpha Editions

This edition published in 2024

ISBN : 9789364730549

Design and Setting By
Alpha Editions
www.alphaedis.com
Email - info@alphaedis.com

As per information held with us this book is in Public Domain.
This book is a reproduction of an important historical work. Alpha Editions uses the best technology to reproduce historical work in the same manner it was first published to preserve its original nature. Any marks or number seen are left intentionally to preserve its true form.

Contents

PART I..- 1 -

PART II...- 11 -

THE FREQUENCY TABLES..- 197 -

APPENDIX TO THE FREQUENCY TABLES..................- 299 -

PART I.

ASSOCIATION IN NORMAL SUBJECTS.

Among the most striking and commonly observed manifestations of insanity are certain disorders of the flow of utterance which appear to be dependent upon a derangement of the psychical processes commonly termed association of ideas. These disorders have to some extent been made the subject of psychological experimentation, and the object of this investigation is to continue and extend the study of these phenomena by an application of the experimental method known as the association test.

§ 1. METHOD OF INVESTIGATION.

In this investigation we have followed a modified form of the method developed by Sommer,[1] the essential feature of which is the statistical treatment of results obtained by uniform technique from a large number of cases.

[Footnote 1: Diagnostik der Geisteskrankheiten, p. 112.]

The stimulus consists of a series of one hundred spoken words, to each of which the subject is directed to react by the first word which it makes him think of. In the selection of the stimulus words, sixty-six of which were taken from the list suggested by Sommer, we have taken care to avoid such words as are especially liable to call up personal experiences, and have so arranged the words as to separate any two which bear an obviously close relation to one another. After much preliminary experimentation we adopted the following list of words:

01 Table 02 Dark 03 Music 04 Sickness 05 Man 06 Deep 07 Soft 08 Eating 09 Mountain 10 House 11 Black 12 Mutton 13 Comfort 14 Hand 15 Short 16 Fruit 17 Butterfly 18 Smooth 19 Command 20 Chair 21 Sweet 22 Whistle 23 Woman 24 Cold 25 Slow 26 Wish 27 River 28 White 29 Beautiful 30 Window 31 Rough 32 Citizen 33 Foot 34 Spider 35 Needle 36 Red 37 Sleep 38 Anger 39 Carpet 40 Girl 41 High 42 Working 43 Sour 44 Earth 45 Trouble 46 Soldier 47 Cabbage 48 Hard 49 Eagle 50 Stomach

No attempt is made to secure uniformity of external conditions for the test; the aim has been rather to make it so simple as to render strictly experimental conditions unnecessary. The test may be made in any room that is reasonably free from distracting influences; the subject is seated with his back toward the experimenter, so that he cannot see the record; he is requested to respond to each stimulus word by one word, the first word that occurs to him other than the stimulus word itself, and on no account more than one word. If an untrained subject reacts by a sentence or phrase, a compound word, or a different grammatical form of the stimulus word, the reaction is left unrecorded, and the stimulus word is repeated at the close of the test.

In this investigation no account is taken of the reaction time. The reasons for this will be explained later.

The general plan has been first to apply the test to normal persons, so as to derive empirically a normal standard and to determine, if possible, the nature and limits of normal variation; and then to apply it to cases of various forms of insanity and to compare the results with the normal standard, with a view to determining the nature of pathological variation.

§ 2. THE NORMAL STANDARD.

In order to establish a standard which should fairly represent at least all the common types of association and which should show the extent of such variation as might be due to differences in sex, temperament, education, and environment, we have applied the test to over one thousand normal subjects.

Among these subjects were persons of both sexes and of ages ranging from eight years to over eighty years, persons following different occupations, possessing various degrees of mental capacity and education, and living in widely separated localities. Many were from Ireland, and some of these had but recently arrived in this country; others were from different parts of Europe, but all were able to speak English with at least fair fluency. Over two hundred of the subjects, including a few university professors and other highly practiced observers, were professional men and women or college students. About five hundred were employed in one or another of the New York State hospitals for the insane, either as nurses and attendants or as workers at various trades; the majority of these were persons of common school education, but the group includes also, on the one hand, a considerable number of high school graduates; and on the other hand, a few laborers who were almost or wholly illiterate. Nearly one hundred and fifty of the subjects were boys and girls of high school age, pupils of the Ethical Culture School, New York City. The remaining subjects form a miscellaneous group, consisting largely of clerks and farmers.

§ 3. THE FREQUENCY TABLES.

From the records obtained from these normal subjects, including in all 100,000 reactions, we have compiled a series of tables, one for each stimulus word, showing all the different reactions given by one thousand subjects in response to that stimulus word, and the frequency with which each reaction has occurred. [1] These tables will be found at the end of this paper.

[Footnote 1: A similar method of treating associations has been used by Cattell (Mind, Vol. XII, p. 68; Vol. XIV, p. 230), and more recently by Reinhold (Zeitschr. f. Psychol., Vol. LIV, p. 183), but for other purposes.]

With the exception of a few distinctive proper names, which are indicated by initials, we have followed the plan of introducing each word into the table exactly as it was found in the record. In the arrangement of the words in each table, we have placed together all the derivatives of a single root, regardless of the strict alphabetical order.[1]

[Footnote 1: It should be mentioned that we have discovered a few errors in these tables. Some of these were made in compiling them from the records, and were evidently due to the assistant's difficulty of reading a strange handwriting. Other errors have been found in the records themselves. Each of the stimulus words *butter*, *tobacco* and *king* appears from the tables to have been repeated by a subject as a reaction; such a reaction, had it occurred, would not have been accepted, and it is plain that the experimenter wrote the stimulus word in the space where the reaction word should have been written. Still other errors were due to the experimenter's failure to speak with sufficient distinctness when reading off the stimulus words; thus, the reaction *barks* in response to *dark* indicates that the stimulus word was probably understood as *dog*; and the reactions *blue* and *color* in response to *bread* indicate that the stimulus word was understood as *red*.]

The total number of different words elicited in response to any stimulus word is limited, varying from two hundred and eighty words in response to *anger* to seventy-two words in response to *needle*. Furthermore, for the great majority of subjects the limits are still narrower; to take a striking instance, in response to *dark* eight hundred subjects gave one or another of the following seven words: *light, night, black, color, room, bright, gloomy;* while only two hundred gave reactions other than these words; and only seventy subjects, out of the total number of one thousand, gave reactions which were not given by any other subject.

If any record obtained by this method be examined by referring to the frequency tables, the reactions contained in it will fall into two classes: the *common* reactions, those which are to be found in the tables, and the *individual* reactions, those which are not to be found in the tables. For the sake of accuracy, any reaction word which is not found in the table in its identical form, but which is a grammatical variant of a word found there, may be classed as *doubtful.*

The value of any reaction may be expressed by the figure representing the percentage of subjects who gave it. Thus the reaction, *table—chair*, which was given by two hundred and sixty-seven out of the total of our one thousand subjects, possesses a value of 26.7 per cent. The significance of this value from the clinical standpoint will be discussed later.

§ 4. NORMAL ASSOCIATIONAL TENDENCIES

The normal subjects gave, on the average. 6.8 per cent of individual reactions, 1.5 per cent of doubtful ones, and 91.7 cent of common ones. The range of variation was rather wide, a considerable number of subjects giving no individual reactions at all, while a few gave over 30 per cent.[1]

[Footnote 1: In the study of the reactions furnished by our normal subjects it was possible to analyze the record of any subject only by removing it from the mass of material which forms our tables, and using as the standard of comparison the reactions of the remaining 999 subjects.]

In order to determine the influence of age, sex, and education upon the tendency to give reactions of various values, we have selected three groups of subjects for special study: (1) one hundred persons of collegiate or professional education; (2) one hundred persons of common school education, employed in one of the State hospitals as attendants, but not as trained nurses; and (3) seventy-eight children under sixteen years of age. The reactions given by these subjects have been classified according to frequency of occurrence into seven groups: (a) individual reactions (value 0); (b) doubtful reactions (value ±); (c) reactions given by one other person (value 0.1 per cent); (d) those given by from two to five others (value 0.2—0.5 per cent); (e) those given by from six to fifteen others (value 0.6-1.5 per cent); (f) those given by from sixteen to one hundred others (value 1.6—10.0 per cent); and (g) those given by more than one hundred others (value over 10.0 per cent). The averages obtained from these groups of subjects are shown in Table 1, and the figures for men and women are given separately.

TABLE I

Value of reaction 0 ± 0.1 0.2-0.5 0.6-1.5 1.6-10 >10
　　　　Sex Number % % % % % % %
　　　　　of cases

Persons of M.. 60 9.2 1.8 5.2 9.7 11.0 27.8 85.5
　collegiate F... 40 9.5 1.8 8.0 9.8 11.7 28.0 83.4
　education Both 100 9.3 1.8 4.7 8.7 11.8 28.2 34.4

Persons of M.. 50 5.8 1.6 8.6 8.3 10.2 81.6 88.7
 common school F.. 50 4.6 1.8 8.8 7.1 9.4 82.0 42.1
 education Both 100 5.2 1.4 3.5 7.7 9.8 81.8 40.4
School children M... 33 5.9 0.8 4.2 8.7 10.0 28.6 88.5
 under 16 Jr. F.. 45 5.0 1.0 4.6 9.8 11.0 80.1 36.7
 years of age Both 78 5.7 1.4 4.6 9.8 11.2 29.4 87.4
General average. Both.1000 6.8 1.5

It will be observed that the proportion of individual reactions given by the subjects of collegiate education is slightly above the general average for all subjects, while that of each of the other classes is below the general average. In view, however, of the wide limits of variation, among the thousand subjects, these deviations from the general average are no larger than might quite possibly occur by chance, and the number of cases in each group is so small that the conclusion that education tends to increase the number of individual reactions would hardly be justified.

It will be observed also that this comparative study does not show any considerable differences corresponding to age or sex.

With regard to the type of reaction, it is possible to select groups of records which present more or less consistently one of the following special tendencies: (1) the tendency to react by contrasts; (2) the tendency to react by synonyms or other defining terms; and (3) the tendency to react by qualifying or specifying terms. How clearly the selected groups show these tendencies is indicated by Table II. The majority of records, however, present no such tendency in a consistent way; nor is there any evidence to show that these tendencies, when they occur, are to be regarded as manifestations of permanent mental characteristics, since they might quite possibly be due to a more or less accidental and transient associational direction. No further study has as yet been made of these tendencies, for the reason that they do not appear to possess any pathological significance.

TABLE II.

Special group values.

Stimulus Reaction General Contrasting Defining Specifying
 word.   word.   value. group 49 group 73 group 84
                        | subjects subjects subjects
                        |——— % No. % No. % No. %

         chair.......... 26.7 25 51.0 11 15.1 10 11.9
1. Table....{ furniture....... 7.5 0 0 13 17.8 4 4.8

	round.......... 1.0 1 2.0 0 0 4 4.5
	wood........... 7.6 2 4.1 9 12.3 10 11.9
	cotton......... 2.8 0 0 1 1.4 5 6.0
	easy............ 3.4 0 0 8 11.0 1 1.2
	feathers....... 2.4 0 0 1 1.4 5 6.0
7. Soft.....{	hard............ 36.5 34 69.4 14 19.2 18 21.4
	silk............ 1.0 0 0 0 0 2 2.4
	sponge......... 2.2 0 0 0 0 4 4.8
	cloth.......... 1.7 1 2.0 0 0 3 3.6
	color.......... 12.9 0 0 20 27.4 6 7.1
11. Black...{	dress.......... 2.9 1 2.0 1 1.4 9 10.7
	ink............. 1.4 0 0 1 1.4 4 4.8
	white.......... 33.9 31 63.3 17 23.3 18 21.4
	desire......... 19.7 7 14.3 21 28.8 10 11.9
26. Wish....{	longing......... 1.9 1 2.0 6 8.2 2 2.4
	money.......... 3.2 0 0 1 1.4 3 3.6
	flowers........ 4.2 0 0 1 1.4 7 8.3
	girl............ 2.4 0 0 0 0 5 0.0
29. Beau-	homely.......... 2.7 3 6.1 0 0 0 0
tiful..{	lovely.......... 6.4 2 4.1 7 9.6 2 2.4
	pleasing........ 1.6 0 0 3 4.1 0 0
	sky............. 1.6 0 0 0 0 3 3.6
	ugly............ 6.6 13 26.5 3 4.1 0 0
	court.......... 6.4 2 4.1 5 6.8 10 11.9
56. Justice.{	injustice....... 2.6 6 12.2 1 1.4 0 0
	right.......... 15.7 3 6.1 20 27.4 13 15.5
	comfort......... 2.6 0 0 5 6.8 1 1.2
	disease......... 0.9 2 4.1 0 0 1 1.2
59. Health..{	good............ 9.4 2 4.1 8 11.0 18 21.4
	sickness........ 15.3 23 46.9 6 8.2 1 1.2
	strength........ 11.2 2 4.1 12 16.4 4 4.8
	arrow........... 1.3 0 0 0 0 2 2.4
	fast............ 22.2 0 0 25 34.2 15 17.9
	horse........... 2.8 1 2.0 1 1.4 6 7.1
65. Swift...{	quick........... 11.7 1 2.0 22 30.1 2 2.4
	run............. 1.9 0 0 0 0 4 4.8
	runner.......... 1.3 0 0 0 0 1 1.2
	slow............ 19.0 30 61.2 2 2.7 4 4.8
	speed.......... 2.9 1 2.0 5 6.8 0 0

```
              disagreeable.... 1.0 0 0 2 2.7 0 0
              distasteful..... 1.0 0 0 4 5.5 0 0
              gall............ 4.2 0 0 2 2.7 8 9.5
76. Bitter..{ medicine........ 3.7 0 0 0 0 3 3.6
              quinine......... 2.3 0 0 0 0 6 7.1
              sweet........... 30.5 31 63.3 8 11.0 12 14.3
              taste........... 6.6 1 2.0 17 23.3 3 3.6

bread........... 20.6 17 34.7 4 5.5 18 21.4

              eatable......... 1.2 0 0 9 12.3 0 0
81. Butter..{ food............ 6.3 1 2.0 14 19.2 3 3.6
              sweet........... 1.2 0 0 0 0 3 3.6
              yellow.......... 8.0 0 0 0 0 18 21.4

              gladness........ 4.4 0 0 7 9.6 1 1.2
              grief........... 1.8 4 8.2 0 0 0 0
86. Joy.....{ pleasure........ 12.1 1 2.0 13 17.8 7 8.3
              sadness......... 1.3 2 4.1 0 0 0 0
              sorrow.......... 13.5 23 46.9 2 2.7 2 2.4
```

§ 5. PRACTICAL CONSIDERATIONS.

This method is so simple that it requires but little training on the part of the experimenter, and but little co-operation on the part of the subject. It is not to be assumed that every reaction obtained by it is a true and immediate association to the corresponding stimulus word; but we have found it sufficient for the purpose of the test if the subject can be induced to give, in response to each stimulus word, any one word other than the stimulus word itself. No attempt is made to determine the exact degree of co-operation in any case.

In the early stages of this investigation the reaction time was regularly recorded. The results showed remarkable variations, among both normal and insane subjects. In a series of twenty-five tests, made more recently upon normal subjects, ninety reactions occupied more than ten seconds, and fifty-four of the stimulus words elicited a ten-second response from at least one subject.[1]

[Footnote 1: These tests were made by Dr. F. Lyman Wells, of the McLean Hospital, Waverley, Mass., and he has kindly furnished these data.]

It is noteworthy that these extremely long intervals occur in connection with reactions of widely differing values. That they are by no means limited to individual reactions is shown in Table III. by a group of selected reactions, all given by normal subjects.

TABLE III.

Word combination Reaction time Value of in seconds. reaction. comfort—happiness 20 5.0% short—long 11 27.9% smooth—plane 16 2.3% woman—lady 40 4.1% hard—iron 12 2.4% justice—judge 20 9.1% memory—thought 20 8.1% joy—pleasure 18 12.1%

It is apparent, even from a superficial examination of the material, that the factors which cause variations of reaction time, both in the normal state and in pathological states, are numerous and complex.

It has been the purpose of this study to establish as far as possible strictly objective criteria for distinguishing normal from abnormal associations, and for this reason we have made no attempt to determine by means of introspection the causes of variations of reaction time.

It would seem that the importance and magnitude of the problem of association time are such as to demand not merely a crude measurement of the gross reaction time in a large number of cases, but rather a special investigation by such exact methods as have been used by Cattell [1] and others in the analysis of the complex reaction. It would be impracticable for us to employ such methods in a study so extensive as this.

[Footnote 1: Mind, Vol. XI, 1886.]

In view of these considerations we discontinued the recording of the reaction time.

If the association test is to be useful in the study of pathological conditions, it is of great importance to have a reliable measure of the associational value of a pair of ideas. Many attempts have been made to modify and amplify the classical grouping of associations according to similarity, contrast, contiguity, and sequence, so as to make it serviceable in differentiating between normal and abnormal associations.

In this study we attempted to apply Aschaffenburg's [1] classification of reactions, but without success. Our failure to utilize this system of classification is assigned to the following considerations: (1) Distinctions between associations according to logical relations are extremely difficult to define; in many cases there is room for difference of opinion as to the proper place for an association, and thus the application of a logical scheme depends largely upon the personal equation of the observer; that even experienced observers cannot, in all cases, agree in placing an association is shown by Aschaffenburg's criticisms of the opinions of other observers on this point.[2] (2) Logical distinctions do not bring out clearly the differences between the reactions of normal subjects and those of insane subjects; logically, the reaction *bath—ink*, which was given by a patient, might be placed in the class with the reaction *bath—water*, although there is an obvious difference between the two reactions. (3) Many of the reactions given by insane subjects possess no obvious logical value whatever; but since any combination of ideas may represent a relationship, either real or imagined, it would be arbitrary to characterize such a reaction as incoherent.

[Footnote 1: Experimentelle Studien uber Association. Psychologische Arbeiten, Vol. I, p. 209; Vol. II, p. 1; Vol. IV, p. 235.]

[Footnote 2: Loc. cit, Vol. 1, pp. 226-227.]

The criterion of values which is used in this study is an empirical one. As has already been explained (p. 8), every word contained in the frequency tables possesses a value of at least 0.1 per cent, and other words have a zero value. With the aid of our method the difficulty of classifying the reactions quoted above is obviated, as it is necessary only to refer to the table to find their proper values: the value of the reaction *bath—water* is 33.9 per cent, while that of the reaction *bath—ink* is 0.

Logically the combination *health—wealth* may be placed in any one of four classes, as follows:

```
                / intrinsic / causal dependence
health—wealth /  \ coordination
              \
               \ extrinsic / speech reminiscence
                          \ sound similarity
```

But since our table shows this association to have an empirical value of 7.6 per cent, it becomes immaterial which of its logical relations is to be considered the strongest. It is mainly important, from our point of view, to separate reactions possessing an empirical value from those whose value is zero.

§ 6. AN EMPIRICAL PRINCIPLE OF NORMAL ASSOCIATION.

On a general survey of the whole mass of material which forms the basis of the first part of this study, we are led to observe that *the one tendency which appears to be almost universal among normal persons is the tendency to give in response to any stimulus word one or another of a small group of common reactions.*

It appears from the pathological material now on hand that this tendency is greatly weakened in some cases of mental disease. Many patients have given more than 50 per cent of individual reactions.

It should be mentioned that occasionally a presumably normal subject has given a record very similar to those obtained from patients, in respect to both the number and the nature of the individual reactions. A few subjects who gave peculiar reactions were known to possess significant eccentricities, and for this reason we excluded their records from the thousand records which furnished the basis for the frequency tables; we excluded also a few peculiar records obtained from subjects of whom nothing was known, on the ground that such records would serve only to make the tables more cumbersome, without adding anything to their practical value. The total number of records thus excluded was seventeen.

It will be apparent to anyone who examines the frequency tables that the reactions obtained from one thousand persons fall short of exhausting the normal associational possibilities of these stimulus words. The tables, however, have been found to be sufficiently inclusive for the practical purpose which they were intended to serve. Common reactions, whether given by a sane or an insane subject, may, in the vast majority of instances, safely be regarded as normal. As to individual reactions, they cannot all be regarded as abnormal, but they include nearly all those reactions which are worthy of special analysis in view of their possible pathological significance. What can be said further of individual reactions, whether normal or abnormal, will appear in the second part of this contribution.

PART II.

ASSOCIATION IN INSANE SUBJECTS.

§ 1. GENERAL SURVEY OF PATHOLOGICAL MATERIAL.

The pathological material which forms the basis of the present part of our study consists mainly of two hundred and forty-seven test records obtained for the most part from patients at the Kings Park State Hospital.

The different groups from which the cases were selected, together with the number from each group, are shown in Table I.

TABLE I.

Dementia præcox 108 cases.
Paranoic conditions 33 "
Epilepsy 24 "
General Paresis 32 "
Manic-depressive insanity 32 "
Involuntary melancholia 8 "
Alcoholic psychoses 6 "
Senile dementia 4 "

A comparison of our pathological with our normal material *en masse* reveals in the former evidence of a weakening of the normal tendency to respond by common reactions. This is shown in Table II.

TABLE II.

Common Doubtful Individual
reactions. reactions. reactions.
1,000 normal subject 91.7% 1.5% 6.8%

247 insane subjects 70.7% 2.5% 26.8%

It seems evident from this that pathological significance attaches mainly to individual reactions, so that our study resolves itself largely into (1) an analysis and classification of individual reactions and (2) an attempt to determine what relationship, if any, exists between the different types of reactions and the different clinical forms of mental disease.

§ 2. CLASSIFICATION OF REACTIONS.

Those who have attempted to use the association test in the study of insanity have felt the need of a practical classification of reactions, and have at the same time encountered the difficulty of establishing definite criteria for distinguishing the different groups from one another. It is a comparatively simple matter to make these distinctions in a general way and even to formulate a more or less comprehensive theoretical classification, but there still remains much difficulty in practice. We have made repeated attempts to utilize various systems of classification which involve free play of personal equation in their application. Although for us the matter is greatly simplified by the elimination of all the common reactions with the aid of the frequency tables, we have nevertheless met with no success. The distinctions made by either of us have on no occasion fully satisfied, at the second reading, either the one who made them or the other, while a comparison of the distinctions made by each of us independently has shown a disagreement to the extent of 20-35 per cent.

We sought, therefore, to formulate a classification in which the various groups should be so defined as to obviate the interference of personal equation in the work of applying it, hoping thus to achieve greater accuracy. In this we can lay claim to only partial success; for, in the first place, having satisfactorily defined a number of groups, we found it necessary in the end to provide a special group for unclassified reactions, into which falls more than one-third of the total number of individual reactions; and, in the second place, in at least two of our groups the play of personal equation has not been entirely eliminated, so that there is still a possibility of error to the extent of five per cent of individual reactions, which means approximately one per cent of the total number of reactions. We have found, however, that in spite of these shortcomings the classification here proposed is more serviceable than others which, though more comprehensive, are at the same time lacking in definiteness.

Our classification consists of the following classes, groups and subdivisions:

I. *Common reactions*. 1. Specific reactions. 2. Non-specific reactions.

II. *Doubtful reactions*.

III. *Individual reactions*.
 1. Normal reactions.
 2. Pathological reactions:
  A. Derivatives of stimulus words.
  B. Partial dissociation:
   (a) Non-specific reactions.
   (b) Sound reactions:
    a. Words.
    b. Neologisms.

(c) Word complements.
   (d) Particles of speech.
  C. Complete dissociation:
   (a) Perseveration:
      a. Association to preceding stimulus.
      b. Association to preceding reaction.
      c. Repetition of preceding stimulus.
      d. Repetition of previous stimulus.
      e. Repetition of preceding reaction.
      f. Repetition of previous reaction.
      g. Reaction repeated five times (stereotypy).
   (b) Neologisms without sound relation.
 3. Unclassified.

§ 3. NON-SPECIFIC REACTIONS; DOUBTFUL REACTIONS.

Non-specific Reactions.—It has already been intimated that common reactions are in the vast majority of instances to be regarded as normal. From amongst them, however, a fairly definite group can be separated out which seems to possess some pathological significance, namely, the group which we have termed non-specific.

In this group are placed words which are so widely applicable as to serve as more or less appropriate reactions to almost any of our stimulus words. That such reactions are in value inferior to the remaining group of common reactions, which we have termed, in contradistinction, *specific reactions*, is perhaps sufficiently obvious; we shall speak later, however, of their occurrence in both normal and insane cases.

It is not always easy to judge whether or not a given reaction should be classed as non-specific. A study of our material made with special reference to this type of reactions has enabled us to select the following list of words, any of which, occurring in response to any stimulus word, is classed as a non-specific reaction:

article, articles bad beautiful, beauty fine good, goodness great happiness, happy large man necessary, necessity nice

object (noun) people person pleasant, pleasantness, pleasing, pleasure pretty small thinking, thought, thoughts unnecessary unpleasant use, used, useful, usefulness, useless, uselessness, uses, using woman work

It should be mentioned that some of these words occur as reactions to one or several stimulus words with such frequency (*citizen—man*, value 27.8 per cent; *health—good*, value 9.4 per cent) as to acquire in such instances a value as high as that of strictly specific reactions.

Doubtful Reactions have already been defined (p.40): any reaction word which is not found in the table in its identical form, but which is a grammatical variant or derivative of a word found there, is placed in this group.

§ 4. INDIVIDUAL REACTIONS; EXPLANATION OF GROUPS AND METHODS OF APPLICATION.

Normal Reactions.—Inasmuch as the frequency tables do not exhaust all normal possibilities of reaction, a certain number of reactions which are essentially normal are to be found among the individual reactions. In order to separate these from the pathological reactions, we have compiled an appendix to the frequency tables, consisting mainly of specific definitions of groups of words to be included under each stimulus word in our list. This appendix will be found at the end of this paper.

A word of explanation is perhaps due as to the manner in which the appendix has been compiled. It was developed in a purely empirical way, the basis being such individual reactions, given by both normal and insane subjects, as seemed in our judgment to be obviously normal.

It must be acknowledged that the appendix falls short of all that might be desired. In the first place, its use involves to some slight extent the play of personal equation, and it therefore constitutes a source of error; in the second place, it is in some respects too inclusive while in other respects it is not sufficiently so. However, the error due to personal equation is slight; the inclusion of certain "far-fetched" or even frankly pathological reactions may be discounted by bearing in mind that the general value of this group is not equal to that of the group of common reactions; and the number of strictly normal reactions which are not included is after all small. Our experience has shown us that the appendix constitutes an important aid in the analysis of individual reactions.

Pathological Reactions. Derivatives of Stimulus Words.—We place here any reaction which is a grammatical variant or derivative of a stimulus word. The tendency to give such reactions seems to be dependent upon a suspension or inhibition of the normal process by which the stimulus word excites the production of a new concept, for we have here not a production of a new concept but a mere change in the form of the stimulus word. As examples of such reactions may be mentioned: *eating—eatables, short—shortness, sweet—sweetened, quiet—quietness*.

Partial Dissociation.—We have employed the term dissociation to indicate a rupture of that bond—whatever be its nature-which may be supposed to exist normally between stimulus and reaction and which causes normal persons to respond in the majority of instances by common reactions. And we speak of partial dissociation where there is still an obvious, though weak and superficial, connection. Under this heading we can differentiate four types:

Non-specific Reactions have already been defined; we distinguish those in this class from those in the class of common reactions by means of the frequency tables.

Sound Reactions.—This type requires no explanation; the main difficulty is to decide what degree of sound similarity between stimulus and reaction should be deemed sufficient for placing a reaction under this heading. The total number of different sounds used in language articulation is, of course, small, so that any two words are liable to present considerable chance similarity. Some time ago we estimated the average degree of sound similarity between stimulus words and reaction words in a series of one hundred test records obtained from normal persons; we found that on the average 14.53 per cent of the sounds of the stimulus words were reproduced, in the same order, in the reaction word. Our experience finally led us to adopt the following general rule: A reaction is to be placed under this heading when fifty per cent of the sounds of the shorter word of the pair are identical with sounds of the longer word and are ranged in the same order.

Among sound reactions we occasionally find *neologisms*; for these a separate heading is provided. Possibly their occurrence may be taken as an indication of an exaggerated tendency to respond by sound reactions.

Word Compliments.—Here we include any reaction which, added to the stimulus word, forms a word, a proper name, or a compound word in common use.

Particles of Speech.—Under this heading we include articles, numerals, pronouns, auxiliary verbs, adverbs of time, place and degree, conjunctions, prepositions, and interjections.

Complete Dissociation.—Here are included reactions which appear to be entirely unrelated to the corresponding stimulus words; in the case of such reactions the stimulus words seem to act, as Aschaffenburg has pointed out, merely as signals for discharge. This subdivision contains several types of reactions which seem to be dependent upon the phenomenon of perseveration; it contains also the rather important type of neologisms.

The phenomenon of *preservation* occurs in cases in which one may observe an abnormal immobility of attention. To react normally to a series of stimulus words requires on the part of the subject, in the first place, a certain alertness in order that he may grasp quickly and clearly the meaning of each word, and, in the second place, a prompt shifting of the mind from one reaction to the next. When such mental mobility is lacking the subject is liable to react not by a response adjusted to the stimulus word, but either by repeating a previous stimulus or reaction, or by giving a word associated to the preceding stimulus or reaction.

The names of the different types of reactions included under the heading of perseveration are sufficiently descriptive; we shall here refer only to those which require further definition.

Association to Preceding Stimulus.—Here is placed any reaction that is shown by the frequency tables to be related to the stimulus preceding the one in question. Seeming or even obvious relationship, if not established by reference to the frequency tables, is disregarded. In the tables, however, the combination may not exist in direct order but only in reverse order, in which case the reaction is included here. The following examples may serve as illustrations:

thief—night lion—pocket-book

Lion—pocket-book is not found in the frequency tables, and is, therefore, an individual reaction; *thief—pocket-book*, however, is found there; *pocket-book* is, therefore, classed in this case as an association to preceding stimulus.

table—fork dark—mutton

Dark—mutton is not found in the frequency tables; *table—mutton* is also not found there in the direct order, but is found in the reverse order, viz.: *mutton—table; mutton* is, therefore, classed in this case as an association to preceding stimulus.

Association to Preceding Reaction.—If either the reaction in question or the preceding reaction happens to be one of the stimulus words in our list, and a relationship between the two be found to exist by reference to the frequency tables—whether in direct or in reverse order—the reaction in question is classed as an association to preceding reaction. This is illustrated by the following examples:

eating—table mountain—floor

Mountain—floor is an individual reaction; *table—floor*

is found in the frequency tables; *floor* is, therefore, classed as an association to preceding reaction.

beautiful—flowers window—red

Window—red is an individual reaction; *red—flowers* is found in the frequency tables; therefore, *red* is classed as an association to preceding reaction.

In cases in which neither the reaction in question nor the preceding reaction happens to be one of our stimulus words, but a relationship between them may be judged to exist without considerable doubt, the reaction in question is also classed here. Example:

priest—father ocean—mother

Ocean—mother is an individual reaction; neither the word *father* nor the word *mother* is among our stimulus words; but the association between the words *father* and *mother* may be judged to exist without considerable doubt; therefore, in this case *mother* is classed as an association to preceding reaction.

In such cases as this personal equation must necessarily come into play; comparative uniformity of judgment may, however, be attained by systematically excluding any reaction the relationship of which to the preceding reaction is subject to any considerable doubt and by placing any such reaction in the unclassified group.

Repetition of Previous Stimulus.—Here we place any reaction which is a repetition of any previous stimulus from amongst the ten next preceding, at the same time placing *repetition of preceding stimulus* under a separate heading.

Neologisms.—Here we place the newly coined words, so commonly given by the insane, excepting such as possess a sound relationship to the stimulus word, for which, as already stated, a special place in the classification has been provided.

Neologisms might be divided into three types, as follows: (1) those which arise from ignorance of language (*comfort—uncomfort, short—diminiature*); (2) distortions of actual words, apparently of pathological origin and not due to ignorance (*hungry—foodation, thief—dissteal*); and (3) those which seem to be without any meaning whatever (*scack, gehimper, hanrow, dicut*). It is, however, impossible to draw clear-cut distinctions between these types, and for this reason we have made no provision in our classification for such division.

Unclassified Reactions.—This group is important, in the first place, because it is numerically a large one, and in the second place, because it contains certain fairly definite types of reactions which are placed here for the sole reason that we have not been able to find strictly objective criteria for their differentiation from other types.

It has already been stated that the frequency tables, even together with the appendix, fail to exhaust all normal possibilities of association, so that a certain small number of perfectly normal reactions must fall into the unclassified group. We submit the following examples:

music—listen smooth—suave sour—curdled earth—mound

Another type of reactions found in the unclassified group, though also normal, yet not obviously so until explained by the subject, is represented by those which originate from purely personal experiences, such as the following, given by normal subjects:

blossom—T..... hammer—J.....

The first of these reactions is explained by the subject's acquaintance with a young lady, Miss T...., who has been nick-named "Blossom," and the second is explained by the subject's having among her pupils at school a boy by the name of J.... Hammer.

It would be difficult to estimate the proportion of such reactions in the unclassified group, but we have gained the general impression that it is small. An attempt to place them in a separate group could be made only with the aid of explanations from the subjects; such aid in the case of insane subjects is generally unreliable. Moreover, to class these reactions as strictly normal would perhaps be going too far, since their general value is obviously inferior to that of the common reactions; and in any case in which they are given in unusually large numbers they must be regarded as manifestation of a tendency to depart from the normal to the extent to which they displace common reactions. The next type of reactions met with in the unclassified group is characterized by a peculiarly superficial, or non-essential, or purely *circumstantial* relationship to the stimulus. Such reactions, though occasionally given by normal subjects, are more often given by insane ones, and seem to be somewhat characteristic of states of mental deterioration which are clinically rather loosely described as puerilism. We offer the following examples, given by normal subjects:

music—town sickness—summer child—unknown house—enter

Still another type of reactions to be considered in this connection consists of words which are in no way related to the corresponding stimulus words, but which arise from *distraction* of the subject by surrounding objects, sounds, and the like. In some cases the experimenter may be able to judge from the direction of the subject's gaze, from a listening attitude, and so on, that certain reactions are due to distraction. In other cases, particularly in cases of normal subjects, the fact that certain reactions are due to distraction may be determined by questioning the subject on this point immediately after making the test; In work with insane subjects, as we have several times had occasion to point out, such aid is generally not available.

The group of unclassified reactions includes also one more type of reactions which are of great importance both numerically and otherwise. These are the *incoherent reactions*, that is to say, reactions which are determined neither by the stimulus words, nor by the agency of perseveration, nor by distraction.

Although the occurrence of incoherent reactions is hardly subject to doubt, yet in no instance is it possible to establish with certainty that a given reaction is of this type, for in no instance can a remote, or an imagined, or a merely symbolic relationship between stimulus and reaction be positively excluded. Some, indeed, would assert that some such relationship must necessarily exist in every instance, at least in the domain of the subconscious. This circumstance necessitates the placing of this type of reactions in the unclassified group.

In practice it may be found advisable in some cases to analyze the unclassified reactions with a view to ascertaining to what extent each of the various types is represented among them. But one here treads on slippery ground, and one must be continually warned against the danger of erroneous conclusions.

§ 5. ORDER OF PREFERENCE.

After having developed the classification here proposed we found that there was still considerable room for difference of opinion in the placing of many reactions, owing to the circumstance that in many cases a reaction presents features which render it assignable under any one of two or more headings. To leave the matter of preference in grouping to be decided in each case according to the best judgment of the experimenter would mean introducing again the play of personal equation, and would thus court failure of all our efforts to accomplish a standardization of the association test. Therefore, the necessity of establishing a proper order of preference for guidance in the application of the classification became to us quite apparent.

In the arrangement of the order of preference we were guided mainly by two principles, namely: (1) as between two groups of unequal definition, the one which is more clearly defined and which, therefore, leaves less play for personal equation is to be preferred; (2) as between two groups of equal definition, the one which possesses the greater pathological significance is to be preferred. In accordance with these principles we have adopted the order of preference shown in Table III., placing every reaction under the highest heading on the list under which it may be properly classed.

TABLE III

1. Non-specific (common). 2. Doubtful reactions. INDIVIDUAL REACTIONS. 3. Sound reactions (neologisms). 4. Neologisms without sound relation. 5. Repetition of preceding reaction. 6. Reaction repeated five times. 7. Repetition of preceding stimulus. 8. Derivatives. 9. Non-specific reactions. 10. Sound reactions (words). 11. Word complements. 12. Particles of speech. 13. Association to preceding stimulus. 14. Association to preceding reaction (by frequency tables). 15. Repetition of previous reaction. 16. Repetition of previous stimulus. 17. Normal (by appendix). 18. Association to preceding reaction (without frequency tables). 19. Unclassified.

§ 6. ERRORS INVOLVED IN THE USE OF ARBITRARY OBJECTIVE STANDARDS.

It may readily be seen that such definiteness and uniformity as this classification possesses results from the introduction of more or less arbitrary criteria for the differentiation of the various types of reactions. The question might arise, To what extent do the distinctions thus made correspond to reality? To consider, for instance, our rule for the placing of sound reactions (50 per cent of the sounds of the shorter word to be present, in the same order, in the other word): when a given reaction (*man—minstrel*) is in accordance with the rule assigned under the heading of sound reactions, can it be assumed that sound similarity and not some other relationship is the determining factor of the association in question? Or when in, a given instance (*cabbage—cobweb*) the sound similarity falls somewhat short of the standard required by the rule, can it be assumed that sound similarity is not, after all, the determining factor?

Similar questions may, of course, arise in connection with other subdivisions.

It must, indeed, be conceded that objective methods can reveal but indirectly and with uncertainty the inner mechanism which produces any association and that in any given instance it would be impossible to establish the correctness of grouping in accordance with such

methods. However, to decide that question for any given reaction is really not necessary in practice, since an error made through wrongly placing one, two, or three reactions tinder any heading is of no significance; the types acquire importance only when represented by large numbers in a record under consideration; and when many reactions fall tinder a single heading the likelihood of error, as affecting the record as a whole, is by that fact alone greatly reduced.

The whole question might more profitably be approached from another point of view: To what extent are the distinctions of this classification useful? An answer to this question can be found only in the results.

§ 7. ANALYSIS OF PATHOLOGICAL MATERIAL

We present in Table IV, the results of a statistical examination of the records obtained from certain groups of normal subjects and from some groups of insane subjects.

The normal groups have been studied for the purpose of determining the frequency and manner of occurrence among normal subjects of the various of abnormal reactions. It seemed best for this purpose to consider separately the records of those subjects who gave an unusually large number of individual reactions. Fifty-three records containing fifteen or more individual reactions were found after a fairly diligent search among our normal test records. In the other groups of subjects—persons of common school education, persons of collegiate education, and children—we included no records containing more than ten individual reactions.

The more striking departures from average normal figures are indicated in the table by the use of heavy type.

This table reveals associational tendencies as occurring in connection with the psychoses studied. A better insight into the nature of these tendencies can be gained by a special analysis of the test of each clinical group.

DEMENTIA PRÆCOX

In this psychosis we find the number of individual reactions far exceeding not only that of the normal but that of any other psychosis which we studied. To a corresponding extent we find the number of the highest type of normal reactions—the common specific reactions—reduced.

TABLE IV.

TYPES OF REACTION
                        A B C D E F G H I J K L M N O P Q R S T U V W X Y Z AA

+—+——+——+——+—+——+——+——+—+——+—
—+—+——+——+—+——+——+—+——+——+—+——+——+—
+—+——+——+—+—+——+——+

Common reactions: | | | | | | | | | | | | | | | | | | | | | | | |
  Specific reactions................|90|89.8|....|90|89.7|....|91|89.4|....|72|71.4|

....|631/2|58.9|....|82|71.3|....|71|63.7|....|78 |71.8|....|80 |71.2|....|

Non-specific reactions............| 4| 4.9|....| 4| 4.1|....| 5| 5.7|....| 3| 4.8|....| 3 | 4.2|....| 4| 4.8|....| 5| 6.0|....|41/2 | 5.3|....|31/2 | 4.6|....|

| | | | | | | | | | | | | | | | | | | | | | | | | | |

Doubtful reactions................| 1| 1.1|....| 1| 0.6|....| 0| 0.7|....| 2| 2.3|....| 2 | 2.5|....| 2| 3.0|....| 3| 3.0|....| 2 | 2.2|....| 2 | 3.0|....|

| | | | | | | | | | | | | | | | | | | | | | | | | | |

Individual reactions: | | | | | | | | | | | | | | | | | | | | | | | | | |

Normal reactions................| 2| 1.8|41.8| 1| 1.8|35.8| 1| 1.6|42.0| 7| 7.3|33.4| 4 | 4.8|13.9| 3| 3.5|16.3|31/2| 3.4|12.6| 3 | 3.6|17.4|41/2 | 5.3|24.3|

Derivatives of stimulus words.....| 0|0.01| 0.3| 0|0.02| 0.3| 0| 0| 0 | 0|0.04| 0.2| 0 |0.16|0.46| 0|0.10|0.40| 0|0.04|0.15| 0 |0.09|0.45| 0 |0.09|0.43|

Non-specific Reactions............| 0| 0.1| 3.3| 0|0.1 | 1.2| 0|0.2 | 5.3| 0|0.4 | 2.0| 0 |0.6 |1.7 | 0|0.4 |1.7 | 0|0.5 |1.8 | 1 |0.5 |2.4 | 0 |0.3 |1.6 |

Sound reactions (words)...........| 0|0.08| 1.9| 0|0.05| 0.9| 0| 0 | 0 | 0|0.11| 0.5| 0 |1.62|4.7 | 1|1.60|7.4 | 0|0.54|2.0 | 0 |0.22|1.0 | 1 |1.53|7.1 |

Sound reactions (neologisms)......| 0|0.01| 0.3| 0|0.02| 0.3| 0| 0 | 0 | 0| 0 | 0 | 0 |0.07|0.2 | 0|1.0 |4.7 | 0|0.17|0.6 | 0 |0.06|0.3 | 0 |0.03|0.1 |

Word complements..................| 0|0.01| 0.3| 0|0.03| 0.6| 0| 0 | 0 | 0|0.08| 0.3| 0 |0.06|0.2 | 0|0.03|0.1 | 0| 0 | 0 | 0 |0.06|0.3 | 0 |0.10|0.9 |

Particles of speech...............| 0|0.09| 2.2| 0|0.06| 1.2| 0|0.06| 1.6| 0|0.68| 3.1| 0 |1.06|3.1 | 0|0.50|2.2 | 0|1.53|5.3 | 0 |1.22|5.3 | 0 |1.32|6.1 |

Association to preceding stimulus.| 0|0.06| 1.4| 0|0.06| 1.2| 0|0.04| 1.1| 0|0.49| 2.2| 0 |0.92|2.7 | 0|0.60|2.7 | 1|1.04|3.8 | 0 |0.75|3.6 | 0 |0.53|2.5 |

Association to preceding reaction.| 0| 0 | 0 | 0| 0 | 0 | 0|0.04| 1.0| 0|0.09| 0.4| 1 |1.29|3.8 | 0|0.40|2.0 | 1|2.50|9.2 | 1 |3.69|17.7| 0 |0.37|1.7 |

Repetition of preceding stimulus..| 0| 0 | 0 | 0|0.03| 0.6| 0| 0 | 0 | 0| 0 | 0 | 0 |0.06|0.2 | 0| 0 | 0 | 0|0.08|0.3 | 0 | 0 | 0 | 0 | 0 | 0 |

Repetition of previous stimulus...| 0| 0 | 0 | 0|0.01| 0.3| 0| 0 | 0 | 0|0.02| 0.1| 0 |0.12|0.4 | 0|0.10|0.4 | 0|0.29|1.1 | 0 |0.28|1.4 | 0

|0.22|1.0 |
Repetition of preceding reaction..| 0| 0 | 0 | 0|0.03| 0.6| 0|0.02| 0.5| 0|0.08| 0.3| 0 |1.16|3.4 | 0|0.12|0.6 | 0|0.58|2.1 | 0 |2.28|10.9| 0 |0.73|3.6 |
Repetition of previous reaction...| 0|0.21| 4.7| 0|0.31| 6.3| 0|0.23| 5.8| 0|0.92| 4.2| 1 |2.72|7.9 | 1|1.51|7.1 | 3|3.46|12.7| 0 |0.87|4.2 | 0 |0.91|4.2 |
Reaction repeated five times......| 0| 0 | 0 | 0|0.05| 0.9| 0|0.08| 2.1| 0|0.32| 1.5| 0 |1.52|4.4 | 0|1.21|5.5 | 0|4.58|16.8| 0 |1.28|6.1 | 0 |0.81|3.8 |
Neologisms without sound relation.| 0| 0 | 0 | 0| 0 | 0 | 0|0.02| 0.5| 0| 0 | 0 | 0 |1.90|5.5 | 0|0.81|3.7 | 0|0.58|2.1 | 0 |0.09|0.4 | 0 |0.31|1.5 |
Unclassified......................| 2| 1.8|43.4| 2|2.5 |50.3| 1|1.5 |39.4|11|11.1|51.2|11 |16.2|47.2| 5|9.3 |43.5| 6|7.7 |28.5| 5 |5.9 |28.4| 4 |8.6 |40.1|

Total individual reactions | 4| 4.2|....| 5|5.1 |....| 9|3.9 |....|21|21.8|....|261/2|34.3|....|10|21.3|....|19|27.2|....|141/2|20.8 |....|111/2|21.5|....|

86 normal subjects, common school education; records containing not over 10 individual reactions.

   A. Median per cent of all reactions.
   B. Average per cent of all reactions.
   C. Average per cent of individual reactions.

66 normal subjects, collegiate education; records containing not over 10 individual reactions.

   D. Median per cent of all reactions.
   E. Average per cent of all reactions.
   F. Average per cent of individual reactions.

46 normal subjects, school children; records containing not over 10 individual reactions.

   G. Median per cent of all reactions.
   H. Average per cent of all reactions.
   I. Average per cent of individual reactions.

53 normal subjects; records containing not under 15 individual reactions.

  J. Median per cent of all reactions.
  K. Average per cent of all reactions.
  L. Average per cent of individual reactions.

108 cases of dementia præcox.

  M. Median per cent of all reactions.
  N. Average per cent of all reactions.
  O. Average per cent of individual reactions.

33 cases of paranoic conditions.

  P. Median per cent of all reactions.
  Q. Average per cent of all reactions.
  R. Average per cent of individual reactions.

24 cases of epilepsy.

  S. Median per cent of all reactions.
  T. Average per cent of all reactions.
  U. Average per cent of individual reactions.

32 cases of general paresis.

  V. Median per cent of all reactions.
  W. Average per cent of all reactions.
  X. Average per cent of individual reactions.

32 cases of manic-depressive insanity.

  Y. Median per cent of all reactions.
  Z. Average per cent of all reactions.
  AA. Average per cent of individual reactions.

While almost every type of individual reactions shows here an increase over the normal averages, the most striking increases are shown by the table to be in the groups of unclassified reactions, neologisms, sound reactions, and some types of perseveration. A further examination of the individual test records shows that there is no uniformity of associational tendencies in this clinical group, but that several tendencies are more or less frequently met with either alone or in various combinations. Yet some of these tendencies, when appearing at all prominently, are so highly characteristic of dementia præcox as to be almost pathognomonic. Among these may be mentioned: (1) the tendency to give *neologisms*, particularly those of the senseless type; (2) the tendency to give unclassified reactions largely of the *incoherent* type; and (3) the tendency toward *stereotypy* manifested chiefly by abnormally frequent repetitions of the same reaction. Fairly characteristic also is the occasional tendency to give sound reactions. Again, occasionally one encounters pronounced *perseveration*, and at least two of our subjects gave a good many unclassified reactions obviously due to *distraction*.

It must be noted that not infrequently cases of dementia præcox give test records that cannot be distinguished from normal. It seems that the pathological associational tendencies constitute merely a special group of symptoms, some of which may be expected to be manifest in cases which have reached a state of advanced mental deterioration, but may not necessarily be present in the early stages of the disease. On the other hand there is evidence to show that these tendencies may in some cases appear among the earliest manifestations. This matter will be referred to again.

Thus the test records of dementia præcox depart from the normal not sharply but by a gradual shading off. We find similar gradual transitions between dementia præcox and other psychoses. For this work we selected cases in which the diagnoses were established with reasonable certainty. Whether or not in cases of doubtful clinical classification this association test may be of aid in determining the diagnosis, is a question that must for the present remain open.

We submit herewith copies of test records. The numbers which appear after the reactions indicate in each case the reaction type, in accordance with Table III. (p. 27); common specific reactions are not numbered.

CASE No. 4752.—H.J. Neologisms; some unclassified reactions, mostly incoherent.

Table—meadow.........19
Dark—black...........
Music—sweet..........
Sickness—dead........ 2
Man—manion.......... 3
Deep—near............19
Soft—sooner..........19
Eating—formble....... 4
Mountain—gair........ 4
House—temble......... 4
Black—benched........ 4
Mutton—ranched....... 4
Comfort—bumble....... 4
Hand—semble.......... 4
Short—simber......... 4
Fruit—narrow.........13
Butterfly—Ben........19
Smooth—gum...........19

Command—bramble......19
Chair—low............
Sweet—temper.........19
Whistle—bensid....... 4
Woman—hummery........ 4
Cold—gunst........... 4
Slow—bemper.......... 4
Wish—tip.............19
River—gumper......... 4
White—Andes..........19
Beautiful—giinper.... 4
Window—hummer........ 4
Rough—geep........... 4
Citizen—humper....... 4
Foot—zuper........... 4
Spider—gumper........ 4
Needle—himper........ 4
Red—gumper........... 4
Sleep—moop........... 4
Anger—rumble.........19
Carpet—slamper....... 4
Girl—Mnker........... 4
High—bumper.......... 4
Working—gumpip....... 4
Sour—imper........... 4
Earth—gumper......... 4
Trouble—humper....... 4
Soldier—guipper...... 4
Cabbage—phar......... 4
Hard—her.............12
Eagle—damnornott..... 4
Stomach—dumper....... 4
Stem—gumper.......... 4
Lamp—huntenit........ 4
Dream—hungnot........ 4
Yellow—bampir........ 4
Bread—gumper......... 4
Justice—sidnerber.... 4
Boy—eeper............ 4
Light—huntznit....... 4
Health—geeper........ 4
Bible—himpier........ 4
Memory—hummer........19

Sheep—hunner………. 4
Bath—bemnitper……. 4
Cottage—gumper……. 4
Swift—dumper………. 4
Blue—dipper………..19
Hungry—hummer…….. 3
Priest—rump………..19
Ocean—himmer………. 4
Head—hiniper………. 4
Stove—gamper………. 4
Long—humble………..19
Religion—gumper…… 4
Whiskey—numper……. 4
Child—himmer………. 4
Bitter—gehimper…… 3
Hammer—gueep………. 4
Thirsty—humper……. 4
City—deeper………..19
Square—bummer…….. 4
Butter—bimper…….. 3
Doctor—harner…….. 4
Loud—harner……….. 4
Thief—himmer………. 4
Lion—humor………...19
Joy—gumpier……….. 4
Bed—hoomer………... 4
Heavy—doomer………. 4
Tobacco—per………..12
Baby—hoomer……….. 4
Moon—gumper……….. 4
Scissors—gumper…… 4
Quiet—humper………. 4
Green—gueet……….. 3
Salt—rummer……….. 4
Street—numper…….. 4
King—himper……….. 4
Cheese—guinter……. 4
Blossom—yunger……. 4
Afraid—yunger…….. 4

CASE No. 5183.—G. D. Neologisms; numerous unclassified reactions, mostly incoherent; some sound neologisms.

Table—muss………19
Dark—gone…………19
Music—caffa………. 4
Sickness—monk……..19
Man—boy…………..
Deep—lesson……….19
Soft—ness………… 4
Eating—pie…………
Mountain—Gus………19
House—muss………..15
Black—court……….19
Mutton—beef……….
Comfort—ness……… 4
Hand—koy…………. 4
Short—ness……….. 4
Fruit—dalb……….. 4
Butterfly—flack…… 4
Smooth—mess……….19
Command—cork………19
Chair—ness……….. 4
Sweet—Bess………..17
Whistle—toy……….
Woman—girl………..
Cold—cork…………15
Slow—mass…………19
Wish—veil………… 4
River—mouth……….17
White—cast………..17
Beautiful—ness……. 4
Window—crow……….19
Rough—ratter………19
Citizen—zide……… 4
Foot—malloy………. 4
Spider—straw………19
Needle—cast……….15
Red—Roman…………19
Sleep—scack………. 4
Anger—gois……….. 4
Carpet—noise………13
Girl—call…………18
High—hort………… 4
Working—kaffir…….19
Sour—romerscotters… 4

- 28 -

Earth—bell………..19
Trouble—tramine…… 4
Soldier—gas……….19
Cabbage—cor……….. 4
Hard—kalbas……….. 4
Eagle—bell………..15
Stomach—chenic……. 4
Stem—trackstar……. 3
Lamp—loss…………19
Dream—melso……….. 4
Yellow—ormondo……. 4
Bread—life………..
Justice—quartz…….19
Boy—nellan……….. 4
Light—cor…………. 4
Health—hallenbee….. 4
Bible—book………..
Memory—bike……….19
Sheep—armen……….. 4
Bath—cor…………. 4
Cottage—callan……. 4
Swift—swar……….. 3
Blue—blacksen…….. 4
Hungry—scatterbuck… 4
Priest—canon………17
Ocean—men…………19
Head—will…………19
Stove—somen……….. 4
Long—lass…………19
Religion—cor………. 4
Whiskey—hanrow……. 4
Child—vand……….. 4
Bitter—bike……….15
Hammer—hemmel…….. 3
Thirsty—cass………. 4
City—cor…………. 4
Square—malice……..19
Butter—back……….19
Doctor—ness……….. 4
Loud—arman……….. 4
Thief—cast………..15
Lion—loss…………15
Joy—kaffir………..15

Bed—banrow………. 4
Heavy—cast………..15
Tobacco—colrow……. 4
Baby—boil…………19
Moon—padoc……….. 4
Scissors—kantow…… 4
Quiet—kilroe……… 4
Green—graft……….10
Salt—semen………..19
Street—pess………. 4
King—guess………..19
Cheese—tiffer…….. 4
Blossom—cad……….19
Afraid—mellows…….19

CASE No. 1500.—D.V. Considerable number of neologisms; stereotypy manifested partly in a tendency toward frequent repetition of certain reactions but mainly in a persistent tendency to make use of the grammatical form of present participle, giving rise to numerous doubtful reactions.

Table—stand……….
Dark—lonesome……..
Music—playing……..
Sickness—disease…..
Man—hiding………..19
Deep—unreckless…… 4
Soft—beginning…….19
Eating—plenty……..
Mountain—high……..
House—standing……. 6
Black—grivelling….. 4
Mutton—plenty……..15
Comfort—laying…….19
Hand—disease………15
Short—writing……..13
Fruit—coming………19
Butterfly—flying…..
Smooth—glimming…… 4
Command—master…….
Chair—standing……. 6
Sweet—sugar……….
Whistle—blowing……
Woman—loving………

Cold—cellar..........19
Slow—coming..........15
Wish—dreaming........ 2
River—divided........19
White—wall...........
Beautiful—pleasant... 1
Window—breaking...... 2
Rough—tumble.........
Citizen—gentleman....
Foot—sweating........19
Spider—biting........ 2
Needle—stinging...... 2
Red—coloring.........
Sleep—dreaming.......
Anger—widing......... 4
Carpet—cleaning......
Girl—pretty.......... 1
High—degrace......... 4
Working—nobody.......19
Sour—holling......... 4
Earth—disgrace.......19
Trouble—plenty.......
Soldier—shooting.....13
Cabbage—welldebell... 4
Hard—earning......... 4
Eagle—setting........19
Stomach—degrivel..... 4
Stem—biting..........19
Lamp—burning.........
Dream—walking........19
Yellow—blowing.......15
Bread—making.........
Justice—unpossible... 4
Boy—growing.......... 2
Light—stand.......... 6
Health—raising.......19
Bible—teaching....... 2
Memory—together......12
Sheep—weeding........19
Bath—held............19
Cottage—standing..... 2
Swift—incuriossable.. 4
Blue—smooven......... 4

- 31 -

Hungry—uncareless.... 4
Priest—going.........19
Ocean—moving......... 2
Head—setting.........15
Stove—warm...........
Long—slowly.......... 2
Religion—everything..19
Whiskey—burning......
Child—born...........
Bitter—taking........19
Hammer—hitting....... 2
Thirsty—drinking.....
City—welldebell...... 4
Square—taking........15
Butter—soft..........
Doctor—instrument....19
Loud—speaking........ 2
Thief—gitting........ 4
Lion—scared..........17
Joy—playing.......... 2
Bed—laying........... 2
Heavy—raisen......... 4
Tobacco—eating.......19
Baby—born............
Moon—shining.........
Scissors—cutting.....

Quiet—hitting........15
Green—landed.........19
Salt—throwing........19
Street—walking.......
King—tension.........19
Cheese—eating........
Blossom—growing...... 2
Afraid—nobody........

CASE No. 5138.—C.J. Unclassified reactions, mostly incoherent.

Table—tablecloth.....
Dark—forward.........19
Music—instrument.....
Sickness—fluid.......19
Man—hemale........... 4
Deep—steep...........
Soft—hard............

- 32 -

Eating—mountain......19
Mountain—raven.......19
House—shutter........17
Black—blue...........
Mutton—beef..........
Comfort—discomfort...
Hand—wrist...........
Short—tall...........
Fruit—vegetable......
Butterfly—bee........
Smooth—rough.........
Command—orders.......
Chair—sofa...........
Sweet—sour...........
Whistle—fife.........
Woman—girl...........
Cold—warm............
Slow—faster.......... 2
Wish—not............. 2
River—neck...........17
White—blue...........
Beautiful—homely.....
Window—sill..........
Rough—paint..........19
Citizen—pedestrian...19
Foot—rose............19
Spider—towel.........19
Needle—lifter........19
Red—dove.............19
Sleep—coat...........13
Anger—smile..........19
Carpet—gas...........19
Girl—kite............19
High—cow.............19
Working—candy........19
Sour—peach...........17
Earth—balloon........19
Trouble—grass........13
Soldier—brass........17
Cabbage—flea.........19
Hard—cat.............19
Eagle—negro..........10
Stomach—winter.......19

- 33 -

Stem—leaf............
Lamp—cloth..........19
Dream—slumber........
Yellow—pink..........
Bread—glass..........19
Justice—coal.........19
Boy—maid.............
Light—shine..........
Health—pale..........17
Bible—leaf...........
Memory—grief.........19
Sheep—giraffe........19
Bath—soap............
Cottage—scene........19
Swift—slow...........
Blue—piece...........19
Hungry—food..........
Priest—minister......
Ocean—waves..........
Head—black...........
Stove—lid............
Long—short...........
Religion—Christian...
Whiskey—malt.........
Child—baby...........
Bitter—sweet.........
Hammer—nail..........
Thirsty—water........
City—steeple.........19
Square—marble........19
Butter—bread.........
Doctor—aster.........19
Loud—fog.............19
Thief—Mary...........19
Lion—tiger...........
Joy—glad.............
Bed—sheet............
Heavy—light..........
Tobacco—smoke........
Baby—powder..........
Moon—sky.............
Scissors—handle......
Quiet—sing...........19

Green—pink………..
Salt—chimney………19
Street—block………
King—crown………..
Cheese—tea………..17
Blossom—leaves…….
Afraid—frighten……

CASE No. 17979.—R.T. Unclassified reactions, mostly incoherent.

Table—full………..19
Dark—coldness…….. 2
Music—aeronaut…….19
Sickness—better……
Man—extension……..19
Deep—electrician…..19
Soft—harden……….. 2
Eating—stomach…….
Mountain—Lord……..19
House—roof………..
Black—darkness…….
Mutton—working…….19
Comfort—ahead……..12
Hand—mercury………19
Short—have………..12
Fruit—flavor………19
Butterfly—plant……13
Smooth—level………
Command—obedient…..
Chair—rest………..
Sweet—polish………19
Whistle—note………
Woman—comfort……..
Cold—pleasant…….. 1
Slow—move…………
Wish—wealth……….
River—shell……….19
White—change………19
Beautiful—sat……..19
Window—temperature…39
Rough—shell……….15
Citizen—soldier……
Foot—travel……….
Spider—web………..

- 35 -

Needle—point.........
Red—temperature......15
Sleep—rest...........
Anger—temper.........
Carpet—court.........10
Girl—birth...........10
High—dirt............19
Working—ease.........
Sour—bait........... 4
Earth—vexation.......19
Trouble—business.....
Soldier—obedient..... 2
Cabbage—fell.........19
Hard—solid...........
Eagle—government.....19
Stomach—chest........
Stem—wish............19
Lamp—brilliancy......17
Dream—unso........... 4
Yellow—color.........
Bread—crust..........
Justice—truth........
Boy—obedient.........
Light—heart.......... 2
Health—feeling.......
Bible—scripture......
Memory—saying........19
Sheep—wool...........
Bath—get.............19
Cottage—morrell...... 4
Swift—good........... 1
Blue—look............19
Hungry—have..........12
Priest—scripture.....15
Ocean—supply.........19
Head—manager.........17
Stove—shake..........19
Long—journey.........
Religion—thought..... 1
Whiskey—lusk......... 4
Child—wish...........15
Bitter—enmalseladiga. 4
Hammer—efface........19

Thirsty—want.........
City—comforts........15
Square—crown.........19
Butter—flavor........15
Doctor—dram..........19
Loud—temper..........15
Thief—catched........ 2
Lion—crown...........15
Joy—pleasure......... 1
Bed—comforts.........
Heavy—thoughts....... 1
Tobacco—changes......15
Baby—pleasure........ 1
Moon—brilliancy...... 2
Scissors—edge........
Quiet—baptism........19
Green—autumn.........19
Salt—gather..........19
Street—thoroughfare..
King—crown...........
Cheese—flavor........15
Blossom—wood.........17
Afraid—downhearted...17

CASE No. 3307.—G.F. Unclassified reactions, mostly incoherent; slight tendency to respond by sound reactions.

Table—desk...........
Dark—blue............
Music—stars..........13
Sickness—trees.......19
Man—menace...........10
Deep—soap............19
Soft—excited.........19
Eating—spelling......10
Mountain—marbles.....19
House—train..........19
Black—bed............19
Mutton—button........10
Comfort—steak........13
Hand—flexible........19
Short—umbrella.......17
Fruit—blanket........19
Butterfly—grass......

Smooth—sheet………19
Command—carpet…….19
Chair—store……….19
Sweet—flower………
Whistle—linen……..19
Woman—water……….19
Cold—coal…………
Slow—ferry………..17
Wish—sample……….19
River—shades………19
Whiter—blue……….
Beautiful—suspender..19
Window—wood……….
Rough—chisel………19
Citizen—ruler……..
Foot—snake………..19
Spider—fly………..
Needle—bird……….13
Red—green…………
Sleep—opening……..19
Anger—angry……….
Carpet—stitching…..19
Girl—madam………..17
High—ceiling………
Working—easy………
Sour—warm…………19
Earth—heaven………
Trouble—astonished…19
Soldier—man……….1
Cabbage—carrot…….
Hard—softness……..2
Eagle—parrot………
Stomach—mind………19
Stem—stable……….10
Lamp—oil………….
Dream—awake……….
Yellow—darkness……2
Bread—rough……….19
Justice—male………19
Boy—buoy………….10
Light—standing…….19
Health—very……….12
Bible—ashamed……..19

Memory—staring……19
Sheep—stock……….
Bath—sponge……….
Cottage—house……..
Swift—mouse……….19
Blue—fall…………19
Hungry—appetite……
Priest—pastor……..
Ocean—waves……….
Head—hat………….
Stove—blackening….. 2
Long—garden……….19
Religion—goodness…. 1
Whiskey—Kummell……17
Child—woman………. 1
Bitter—coughing……19
Hammer—sofa……….19
Thirsty—pillow…….18
City—united……….19
Square—oblong……..
Butter—lard……….
Doctor—physician…..
Loud—easy…………
Thief—burglar……..
Lion—tiger………..
Joy—healthy………. 2
Bed—thread………..10
Heavy—gloves………17
Tobacco—cigar……..
Baby—hood…………11
Moon—stars………..
Scissors—knife…….
Quiet—recollect……17
Green—ring………..19
Salt—pencil……….19
Street—bushes……..19
King—Germany………17
Cheese—rice……….17
Blossom—pepper…….19
Afraid—allspice……18

CASE NO. 971.—O.M. Unclassified reactions, mostly incoherent.

Table—vote………..19
Dark—plenty……….19
Music—health………19
Sickness—fright……
Man—manager……….10
Deep—slow…………19
Soft—pepper……….19
Eating—vanity……..19
Mountains—slept……19
House—courage……..19
Black—funeral……..
Mutton—age………..19
Comfort—slide……..19
Hand—credit……….19

Short—Simpson……..17
Fruit—physician……19
Butterfly—torment….19
Smooth—button……..17
Command—scarf……..19
Chair—rage………..19
Sweet—cider……….17
Whistle—lace………19
Woman—debt………..19
Cold—powderly…….. 4
Slow—telephone…….19
Wish—regret……….17
River—herald………19
White—black……….
Beautiful—jolly……19
Window—pane……….
Rough—duty………..19
Citizen—ward………17
Foot—minister……..19
Spider—handsome……19
Needle—pin………..
Red—white…………
Sleep—apple……….13
Anger—sour………..19
Carpet—wood……….
Girl—boy………….
High—low………….
Working—height…….13
Sour—pitcher………19

- 40 -

Earth—clam……….19
Trouble—necessity…. 9
Soldier—marine…….
Cabbage—watermelon…17
Hard—cracker………17
Eagle—bright………19
Stomach—back………
Stem—stimulant…….10
Lamp—hair…………19
Dream—knees……….19
Yellow—amen……….12
Bread—general……..19
Justice—no……….. 2
Boy—grass…………19
Light—thought…….. 9
Health—depression….17
Bible—judger……… 4
Memory—stomach…….19
Sheep—crusade……..19
Bath—labor………..19
Cottage—cotton…….10
Swift—depth……….19
Blue—crimson………17
Hungry—alloyed…….19
Priest—politicians…17
Ocean—sea…………
Head—cranium………
Stove—soft………..19
Long—biles……….. 4
Religion—bunion……10
Whiskey—vinegar……17
Child—edge………..19
Bitter—born……….10
Hammer—wood……….
Thirsty—cradle…….19
City—flames……….19
Square—eating……..19
Butter—dirt……….19
Doctor—malefactor….19
Loud—quinine………19
Thief—joy…………19
Lion—sage…………19
Joy—thorn…………19

- 41 -

Bed—draper………..19
Heavy—close………..19
Tobacco—weed………
Baby—stop…………19
Moon—starch………..19
Scissors—crepe…….17
Quiet—bustle………19
Green—color………..
Salt—throw………..19
Street—ferment…….19
King—jaunce……….. 4
Cheese—tepid………19
Blossom—woman…….. 9
Afraid—shame………17

CASE No. 01665.—E.H. Unclassified reactions, mostly incoherent.

Table—cent………..19
Dark—sweet………..19
Music—delighted…… 2
Sickness—pop………19
Man—change………..19
Deep—pass…………19
Soft—drop…………19
Eating—fair………..19
Mountains—heavy……19
House—fate………..19
Black—right………..19
Mutton—with………..12
Comfort—indeed…….12
Hand—span…………10
Short—stop………..
Fruit—dip…………19
Butterfly—home…….19
Smooth—days………..19
Command—stop………15
Chair—pledge………19
Sweet—right………..15
Whistle—home………15
Woman—Louisa………17
Cold—chair………..16
Slow—aid………….19
Wish—book………… 2
River—shoes………..19

- 42 -

White—ouch………..12
Beautiful—not……..12
Window—papers……..19
Rough—lettuce……..19
Citizen—money……..17
Foot—stand………..
Spider—socks……….19
Needle—drops……….15
Red—glass…………17
Sleep—suits………..19
Anger—suits……….5
Carpet—hat………..19
Girl—president……..19
High—pass…………19
Working—knock…….19
Sour—cake…………19
Earth—home………..
Trouble—news……….17
Soldier—name……….19
Cabbage—rule……….19
Hard—rope………….19
Eagle—in………….12
Stomach—potato…….17
Stem—pick…………
Lamp—berry………..18
Dream—book………..
Yellow—lettuce…….19
Bread—chews……….17
Justice—night……..15
Boy—bat…………..17
Light—rasp………..19
Health—off………..12
Bible—comforter……2
Memory—candy………19
Sheep—eat…………
Bath—sweet………..19
Cottage—walk………19
Swift—reason……….19
Blue—dot………….19
Hungry—swift……….16
Priest—birth……….19
Ocean—stop………..15
Head—strap………..19

Stove—pot............17
Long—name............
Religion—day.........13
Whiskey—take.........19
Child—jaw............17
Bitter—licorice......17
Hammer—sound.........
Thirsty—cards........19
City—dice............18
Square—muff..........19
Butter—stick.........19
Doctor—perfect.......19
Loud—walk............15
Thief—jail...........
Lion—cow.............
Joy—nail.............19
Bed—new..............19
Heavy—down...........12
Tobacco—prize........19
Baby—new.............15
Moon—new.............
Scissors—teach.......19
Quiet—man............ 1
Green—water..........17
Salt—money...........19
Street—right.........15
King—girl............19
Cheese—house.........19
Blossom—work......... 1
Afraid—jars..........19

CASE M.F. (from Hudson River State Hospital).—Unclassified reactions, mostly incoherent.

Table—heat...........19
Dark—succeed.........19
Music—benefit........19
Sickness—steep.......19
Man—dicut............ 4
Deep—rectify.........19
Soft—bed.............
Eating—dozy..........19
Mountain—tulu........ 4
House—sails..........19

Black—sunrise……..19
Mutton—tuition…….19
Comfort—blasphemous..19
Hand—doing………..
Short—pest………..19
Fruit—charm……….19
Butterfly—doctor…..19
Smooth—border……..19
Command—right……..
Chair—distill……..19
Sweet—noticed……..19
Whistle—stead……..19
Woman—splice………19
Cold—strap………..19
Slow—chief………..19
Wish—shame………..19
River—word………..19
White—color………..
Beautiful—better…..19
Window—dull………..19
Rough—bright………18
Citizen—chum……….19
Foot—relax………..19
Spider—float………19
Needle—action……..19
Red—stout…………19
Sleep—lazy………..17
Anger—anguish……..
Carpet—knowledge…..19
Girl—first………..10
High—hand…………19
Working—power……..17
Sour—mud………….19
Earth—sky…………
Trouble—sorrow…….
Soldier—manhood…… 2
Cabbage—righteous….19
Hard—beaten……….17
Eagle—dog…………19
Stomach—paste……..19
Stem—dust…………10
Lamp—fall…………19
Dream—idle………..17

- 45 -

Yellow—zone..........19
Bread—pan............17
Justice—tricks.......17
Boy—barrel...........19
Light—powers........15
Health—kindness......19
Bible—story..........
Memory—pillow........19
Sheep—veil...........19
Bath—ink.............19
Cottage—paper........19
Swift—arrow..........
Blue—cold............
Hungry—dyes..........19
Priest—cloak.........19
Ocean—pilot..........17
Head—tin.............19
Stove—plate..........17
Long—trouble.........19
Religion—soap........19
Whiskey—starch.......18
Child—night..........19
Bitter—contentment...19

Hammer—shortness.....19
Thirsty—knife........19
City—mind............19
Square—truth......... 2
Butter—biscuit.......
Doctor—piles.........17
Loud—distrust........19
Thief—babies.........19
Lion—hair............
Joy—eyesight.........19

Bed—dievos.......... 4
Heavy—determined.....19
Tobacco—health.......19
Baby—wood............19
Moon—heat............15
Scissors—squeeze.....19
Quiet—tears..........19
Green—fall...........15
Salt—soft............10

- 46 -

Street—wait..........19
King—inches..........19
Cheese—doctor........15
Blossom—fades........19
Afraid—hearts........ 2

CASE No. 01552.—E.J.D. Unclassified reactions, mostly incoherent.

Table—unicorn..........19
Dark—African..........17
Music—love.............
Sickness—slumber.......17
Man—minstrel..........10
Deep—river.............
Soft—highwayman........19
Eating—England.........19
Mountain—pleasure...... 1
House—Christianity.....19
Black—directory........19
Mutton—capers..........19
Comfort—mankind........12
Hand—surface..........19
Short—court............10
Fruit—pleasure.........
Butterfly—dispatcher...19
Smooth—navigation......19
Command—administration. 9
Chair—time.............19
Sweet—office...........13
Whistle—foreign........19
Woman—usefulness.......
Cold—frigid............
Slow—vocation..........19
Wish—longing...........
River—tributary........17
White—island...........
Beautiful—unseen.......19
Window—frugal..........19
Rough—nautical.........19
Citizen—pedestrian.....19
Foot—laugh.............19
Spider—jungle..........19
Needle—man............. 9
Red—monde.............. 4

Sleep—resustication.... 4
Anger—uncared..........19
Carpet—foreign.........15
Girl—celt..............19
High—wine..............10
Working—prayer.........19
Sour—flower............10
Earth—tariff...........19
Trouble—ledger.........19
Soldier—work...........
Cabbage—ancient........19
Hard—provender.........19
Eagle—school...........19
Stomach—bowels.........
Stem—tide..............
Lamp—scientific........19
Dream—somno.............4
Yellow—pain............19
Bread—populous.........19
Justice—thwart.........19
Boy—globe..............19
Light—female...........13
Health—linen...........19
Bible—divine...........17
Memory—current.........19
Sheep—water............
Bath—rain..............18
Cottage—journal........19
Swift—yacht............17
Blue—novel.............19
Hungry—viand........... 2
Priest—pedestrian......15
Ocean—commotion........10
Head—sugar.............19
Stove—writer...........19
Long—mingle............19
Religion—tent..........
Whiskey—copulency...... 4
Child—editor...........19
Bitter—backward........19
Hammer—youth...........19
Thirsty—salt...........17
City—gentler...........19

Square—angelus.........19
Butter—pastry..........17
Doctor—veterinary......17
Loud—muslin............19
Chief—grocer...........19
Lion—trip..............19
Joy—penance............17
Bed—granite............19
Heavy—note.............19
Tobacco—vanese......... 4
Baby—school............15
Moon—element...........19
Scissors—elderly.......19
Quiet—trinity..........19
Green—commissioner.....19
Salt—strength..........19
Street—voyager.........19
King—sorrow............19
Cheese—holiday.........19
Blossom—parks..........19
Afraid—stamina.........17

CASE No. 667.—C.L. Pronounced stereotypy. Following note on test record: "Many attempts were made to secure a reaction other than 'cat,' but usually without success; the reaction *cold—warm* was given spontaneously and with apparent interest; most reactions were given only in response to much urging, or else mechanically, without attention."

Table—cat............ 6
Dark—rat.............18
Music—shoe...........19
Sickness—cat......... 6
Man—boy..............
Deep—cat............. 6
Soft—hat.............19
Eating—cat........... 6
Mountain—hit.........19
House—gold...........19
Black—woman.......... 9
Mutton—get...........19
Comfort—cousin.......19
Hand—Jesus...........19
Short—hat............15
Fruit—hand...........16

Butterfly—going......19
Smooth—hat..........15
Command—boy..........
Chair—hat............15
Sweet—cat............ 6
Whistle—boy..........
Woman—cat............
Cold—warm............
Slow—button..........19
Wish—cat............. 6
River—cat............ 5
White—rat............15
Beautiful—good....... 1
Window—wheel.........19
Rough—good........... 9
Citizen—candy........19
Foot—cat............. 6
Spider—dog...........19
Needle—cat........... 6
Red—button...........15
Sleep—cat............ 6
Anger—go.............15
Carpet—cat........... 6
Girl—in..............12 High—little..........19
Working—cold.........19
Sour—cat............. 6
Earth—tag............19
Trouble—cat.......... 6
Soldier—cat.......... 5
Cabbage—cat.......... 5
Hard—cat............. 5
Eagle—cat............ 5
Stomach—cat..........
Stem—hat.............15
Lamp—cat............. 6
Dream—cat............ 5
Yellow—cat...........
Bread—cat............ 5
Justice—cat.......... 5
Boy—cat.............. 5
Light—cat............ 5
Health—cat........... 5
Bible—cat............ 5

Memory—cat……….. 5
Sheep—cat………… 5
Bath—cat…………. 5
Cottage—cat………. 5
Swift—cat…………
Blue—cat…………. 5
Hungry—cat……….. 5
Priest—cat……….. 5
Ocean—cat………… 5
Head—cat…………. 5
Stove—cat………… 5
Long—cat…………. 5
Religion—cat……… 5
Whiskey—cat………. 5
Child—cat………… 5
Bitter—cat……….. 5
Hammer—cat……….. 5
Thirsty—cat………. 5
City—cat…………. 5
Square—cat……….. 5
Butter—cat……….. 5
Doctor—cat……….. 5
Loud—cat…………. 5
Thief—cat………… 5
Lion—cat………….
Joy—cat………….. 5
Bed—cat………….. 5
Heavy—cat………… 5
Tobacco—cat………. 5
Baby—cat…………. 5
Moon—cat…………. 5
Scissors—cat……… 5
Quiet—cat………… 5
Green—cat………… 5
Salt—cat…………. 5
Street—cat……….. 5
King—cat…………. 5
Cheese—cat……….. 5
Blossom—cat………. 5
Afraid—cat………..

CASE No. 6006.—E.T.S. Stereotypy

Table—eat............
Dark—unkindness......19
Music—beautiful...... 1
Sickness—suffering...
Man—good............. 1
Deep—unkindness......15
Soft—unkindness...... 5
Eating—digesting.....

Mountain—low.........
House—small.......... 1
Black—darkness.......
Mutton—good.......... 1
Comfort—home.........
Hand—useful.......... 1
Short—useful......... 5
Fruit—healthy........
Butterfly—beautiful.. 1
Smooth—unkindness....15
Command—great........ 9
Chair—useful......... 1
Sweet—healthy........15
Whistle—beautiful.... 6
Woman—good........... 1
Cold—unhealthy.......19
Slow—good............ 6
Wish—always..........12
River—needed......... 6
White—pretty......... 1

Beautiful—trees......
Window—needed........ 6
Rough—unneeded....... 4
Citizen—needed....... 6
Foot—needed.......... 2
Spider—needed........ 5
Needle—needed........ 5
Red—beautiful........ 2
Sleep—beautiful...... 1
Anger—needed......... 6
Carpet—needed........ 5
Girl—needed.......... 5
High—height..........
Working—needed....... 6

Sour—needed.......... 5
Earth—needed......... 5
Trouble—trust........10
Soldier—needed....... 6
Cabbage—needed....... 5
Hard—trouble.........
Eagle—beautiful...... 6
Stomach—trouble......
Stem—shoot...........10
Lamp—light...........
Dream—pleasant....... 1
Yellow—pretty........ 1
Bread—good........... 1
Justice—needed....... 6
Boy—needed........... 5
Light—Pretty......... 6
Health—needed........
Bible—needed......... 5
Memory—needed........ 2
Sheep—needed......... 5
Bath—needed.......... 5
Cottage—needed....... 5
Swift—needed......... 5
Blue—pretty.......... 1
Hungry—food..........
Priest—Father........

Ocean—fresh..........19
Head—unhealthy.......15
Stove—warmth.........
Long—length..........
Religion—needed...... 2
Whiskey—needed....... 5
Child—needed.........
Bitter—needed........ 5
Hammer—needed........ 5
Thirsty—water........
City—pretty.......... 6
Square—honest........
Butter—good.......... 1
Doctor—needed........
Loud—needed.......... 5
Thieft—trust.........
Lion—love............19

Joy—laughter………
Bed—comfortable……
Heavy—sleepiness….. 2
Tobacco—needed……. 6
Baby—needed………. 5
Moon—needed………. 5
Scissors—needed…… 5
Quiet—pleasure……. 1
Green—me…………18
Salt—needed……….
Street—needed…….. 5
King—needed………. 5
Cheese—needed…….. 5
Blossom—needed……. 5
Afraid—nervous…….

CASE No. 2292.—C.M. Perseveration: numerous instances of association to preceding reaction; unclassified reactions, mostly incoherent.

Table—tree………..19
Dark—night………..
Music—instrument…..
Sickness—smoke…….19
Man—woman…………. 1
Deep—water………..
Soft—tide…………18
Eating—potato……..
Mountain—milk……..13
House—clay………..17
Black—polish………17
Mutton—goat……….
Comfort—cream……..10
Hand—hay………….19
Short—meat………..19
Fruit—pears……….
Butterfly—flower…..
Smooth—smell………10
Command—drink……..19
Chair—wine………..18
Sweet—honey……….
Whistle—wind………
Woman—whiskey……..19

Cold—fire…………
Slow—speed………..

Wish—go…………..
River—boat………..
White—stem………..13
Beautiful—cloak……17
Window—drift………19
Rough—storm………..
Citizen—citron…….10
Foot—feed………….19
Spider—web………..
Needle—thread……..
Red—sew…………..13
Sleep—rest………..
Anger—health………13
Carpet—carrots…….10
Girl—eat………….19
High—horse………..19
Working—hay………..15
Sour—cut………….19
Earth—machine……..19
Trouble—repair…….18
Soldier—mow………..19
Cabbage—plant……..
Hard—seed………….18
Eagle—bird………..
Stomach—egg………..17
Stem—join…………
Lamp—oil………….
Dream—burn………..13
Yellow—gas………..18
Bread—flour………..
Justices—drink…….19
Boy—girl………….
Light—man………… 9
Health—woman……… 1
Bible—baby………..10
Memory—want……….19
Sheep—lamb………..
Bath—water………..
Cottage—hay………..15
Swift—corn………..18
Blue—eat………….18
Hungry—ham………..17
Priest—pickle……..18

Ocean—turnip.........18
Head—hair............
Stove—coal...........
Long—wood............13
Religion—lemon.......10
Whiskey—wheat........17
Child—rye............18
Bitter—medicine......
Hammer—nail..........
Thirsty—beer.........
City—cake............19
Square—pie...........18
Butter—cream.........
Doctor—herb..........19
Loud—duck............19
Thief—feathers.......18
Lion—animal..........
Joy—peace............
Bed—sleep............
Heavy—rest...........13
Tobacco—chew.........
Baby—chair...........19
Moon—sun.............
Scissors—cut.........
Quiet—hair...........18
Green—grapes.........
Salt—bag.............19
Street—stone.........
King—cement..........18
Cheese—money.........19
Blossom—flower.......
Afraid—fast..........19

CASE No. 17880.—E.D. Numerous repetitions of reactions previously given; unclassified reactions, mostly incoherent; neologisms.

Table—eating.........
Dark—night...........
Music—piano..........
Sickness—stoppery.... 4
Man—manly............
Deep—knowing......... 6
Soft—undoable........ 4
Eating—oblong........19

- 56 -

Mountain—guide.......19
House—residing....... 2
Black—dress..........
Mutton—aiding........19
Comfort—escorted..... 6
Hand—escorted........ 5
Short—unescorted.....18
Fruit—eating.........
Butterfly—interfere..19
Smooth—knowing....... 6
Command—unerrorer.... 4
Chair—seated.........
Sweet—durable........19
Whistle—treated......19
Woman—help........... 2
Cold—stoppery........ 4
Slow—unknowing....... 4
Wish—treated.........15
River—boats..........
White—treasurer......19
Beautiful—form.......
Window—outlook.......
Rough—unescorted.....15
Citizen—residing..... 2
Foot—travel..........
Spider—stoppery...... 4
Needle—clothing...... 2
Red—color............
Sleep—stoppery....... 4
Anger—unguarded......17
Carpet—residence.....15
Girl—help............ 6
High—escorted........ 6
Working—man.......... 1
Sour—form............15
Earth—platformer..... 4
Trouble—unguarded....15
Soldier—sentinel..... 2
Cabbage—dinners...... 2
Hard—escorted........ 6
Eagle—newspaper......17
Stomach—health.......
Stem—winding.........

- 57 -

Lamp—reading………
Dream—guarded……..19
Yellow—aged……….19
Bread—knowing…….. 6
Justice—bar……….17
Boy—help…………. 6
Light—advice………19
Health—doableness…. 4
Bible—church………
Memory—knowing……. 2
Sheep—aided……….15
Bath—stoppery…….. 4
Cottage—seashore…..
Swift—business…….17
Blue—help………… 6
Hungry—unadded……. 4
Priest—Rome……….19
Ocean—help……….. 6
Head—knowing……… 2
Stove—cooking……..
Long—bank…………19
Religion—church……
Whiskey—drink……..
Child—help……….. 6
Bitter—error………16
Hammer—builder……. 2
Thirsty—drink……..
City—building……..
Square—unerrorer….. 4
Butter—eating……..
Doctor—destroyer…..10
Loud—notoriety…….17
Thief—error……….15
Lion—lord…………19
Joy—escorted……… 6
Bed—unescorted…….15
Heavy—unescorted….. 5
Tobacco—chewing……
Baby—help………… 6
Moon—knowing……… 6
Scissors—tailor……
Quiet—form………..15
Green—moneyed……..19

- 58 -

Salt—eating..........
Street—city..........
King—adds............19
Cheese—eating........
Blossom—escorted….. 6
Afraid—unguarded…..15

CASE No. 6065.—A.F. Unclassified reactions, mostly incoherent; perseveration: instances of association to preceding reaction and to preceding stimulus.

Table—stove..........19
Dark—clear..........19
Music—calm...........19
Sickness—exact.......19
Man—particular.......18
Deep—personal........18
Soft—frank..........19
Eating—determined....19
Mountain—idea........19
House—street........
Black—water..........
Mutton—ground........19
Comfort—country......18
Hand—fire............19
Short—straight.......10
Fruit—flowers........
Butterfly—horn.......19
Smooth—farm..........19
Command—forbidden.... 2
Chair—bed............
Sweet—sugar..........
Whistle—noise........
Woman—boy............
Cold—house..........13
Slow—store..........14
Wish—work...........19
River—sound.........17
White—blue..........
Beautiful—fair.......
Window—door..........
Rough—glass.........13
Citizen—dress.......19
Foot—exact..........15

- 59 -

Spider—fly………..
Needle—pins………..
Red—person……….. 9
Sleep—nervous……..17
Anger—determined…..15
Carpet—floor………
Girl—man…………. 1
High—fruit………..19
Working—wear………10
Sour—sweet………..
Earth—early………..10
Trouble—state……..19
Soldier—girl………18
Cabbage—woman…….. 9
Hard—heart………..
Eagle—bird………..
Stomach—friend…….19
Stem—tree…………
Lamp—couch………..19
Dream—desk………..19
Yellow—table………
Bread—chair………..14
Justice—truth……..
Boy—honor…………13
Light—tails………..19
Health—care………..
Bible—book………..
Memory—remembrance…
Sheep—free………..19
Bath—court………..19
Cottage—pitcher……19
Swift—strong………
Blue—delicate……..18
Hungry—bread………
Priest—church……..
Ocean—ship………..
Head—height……….. 2
Stove—people……… 9
Long—heart………..15
Religion—Catholic….
Whiskey—Brooklyn…..19
Child—New York…….18
Bitter—frost………19

- 60 -

Hammer—summer……..10
Thirsty—fall……….18
City—autumn………..18
Square—winter……..18
Butter—daily……….19
Doctor—midnight……19
Loud—forenoon……..18
Thief—afternoon……18
Lion—evening……….18
Joy—sorrow………..
Bed—obstinate……..19
Heavy—indifferent….19
Tobacco—pipe……….
Baby—mother………..
Moon—daughter……..18
Scissors—son……….18
Quiet—sister……….18
Queen—brother……..18
Salt—forward……….19
Street—proper……..19
King—vulgar………..18
Cheese—personal……15
Blossom—tree……….
Afraid—fear………..

CASE No. 17188.—G.B. Sound reactions; unclassified reactions, mostly incoherent

Table—tablet……….10
Dark—dot…………..10
Music—Lizzie……….19
Sickness—Josh……..17
Man—McMahon………..10
Deep—deaf (deef)…..10
Soft—sulphur……….10
Eating—itching…….10
Mountain—mouth…….10
House—horse………..10
Black—back…………10
Mutton—button……..10
Comfort—community….10
Hand—hat…………..10
Short—shore……….10
Fruit—Freehoff…….10

Butterfly—busty…… 3
Smooth—small……… 1
Command—Cummings…..10
Chair—cherries…….10
Sweet—sweeten…….. 8
Whistle—Walters……19
Woman—wayman………10
Cold—laboratory……19
Slow—slaw…………10
Wish—wishbone……..
River—Ontario……..17
White—William……..19
Beautiful—bureau…..10
Window—Weldon……..10
Rough—saw…………17
Citizen—Sendow…….17
Foot—hoof…………17
Spider—web………..
Needle—shoe……….19
Red—book………….
Sleep—sitting……..19
Anger—Freeman……..19
Carpet—longing…….19
Girl—gone…………19
High—law………….19
Working—back………15
Sour—clock………..19
Earth—flower………
Trouble—sensibility..17
Soldier—sodder…….10
Cabbage—Cabot……..10
Hard—done………… 2
Eagle—time………..19
Stomach—mat……….19
Stem—water………..
Lamp—florist………19
Dream—Conners……..19
Yellow—flower……..
Bread—water……….
Justice—Gaynor…….17
Boy—passion……….19
Light—life………..
Health—wealth……..

Bible—gone..........15
Memory—Hans..........19
Sheep—pasture……..
Bath—Rogan...........19
Cottage—house……..
Swift—swim...........10
Blue—Thompson……..19
Hungry—memory……..18
Priest—golden……..18
Green—hat............15
Head—broom...........19
Stove—fan............19
Long—time............
Religion—Yukon.......19
Whiskey—Freeman......15
Child—Hopkins……..17
Bitter—brown.........19
Hammer—hands.........19
Thirsty—thirty.......10
City—sure............19
Square—squire……..10
Butter—Tam O'Shanter.10
Doctor—Dorsan……..10
Loud—law.............15
Thief—child..........19
Lion—dirty...........19
Joy—commerce.........19
Bed—strike...........19
Heavy—Walden.........19
Tobacco—Alice……..19
Baby—water...........15
Moon—handsome……..19
Scissors—comet.......19
Quiet—tiger..........19
Green—tree………..
Salt—salary..........10
Street—prunes……..19
King—kind............19
Cheese—handsome......15
Blossom—pretty....... 1
Afraid—Africa……..10

CASE No. 6238.—M.H. Sound reactions; unclassified reactions, mostly incoherent.

Table—token..........19
Dark—dye.............17
Music—meat...........10
Sickness—sorrow......
Man—mother...........17
Jeep—dark............
Soft—silk............
Eating—elephant......19
Mountain—many........10
House—home...........
Black—brown..........
Mutton—men...........10
Comfort—cat..........10
Hand—hat.............10
Short—shift..........10
Fruit—free...........10
Butterfly—baby.......19
Smooth—soft..........
Command—cat..........10
Chair—comfort........
Sweet—sugar..........
Whistle—wine.........19
Woman—when...........10
Cold—cat.............15
Slow—short...........
Wish—when............12
River—Rhine..........
White—when...........10
Beautiful—baby.......
Window—wide..........
Rough—red............19
Citizen—company......19
Foot—feeling.........19
Spider—speck.........10
Needle—nothing.......18
Red—rose.............
Sleep—should.........12
Anger—after..........10
Carpet—cat...........10
Girl—God.............19
High—heaven..........
Working—will......... 2
Sour—sweet...........

- 64 -

Earth—eaten..........14
Trouble—tea..........10
Soldier—sailor.......
Cabbage—cobweb.......19
Hard—haven't.........12
Eagle—eaten..........15
Stomach—sat..........10
Stem—should..........12
Lamp—little..........19
Dream—did............12
Yellow—you...........10
Bread—butter.........
Justice—Jesus........10
Boy—baby.............
Light—love...........14
Health—heaven........
Bible—bitch..........19
Memory—man........... 1
Sheep—shepherd.......
Bath—both............10
Cottage—cat..........10
Swift—said...........19
Blue—bad............. 9
Hungry—haven't.......12
Priest—Pope..........
Ocean—open...........10
Head—heart...........
Stove—steel..........
Long—little..........15
Religion—right.......
Whiskey—when.........12
Child—chimney........19
Bitter—both..........19
Hammer—heart.........15
Thirsty—think........ 9
City—church..........17
Square—swift.........19
Butter—bread.........
Doctor—debtor........10
Loud—loaf............19
Thief—theatre........10
Lion—liar............10
Joy—jam..............19

Bed—broom............19
Heavy—hard...........
Tobacco—Tom..........19
Baby—brother.........17
Moon—men............. 2
Scissors—shift.......10
Quiet—quilt..........10
Green—grass..........
Salt—said............19
Street—Stevens.......10
King—kite............19
Cheese—cat...........15
Blossom—bad.......... 9
Afraid—anger.........

CASE No. 12720.—J.B. Unclassified reactions, many of which are probably due to distraction; some stereotypy. Note on test record states: "Influenced by sensory impressions, but gave good attention to each stimulus word. Had some difficulty in limiting his response to one word, but made all possible effort to comply with every request. On one occasion he was asked to react with his eyes closed, but was unable, under the unnatural conditions, to respond with one word."

Table—floor..........
Dark—light...........
Music—shoe...........19
Sickness—well........
Man—boy..............
Deep—sea.............
Soft—soap............
Eating—tea...........17
Mountain—forest......17
House—horse..........10
Black—sill..........19
Mutton—tablecloth....17
Comfort—black........16
Hand—fingers.........
Short—wrist..........13
Fruit—soup...........17
Butterfly—grape......13
Smooth—coat..........
Command—vest.........18
Chair—pillow.........19
Sweet—brick..........19

Whistle—knuckles…..19
Woman—wall………..19
Cold—eating………..19
Slow—swift………..
Wish—knob………….19
River—pad………….19
White—book………..19
Beautiful—shadow….. 6
Window—stockings…..19
Bough—stand………..19
Citizen—blue……….19
Foot—brass………...19
Spider—shoelace……19
Needle—name………..19
Red—sunlight……….19
Sleep—flag………...18
Anger—slant………..19
Carpet—rip………...19
Girl—lady………….
High—stripe………..19
Working—steam……..17
Sour—handkerchief….19
Earth—ground………
Trouble—insect…….19
Soldier—army………
Cabbage—sill………15
Hard—washstand…….19
Eagle—blue………..15
Stomach—tap……….19
Stem—sill…………15
Lamp—back………….19
Dream—shadow……… 2
Yellow—blanket…….19
Bread—horizontal…..19
Justice—ink……….19
Boy—taste…………19
Light—yellow………
Health—book………..19
Bible—Joseph………17
Memory—Joe………...18
Sheep—pillow………19
Bath—Mott………….19
Cottage—globe……..19

Swift—continue.......19
Blue—notice..........19
Hungry—Josephine.....19
Priest—sixteen.......12
Ocean—flag...........15
Head—cabbage.........
Stove—rivet..........17
Long—floor...........19
Religion—priest......
Whiskey—tin..........19
Child—shadow......... 6
Bitter—black.........15
Hammer—buttons.......15
Thirsty—shadow....... 6
City—back............15
Square—oval..........
Butter—table.........
Doctor—doorway.......10
Loud—shadow.......... 6
Thief—butter.........16
Lion—difference......19
Joy—ink..............15
Bed—butter...........15
Heavy—shadow......... 6
Tobacco—wood.........13
Baby—wall............15
Moon—lightning.......17
Scissors—book........15
Quiet—yellow.........15
Green—sole...........19
Salt—ink.............15
Street—sides.........19
King—stripes.........19
Cheese—butter........
Blossom—trees........
Afraid—boy...........

CASE No. 5374.—J.F. Perseveration; some stereotypy; sound reactions; unclassified reactions many of which are probably due to distraction. Note on test record states: "Understood what was expected, but could not be induced to give much attention to the stimulus words; sat facing a window, and showed a strong tendency to merely name objects in sight. Reaction time very short, in some cases so short that it is doubtful if he recognized the stimulus word at all."

Table—God............19
Dark—angel...........18
Music—bird..........
Sickness—woman....... 9
Man—male.............
Deep—dove............19
Soft—dog.............19
Eating—horse.........18
Mountain—mule........18
House—dog............
Black—rabbit.........18
Mutton—hen...........18
Comfort—dog..........15
Hand—clock...........
Short—myself.........
Fruit—post...........19
Butterfly—bricks.....19
Smooth—glass.........
Command—sand.........10
Chair—leaf...........19
Sweet—wood...........19
Whistle—earth........19
Woman—grass..........14
Cold—mustard.........19
Slow—kale............19
Wish—lampsquob....... 4
River—ten............12
White—rock...........17
Beautiful—water......17
Window—scene.........
Rough—been...........12
Citizen—house........13
Foot—stable.......... 2
Spider—horse.........13
Needle—pin...........
Red—cushion..........18
Sleep—black..........13
Anger—white..........14
Carpet—vingency...... 4
Girl—noodles.........19
High—macaroni........18
Working—tomatoes.....18
Sour—asparagus.......18

Earth—oakry.......... 4
Trouble—peas.........19
Soldier—beans........18
Cabbage—greens.......
Hard—cow.............19
Eagle—robin..........
Stomach—hawk.........13
Stem—fishes..........19
Lamp—whale...........18
Dream—shark..........18
Yellow—crabs.........18
Bread—red............10
Justice—jam..........19
Boy—be............... 2
Light—girl...........13
Health—filth.........10
Bible—book...........
Memory—bad........... 1
Sheep—dat............ 4
Bath—oval............19
Cottage—nurse........19
Swift—begin..........19
Blue—joy.............19
Hungry—wonder........10
Priest—apostle.......17
Ocean—preacher.......13
Head—dead............10
Stove—store..........10
Long—lone............10
Religion—world.......19
Whiskey—whisper......10
Child—gule........... 4
Bitter—Rugby.........19
Hammer—ball..........18
Thirsty—sun..........19
City—Christ..........10
Square—Jesus.........18
Butter—Joe...........19
Doctor—John..........17
Loud—Luke............18
Thief—St. Matthew....18
Lion—lie.............10
Joy—George...........10

- 70 -

Bed—Beth.............10
Heavy—tither......... 4
Tobacco—iron.........13
Baby—blade...........10
Moon—stars...........
Scissors—sun.........13
Quiet—wired..........10
Green—mean...........10
Salt—Lou.............19
Street—vault.........19
King—sepulchre.......18
Cheese—Presbyterian..19
Blossom—Baptist......18
Afraid—Methodist.....18

CASE No. 1431.—A.L. Sound reactions; particles; unclassified reactions, mostly incoherent.

Table—ammitting...... 4
Dark—cat.............
Music—hello..........12
Sickness—spelling....19
Man—then.............12
Deep—heap............10
Soft—deep............ 7
Eating—people........ 1
Mountain—striking....19
House—pat............19
Black—and............12
Mutton—it............12
Comfort—herself......12
Hand—self............19
Short—length.........
Fruit—long...........13
Butterfly—quick......19
Smooth—edges.........19
Command—first........17
Chair—exact..........19
Sweet—nicest......... 2
Whistle—thistle......10
Woman—pins...........19
Cold—waving..........19
Slow—swift...........
Wish—choice..........17

- 71 -

River—never..........10
White—black..........
Beautiful—much.......19
Window—such..........19
Rough—exact..........15
Citizen—just.........
Foot—root............10
Spider—diving........19
Needle—Hercules......19
Red—green............
Sleep—deep...........
Anger—grief..........
Carpet—cheap.........19
Girl—ink.............19
High—I...............10
Working—loafing......
Sour—hour............10
Earth—hurt...........10
Trouble—bubble.......10
Soldier—yes..........12
Cabbage—garbage......10
Hard—hitting.........17
Eagle—fitting........19
Stomach—pitting......19
Stem—condemned.......10
Lamp—stamp...........10
Dream—stained........19
Yellow—purple........
Bread—pimple.........19
Justice—suit.........17
Boy—ahoy.............12
Light—night..........
Health—wealth........
Bible—indeed.........12
Memory—remembering...
Sheep—cow............
Bath—sponge..........
Cottage—people....... 1
Swift—left...........10
Blue—shift...........19
Hungry—property......19
Priest—judge......... 2
Ocean—river..........

Head—sea............13
Stove—Venus..........19
Long—hog.............19
Religion—pigeon......10
Whiskey—gin..........
Child—thing..........19
Bitter—better........10
Hammer—happy......... 9
Thirsty—whiskey......17
City—fitting.........10
Square—round.........
Butter—shut..........10
Doctor—exercise......19
Loud—accounts........10
Thief—endless........19
Lion—tiger...........
Joy—fast.............19
Bed—grass............19
Heavy—heaving........10
Tobacco—queen........19
Baby—water...........19
Moon—room............19
Scissors—pants.......17
Quiet—razor..........13
Green—steel..........18
Salt—sharp...........
Street—fence.........19
King—bring...........10
Cheese—eggs..........
Blossom—see..........19
Afraid—awaiting......19

CASE No. 6251.—C.D. Some stereotypy; particles; unclassified reactions, mostly incoherent.

Table—doctor.........19
Dark—nigger..........17
Music—violin.........
Sickness—whores......19
Man—Mulcane..........17
Deep—deaf............19
Soft—hearing.........18
Eating—pillow........13
Mountain—sight.......19

- 73 -

House—pure………..19
Black—nigger………
Mutton—plenty…….. 6
Comfort—middle…….19
Hand—left………..17
Short—one………..12
Fruit—up………….12
Butterfly—bird…….
Smooth—never……… 6
Command—commodore….10
Chair—seat………..
Sweet—sugar……….
Whistle—highest……19
Woman—Constance……17
Cold—temperature…..
Slow—walk…………
Wish—wishbone……..
River—love………..19
White—Dr. White……17
Beautiful—pretty….. 1
Window—dove……….19
Rough—fine……….. 1
Citizen—United States
Foot—left…………15
Spider—web………..
Needle—ether………19
Red—pot…………..
Sleep—wake………..
Anger—mad…………
Carpet—pretty…….. 1
Girl—boy………….
High—Heidel……….10
Working—never……..
Sour—sweet………..
Earth—bride……….19
Trouble—mischief…..
Soldier—war……….
Cabbage—head………
Hard—never……….. 6
Eagle—fly…………
Stomach—go………..19
Stem—study………..10
Lamp—light………..

Dream—behave.........19
Yellow—false........19
Bread—plenty......... 6
Justice—just.........
Boy—come.............19
Light—Davie..........19
Health—wealth........
Bible—Constance......15
Memory—fine.......... 1
Sheep—plenty......... 6
Bath—bother..........10
Cottage—mansion......
Swift—hurry..........
Blue—flowers......... 2
Hungry—never.........
Priest—highest....... 2
Ocean—land...........
Head—millionaire.....19
Stove—twenty-five....12
Long—thirty-four.....12
Religion—churches....
Whiskey—plenty....... 6
Child—baby...........
Bitter—sorrow........
Hammer—court.........19
Thirsty—blood........11
City—this............12
Square—I.............12
Butter—plenty........ 6
Doctor—millionaire...15
Loud—tell............17
Thief—rich..........19
Lion—west............19
Joy—ever.............12
Bed—Constance........15
Heavy—fine........... 9
Tobacco—back.........10
Baby—millionaire.....15
Moon—always..........12
Scissors—large....... 9
Quiet—stay...........19
Green—flowers........
Salt—perfume.........18

- 75 -

Street—floor........19
King—Haaken.........19
Cheese—kiss.........19
Blossom—flower.......
Afraid—never........

CASE No. 17607.—P.D. Test record somewhat approaching the normal: 24 individual reactions, of which 16 are unclassified, mostly "far fetched" and not strictly incoherent. Patient is a well-marked case of dementia præcox but only moderately deteriorated; works well at the hospital.

Table—oak..............
Dark—brown.............
Music—falsetto.........17
Sickness—typhoid.......
Man—gender.............19
Deep—feet..............19
Soft—feeling...........
Eating—partaking.......19
Mountain—hunter........19
House—dwelling.........
Black—color............
Mutton—sheep...........
Comfort—coziness....... 2
Hand—anatomy...........
Short—stature..........
Fruit—apples...........
Butterfly—insect.......
Smooth—plain...........
Command—order..........
Chair—furniture........
Sweet—sugar............
Whistle—steam..........
Woman—sex..............
Cold—degree............
Slow—speedless.........
Wish—expression........
River—Amazon...........
White—pulp.............17
Beautiful—description..
Window—opaque..........19
Rough—uncouth..........
Citizen—qualification..19
Foot—anatomy...........

Spider—bug.............
Needle—steel...........
Red—color..............
Sleep—slumber..........
Anger—aroused..........
Carpet—texture......... 2
Girl—female............
High—up................
Working—doing..........
Sour—lemon.............
Earth—dirt.............
Trouble—distress.......
Soldier—uniform........
Cabbage—crop...........19
Hard—metal.............
Eagle—bird.............
Stomach—anatomy........
Stem—pipe..............
Lamp—glass.............
Dream—atmosphere.......19
Yellow—color...........
Bread—flour............
Justice—equality.......
Boy—male...............
Light—sun..............
Health—color...........
Bible—nonsense.........19
Memory—retentiveness... 2
Sheep—quadruped........
Bath—water.............
Cottage—stories........19
Swift—speed............
Blue—navy..............
Hungry—appetite........
Priest—uniform.........15
Ocean—Atlantic.........
Head—stature..........15
Stove—iron.............
Long—inches............17
Religion—creed.........
Whiskey—hops...........
Child—neuter..........19
Bitter—horehound.......17

Hammer—steel..........
Thirsty—degree.........15
City—population........
Square—sides..........
Butter—cream..........
Doctor—physician.......
Loud—noise............
Thief—characterization.19
Lion—menagerie.........
Joy—openness...........19
Bed—furniture..........
Heavy—weight..........
Tobacco—plant..........
Baby—egg...............19
Moon—astronomy.........
Scissors—blades........
Quiet—noiseless........
Green—Paris............11
Salt—crystal...........17
Street—lane............
King—usurper...........19
Cheese—milk............
Blossom—bud............
Afraid—scared..........

CASE No. 5537.—J.H. Test record approaching the normal: 21 individual reactions, 8 classed as normal, 1 non-specific, 12 unclassified, mostly "far fetched" but not strictly incoherent. Well-marked dementia præcox, but of recent origin and but slight deterioration.

Table—eat............
Dark—night..........
Music—pleasure....... 1
Sickness—suffering...
Man—farmer..........17
Deep—low............
Soft—hard............
Eating—life..........
Mountain—earth.......
House—dwelling.......
Black—color..........
Mutton—food..........
Comfort—rest.........
Hand—limb............

Short—small………. 1
Fruit—nourishing…..
Butterfly—flower…..

Smooth—straight……
Command—obey………
Chair—furniture……
Sweet—palate………. 8
Whistle—noise……..
Woman—marriage…….
Cold—indisposed……17
Slow—weary………..19
Wish—work…………. 9
River—tug………….
White—sheets………. 2
Beautiful—rare…….19
Window—ventilation…
Rough—uneven………
Citizen—public…….17
Foot—walk………….
Spider—web………..
Needle—sew………..
Red—marine………… 1
Sleep—repose………
Anger—assault……..17
Carpet—cloth………
Girl—sister……….
High—above………..
Working—labor……..
Sour—bitter……….
Earth—farm………..
Trouble—fight……..
Soldier—duty………
Cabbage—vegetable….
Hard—stone………..
Eagle—large………. 1
Stomach—body………
Stem—leaf…………
Lamp—light………..
Dream—unconsciousness
Yellow—flag……….
Bread—hunger………
Justice—freedom……
Boy—school………..

Light—electricity….
Health—business……19
Bible—religion…….
Memory—brain………
Sheep—pasture……..
Bath—clean………..
Cottage—property…..17
Swift—current……..
Blue—uniform………17
Hungry—appetite……
Priest—church……..
Ocean—commerce…….19
Head—thought……… 1
Stove—iron………..
Long—distance……..
Religion—belief……
Whiskey—alcohol……
Child—parent………
Bitter—taste………
Hammer—trade………19
Thirsty—beverage…..
City—position……..19
Square—block………
Butter—yellow……..
Doctor—profession….
Loud—fiddle……….17
Thief—police………
Lion—Africa……….
Joy—sensation……..
Bed—rest………….
Heavy—burden………
Tobacco—store……..19
Baby—care…………
Moon—atmosphere……
Scissors—dressmaker..
Quiet—lonesome…….
Green—color……….
Salt—house………..19
Street—neighborhood..17
King—beast………..19
Cheese—merchant……19
Blossom—flowers……
Afraid—train………10

- 80 -

CASE No. 6190.—L.L. Test record not distinguishable from normal. Case of recent onset, with little, if any deterioration.

Table—chair..........
Dark—light...........
Music—note...........
Sickness—health......
Man—woman............ 1
Deep—shallow.........
Soft—hard...........
Eating—breakfast.....
Mountain—rock........
House—chimney........
Black—white..........
Mutton—animal........
Comfort—chair........
Hand—foot............
Short—long..........
Fruit—ripe..........
Butterfly—fields.....
Smooth—hard..........
Command—army.........
Chair—straw..........19
Sweet—bitter.........
Whistle—engine.......
Woman—man............ 1
Cold—hot.............
Slow—fast............
Wish—desire..........
River—brook..........
White—black..........
Beautiful—girl.......
Window—glass.........
Rough—smooth.........
Citizen—city.........
Foot—ankle...........
Spider—web...........
Needle—cotton........
Red—brick............
Sleep—night..........
Anger—joy............
Carpet—cloth.........
Girl—mouth..........17
High—low.............

Working—idle………
Sour—vinegar………
Earth—round……….
Trouble—sickness…..
Soldier—gun……….
Cabbage—garden…….
Hard—rock…………
Eagle—fly…………
Stomach—man………. 1
Stem—watch………..
Lamp—oil………….
Dream—sleep……….
Yellow—sunflower…..
Bread—butter………
Justice—peace……..
Boy—girl………….
Light—window………
Health—man……….. 1
Bible—God…………
Memory—mind……….
Sheep—pasture……..
Bath—water………..
Cottage—trees……..
Swift—engine………
Blue—sky………….
Hungry—bread………
Priest—church……..
Ocean—ships……….
Head—mind…………
Stove—chimney……..
Long—wind…………19
Religion—God………
Whiskey—alcohol……
Child—mother………
Bitter—fruit………
Hammer—nails………
Thirsty—water……..
City—cars…………
Square—angles……..
Butter—cow………..
Doctor—sickness……
Loud—noise………..
Thief—sinner……… 2

Lion—jungle..........
Joy—gladness.........
Bed—pillow...........
Heavy—iron………..
Tobacco—leaf.........
Baby—mother..........
Moon—stars………..
Scissors—thread......
Quiet—room………..
Green—grass..........
Salt—ocean………..
Street—men………..15
King—queen………..
Cheese—butter……..
Blossom—bud..........
Afraid—coward……..

CASE No. 1278.—B.B. Test record not distinguishable from normal. Case of several years standing, but showing almost complete remission of all symptoms.

Table—chair..........
Dark—day………….
Music—instrument…..
Sickness—health……
Man—woman…………. 1
Deep—thoughts…….. 1
Soft—apple………..
Eating—food..........
Mountain—rock……..
House—building…….
Black—dark………..
Mutton—meat..........
Comfort—home………
Hand—from…………12
Short—stout..........
Fruit—eating.........
Butterfly—bird…….
Smooth—glossy……..
Command—general……
Chair—floor..........
Sweet—taste..........
Whistle—tune………
Woman—man…………. 1

- 83 -

Cold—chilly..........
Slow—fast...........
Wish—something.......
River—water..........
White—black..........
Beautiful—pretty.....
Window—pane..........
Rough—ugly...........
Citizen—papers.......
Foot—shoe............
Spider—bug...........
Needle—thread........
Red—white............
Sleep—slumber........
Anger—kindness.......
Carpet—mat...........
Girl—boy.............
High—short...........
Working—idle.........
Sour—sweet...........
Earth—land...........
Trouble—sorrow.......
Soldier—hero.........
Cabbage—turnip.......
Hard—soft............
Eagle—owl............
Stomach—head.........
Stem—pipe............
Lamp—cover..........19
Dream—sleep..........
Yellow—brown.........
Bread—biscuit........
Justice—peaceful..... 2
Boy—girl.............
Light—dark...........
Health—well..........
Bible—book...........
Memory—lost.......... 2
Sheep—animal.........
Bath—wash............
Cottage—house........
Swift—movements...... 2
Blue—red.............

Hungry—thirst……..
Priest—minister……
Ocean—sea………….
Head—body…………
Stove—iron………..
Long—length……….
Religion—too……….12
Whiskey—drink……..
Child—baby………..
Bitter—taste………
Hammer—nails……….
Thirsty—drink……..
City—town………….
Square—man……….. 1
Butter—bread………
Doctor—patient…….
Loud—howl………….17
Thief—steal……….
Lion—bear…………
Joy—happiness…….. 1
Bed—blanket……….
Heavy—weight……….
Tobacco—smoke……..
Baby—cradle……….
Moon—sun………….
Scissors—thimble…..
Quiet—stillness……
Green—plaid……….17
Salt—pepper……….
Street—sidewalk……
King—queen………..
Cheese—crackers……
Blossom—leaf………
Afraid—frightened….

PARANOIC CONDITIONS.

The clinical group of psychoses included under the designation paranoic conditions is far from being homogeneous. We have here cases that are more or less closely allied to the paranoid form of dementia præcox, other cases that are apparently dependent upon involutional changes (Kraepelin's *praeseniler Beeinträchtigungswah*), still other cases that are characterized by absence or at least delay of mental deterioration, etc.

In some of these cases disturbance of the flow of utterance is not observed, and the test records obtained from them present no striking abnormalities. Distinctly pathological records are obtained mainly from those cases which clinically resemble dementia præcox; in these records the nature of the pathological reactions would seem to indicate that the diagnosis of dementia præcox would be more justifiable than that of paranoic condition.

The following test records will serve to illustrate the types of reactions met with in this group of psychoses:

CASE No. 3039.—F.A. Normal record.

Table—purpose……..19
Dark—obscure………
Music—pleasant……. 1
Sickness—confinement.17
Man—twenty-one…….12
Deep—down…………
Soft—smooth……….
Eating—nourishment…
Mountain—high……..
House—living………
Black—dark………..
Mutton—eating……..
Comfort—pleasant….. 1
Hand—limb…………
Short—low…………
Fruit—eat…………
Butterfly—miller…..
Smooth—soft……….
Command—obey………
Chair—sitting……..
Sweet—tasting……..
Whistle—noise……..
Woman—female………
Cold—unpleasant…… 1
Slow—easy…………
Wish—want…………
River—water……….
White—colorless……
Beautiful—handsome…
Window—glass………
Rough—unpleasant….. 1
Citizen—vote………
Foot—limb…………

Spider—insect……..
Needle—sewing……..
Red—color…………
Sleep—bed…………
Anger—cross………..
Carpet—floor……….
Girl—young………..
High—up…………..
Working—labor……..
Sour—unpleasant…… 1
Earth—dirt………..
Trouble—worriment….
Soldier—fight……..
Cabbage—vegetable….
Hard—tough………..
Eagle—bird………..
Stomach—anatomy……

Stem—growth………..
Lamp—burn…………
Dream—restlessness…
Yellow—color……….
Bread—eat…………
Justice—right……..
Boy—young…………
Light—see…………
Health—well……….
Bible—religion…….
Memory—thoughtful….
Sheep—animal………
Bath—wash…………
Cottage—house……..
Swift—fast………..
Blue—color………..
Hungry—appetite……
Priest—Christian…..17
Ocean—large……….
Head—trunk………..
Stove—fire………..
Long—distance……..
Religion—Christianity
Whiskey—drinkable….
Child—young……….
Bitter—bad………..

Hammer—knock………
Thirsty—dry……….
City—government……
Square—block………
Butter—eat………..
Doctor—cure……….
Loud—noisy………..
Thief—steal……….
Lion—animal……….
Joy—pleasant………
Bed—laying………..
Heavy—weighty……..
Tobacco—smoking……
Baby—new-born……..
Moon—planet……….
Scissors—cutting…..
Quiet—easy………..
Green—color……….
Salt—preservative….
Street—lane……….
King—monarch………
Cheese—eatable…….
Blossom—budding……
Afraid—fear……….

CASE No. 5803.—D.E.D. Slight tendency to give sound reactions.

Table—tree………..19
Dark—bright……….
Music—song………..
Sickness—health……
Man—woman………….
Deep—shallow………
Soft—hard…………
Eating—digesting…..
Mountain—hill……..
House—horse……….10
Black—red…………
Mutton—tallow……..
Comfort—wealth…….
Hand—arm………….
Short—long………..
Fruit—plate……….17
Butterfly—net……..

1

Smooth—surface.......
Command—obey.........
Chair—table..........
Sweet—sour...........
Whistle—call.........
Woman—lady...........
Cold—lukewarm........19
Slow—not.............12
Wish—receive.........
River—lake...........
White—black..........
Beautiful—graceful...
Window—door..........
Rough—smooth.........
Citizen—city.........
Foot—leg.............
Spider—soap..........10
Needle—pin...........
Red—yellow...........
Sleep—slumber........
Anger—amiable........
Carpet—mat...........
Girl—boy.............
High—hill............
Working—playing......
Sour—sweet...........
Earth—land...........
Trouble—tranquillity.10
Soldier—boy..........
Cabbage—plant........
Hard—easy............
Eagle—bird...........
Stomach—bowels.......
Stem—head............
Lamp—chimney.........
Dream—myth...........17
Yellow—blue..........
Bread—biscuit........
Justice—balance......17
Boy—girl.............
Light—gray...........17
Health—wealth........
Bible—prayerbook.....

Memory—understanding.
Sheep—lamb………..
Bath—swim…………
Cottage—house……..
Swift—slow………..
Blue—yellow……….
Hungry—eat………..
Priest—bishop……..
Ocean—river……….
Head—neck…………
Stove—covers………
Long—short………..
Religion—optional….
Whiskey—wine………
Child—baby………..
Bitter—sweet………
Hammer—gimlet……..
Thirsty—drink……..
City—town…………
Square—compass…….
Butter—butterfly…..
Doctor—lawyer……..
Loud—lord…………
Thief—beggar………
Lion—lioness………
Joy—sorrow………..
Bed—couch…………
Heavy—light……….
Tobacco—cigarette….
Baby—child………..
Moon—stars………..
Scissors—knife…….
Quiet—quilt……….
Green—envy………..
Salt—sewing……….
Street—lane……….
King—queen………..
Cheese—cracker…….
Blossom—flower…….
Afraid—courageous….

CASE No. 2133.—M.F. Unclassified reactions, mostly "far fetched" or incoherent; perseveration.

Table—eat............
Dark—night...........
Music—sing...........
Sickness—sadness.....
Man—home.............
Deep—light...........
Soft—sleep...........13
Eating—drink.........
Mountain—hills.......
House—home...........
Black—stove..........17
Mutton—lamb..........
Comfort—pleasure..... 1
Hand—write...........
Short—short-cake.....10
Fruit—grapes.........
Butterfly—butter.....
Smooth—ironing.......
Command—correct......19
Chair—see............19
Sweet—apples.........
Whistle—happiness.... 1
Woman—girl...........
Cold—warm............
Slow—fast............
Wish—like............
River—water..........
White—blue...........
Beautiful—red........13
Window—light.........
Rough—easy...........
Citizen—spring.......19
Foot—run.............
Spider—fly...........
Needle—Carrie........19
Red—pink.............
Sleep—awake..........
Anger—jolly..........19
Carpet—curtains......
Girl—yellow..........19
High—green...........14
Working—bed..........19
Sour—dishes..........19

Earth—grapes.........13
Trouble—work......... 1
Soldier—sing.........15
Cabbage—potatoes…..
Hard—sewing..........17
Eagle—daisy..........19
Stomach—flowers......18
Stem—vine............
Lamp—flatiron........19
Dream—sleep..........
Yellow—awake.........13
Bread—children.......
Justice—dresses......14
Boy—mother...........
Light—dark...........
Health—wealth........
Bible—commands....... 2
Memory—black.........13
Sheep—chickens.......17
Bath—carpet..........19
Cottage—worsted......14
Swift—silk...........18
Blue—cotton..........18
Hungry—chair.........19
Priest—church........
Ocean—spring.........15
Head—canary..........19
Stove—board..........
Long—dishes..........18
Religion—piano.......19
Whiskey—home.........15
Child—baby...........
Bitter—shoes.........19
Hammer—tacks.........
Thirsty—longing......
City—Flushing........17
Square—store.........10
Butter—butcher.......10
Doctor—hat...........19
Loud—chair...........15
Thief—picture........19
Lion—house...........13
Joy—gladness.........

Bed—sleep...........
Heavy—sick........... 2
Tobacco—album........19
Baby—basket..........17
Moon—stars...........
Scissors—knife.......
Quiet—spoon..........18
Green—scar...........19
Salt—pepper..........
Street—sugar.........18
King—blacking........19
Cheese—meat..........
Blossom—flowers......
Afraid—red...........18

CASE No. 4569.—L.K. Marked stereotypy; unclassified reactions, mostly incoherent.

Table—fruit..........17
Dark—light...........
Music—pleasure....... 1
Sickness—illness.....
Man—parent........... 6
Deep—verse...........19
Soft—fruit...........
Eating—illness.......15
Mountain—parent...... 6
House—privilege......19
Black—colors......... 2
Mutton—parent........ 6
Comfort—family.......18
Hand—comfort......... 7
Short—parent......... 6
Fruit—parent......... 5
Butterfly—insect.....
Smooth—surface.......
Command—privilege....15
Chair—house..........
Sweet—dairy..........19
Whistle—nature.......19
Woman—parent......... 6
Cold—house........... 6
Slow—light...........15
Wish—desire..........

- 93 -

River—house.......... 6
White—suspicion......19
Beautiful—house...... 6
Window—light.........
Rough—surface........
Citizen—parent....... 6
Foot—house...........
Spider—insect........
Needle—house......... 6
Red—colors...........
Sleep—God............ 6
Anger—God............ 5
Carpet—house.........
Girl—God............. 6
High—house...........
Working—parent....... 6
Sour—desire..........15
Earth—God............ 6
Trouble—God.......... 5
Soldier—house........ 6
Cabbage—desire.......15
Hard—vegetable.......
Eagle—animal.........
Stomach—doctor.......
Stem—growth..........
Lamp—house...........
Dream—God............ 6
Yellow—color.........
Bread—God............ 6
Justice—fright.......19
Boy—parent........... 6
Light—God............ 6
Health—God........... 5
Bible—teachings......
Memory—teaching...... 2
Sheep—God............ 6
Bath—cleanness.......
Cottage—home.........
Swift—fear...........19
Blue—color...........
Hungry—appetite......
Priest—servant.......
Ocean—God............ 6

- 94 -

Head—servant......... 6
Stove—house..........
Long—God............. 6
Religion—servant..... 6
Whiskey—doctor.......15
Child—house.......... 6
Bitter—taste.........
Hammer—household.....19
Thirsty—drink........
City—God............. 6
Square—touch.........19
Butter—taste.........
Doctor—servant....... 6
Loud—thought......... 9
Thief—slave..........19
Lion—animal..........
Joy—pleasure......... 1
Bed—household........15
Heavy—weight.........
Tobacco—doctor.......15
Baby—care............
Moon—heavens.........
Scissors—household...15
Quiet—nerve..........19
Green—substance......19
Salt—taste...........
Street—heavens.......15
King—servant......... 6
Cheese—taste.........
Blossom—sight........
Afraid—fear..........

CASE No. 6164.—L.E. Remarkably persistent tendency to give sound reactions; numerous sound neologisms; no reactions given in response to some of the stimulus words on the ground that she had "no word to match."

Table—witchhazel.....10
Dark—frog............19
Music—lessons........ 2
Sickness—badness..... 2
Man—wife.............
Deep—seef............ 4
Soft—shoft.......... 3

- 95 -

Eating—feeding.......
Mountain—sounding....10
House—shmouse........ 3
Black—fake...........19
Mutton—shutton....... 3
Comfort—somfort...... 3
Hand—land............10
Short—court..........10
Fruit—shrewd.........10
Butterfly—shuddergy.. 3
Smooth—slude......... 3
Command—noman........ 3
Chair—sash...........19
Sweet—leaf...........19
Whistle—noshissel.... 3
Woman—lemon..........19
Cold—shoal..........10
Slow—snow............10
Wish—dish............
River—liberty........10
White—size...........10
Beautiful—...........
Window—Hilda.........19
Rough—shoff.......... 3
Citizen—shiffizen.... 3
Foot—shoot...........10
Spider—shider........ 3
Needle—dreedle....... 3
Red—shred............10
Sleep—seef.......... 3
Anger—...............
Carpet—shloppet...... 3
Girl—shirl........... 3
High—fie.............10
Working—shlirking.... 3
Sour—bower...........10
Earth—world..........
Trouble—shuttle......19
Soldier—polster...... 3
Cabbage—sheffies..... 4
Hard—shward.......... 3
Eagle—...............
Stomach—.............

Stem—lamp............19
Lamp—sant............ 4
Dream—leam........... 3
Yellow—cherry........19
Bread—dread..........10
Justice—chestnuts....10
Boy—................
Light—shwife......... 3
Health—felt.......... 2
Bible—...............
Memory—..............
Sheep—sheet..........10
Bath—scab............19
Cottage—foppach...... 3
Swift—shift..........10
Blue—shoe............10
Hungry—angry.........
Priest—sheaf.........19
Ocean—notion.........10
Head—shred...........10
Stove—shove.......... 3
Long—song............10
Religion—switching...19
Whiskey—chiston...... 4
Child—kile........... 3
Bitter—shitter....... 3
Hammer—lemon.........13
Thirsty—flrsten...... 3
City—................
Square—birds.........19
Butter—shudder.......10
Doctor—shoctor....... 3
Loud—souse...........10
Thief—sheaf..........10
Lion—Zion............10
Joy—bloy............. 3
Bed—wading...........19
Heavy—shleavy........ 3
Tobacco—confecker.... 4
Baby—savey........... 3
Moon—shoon........... 3
Scissors—............
Quiet—shiet.......... 3

- 97 -

Green—sheel.......... 4
Salt—shawlt.......... 3
Street—freet......... 3
King—sing............10
Cheese—seefs......... 4
Blossom—pleasant..... 9
Afraid—shraid........ 3

CASE No. 3606.—F.W. Neologisms; some particles; many unclassified reactions, mostly incoherent.

Table—pleasure....... 9
Dark—air.............19
Music—walking........19
Sickness—gloves......19
Man—fields...........19
Deep—courtesy........19
Soft—spoons..........19
Eating—oranges.......
Mountain—ice.........17
House—paintings...... 2
Black—blue...........
Mutton—hemisphere....19
Comfort—flowers......19
Hand—sawdust.........19
Short—peanuts........19
Fruit—autoharp.......19
Butterfly—disease....19
Smooth—ice...........
Command—botheration..19
Chair—tea............19
Sweet—arrangement....19
Whistle—steadfast....19
Woman—flowers........15
Cold—grandeur........19
Slow—present.........19
Wish—mania...........19
River—courtesy.......15
White—ink............17
Beautiful—flowers....
Window—air...........
Rough—enjoyment......19
Citizen—queer........19
Foot—hatred..........19

Spider—carousy....... 4
Needle—pleasant...... 9
Red—permit...........19
Sleep—indeed.........12
Anger—benevolence....19
Carpet—disorder......19
Girl—caterer.........19
High—aside...........10
Working—among........12
Sour—destroy.........19
Earth—confusion......19
Trouble—frivolous....19
Soldier—air..........15
Cabbage—temptation...19
Hard—among...........12
Eagle—quality........19
Stomach—debasteur... 4
Stem—counteract......19
Lamp—testament.......19
Dream—connexus....... 4
Yellow—division......19
Bread—atherey........ 4
Justice—anger........19
Boy—quality..........15
Light—among..........12
Health—frivolous.....15
Bible—permit.........15
Memory—usual.........19
Sheep—astray.........
Bath—conscientious...19
Cottage—texalous..... 4
Swift—patience.......19
Blue—community.......19
Hungry—confusion.....15
Priest—second........19
Ocean—apology........19
Head—trinity.........19
Stove—compartment....19
Long—terminal........19
Religion—abundant....19
Whiskey—approvement.. 4
Child—anger..........15
Bitter—courageous....19

Hammer—correction....19
Thirsty—afterwards...12
City—cataract........19
Square—plenty........19
Butter—accost........19
Doctor—southern......19
Loud—triangular......19
Thief—cannery........19
Lion—practice........19
Joy—summons..........19
Bed—avron............ 4
Heavy—olenthegolis... 4
Tobacco—abundant.....15
Baby—parenthus....... 4
Moon—otherwise.......12
Scissors—cartridge...19
Quiet—outside........12
Green—abounty........ 4
Salt—calonry......... 4
Street—abyss.........19
King—cavenry......... 4
Cheese—perplex.......19
Blossom—cartridge....15
Afraid—stubborn......19

EPILEPSY.

Most of the cases of epilepsy in our collection show advanced dementia and in some the clinical history would indicate also original mental inferiority, that is to say, imbecility or feeble-mindedness.

In these cases the dominant characteristic, so far as shown in the test records, seems to be a narrowing of the mental horizon manifested firstly by a tendency to repeat many times one or another word, and secondly by an abnormally pronounced tendency to make use of non-specific reactions or particles of speech. Occasionally other abnormalities are noted, such as perseveration or distraction.

We submit here copies of some test records.

CASE No. 5410.—W.T.K. Repetition of words previously given; nonspecific reactions.

Table—article........ 1
Dark—light...........

Music—tone………..
Sickness—ill………
Man—person……….. 1
Deep—distant……… 2
Soft—condition……. 6
Eating—chew……….
Mountain—high……..
House—abode……….
Black—color……….
Mutton—meat……….
Comfort—peace……..
Hand—limb…………
Short—distance…….
Fruit—result………
Butterfly—animal…..
Smooth—plain………
Command—order……..
Chair—seat………..
Sweet—pleasant……. 1
Whistle—sound……..
Woman—female………
Cold—chilly……….
Slow—pace…………
Wish—desire……….
River—body………..
White—clear……….
Beautiful—grand……
Window—place………13
Rough—unsmooth……. 4
Citizen—member…….
Foot—member……….
Spider—animal……..
Needle—article……. 1
Bed—color…………
Sleep—rest………..
Anger—condition…… 6
Carpet—covering……
Girl—female……….
High—distance……..
Working—occupation…
Sour—condition……. 6
Earth—planet………
Trouble—condition…. 6

Soldier—member……. 6
Cabbage—vegetable….
Hard—condition……. 6
Eagle—animal………
Stomach—member…….
Stem—branch……….
Lamp—article………. 1
Dream—thinking……. 1
Yellow—shade………
Bread—article…….. 6
Justice—position…..19
Boy—male………….
Light—clear……….
Health—condition…..
Bible—book………..
Memory—condition….. 6
Sheep—animal………
Bath—position……..15
Cottage—house……..
Swift—fast………..
Blue—color………..
Hungry—condition….. 6
Priest—office……..
Ocean—body………..
Head—member……….
Stove—article…….. 1
Long—distance……..
Religion—profession..
Whiskey—liquid…….
Child—person………. 1
Bitter—condition….. 6
Hammer—article……. 1
Thirsty—condition…. 6
City—place………..
Square—honest……..
Butter—article……. 6
Doctor—profession….
Loud—sound………..
Thief—position…….15
Lion—animal……….
Joy—pleasant………. 1
Bed—article………. 6
Heavy—weight………

- 102 -

Tobacco—plant……..
Baby—person………. 1
Moon—planet……….
Scissors—article….. 1
Quiet—peaceful…….
Green—shade……….
Salt—article………. 1
Street—place……….
King—ruler………..
Cheese—article……. 6
Blossom—plant……..
Afraid—fear……….

CASE No. 2208.—J.A. Repetition of words previously given; non-specific reactions.

Table—wood………..
Dark—chairs………..13
Music—wood………..14
Sickness—dropsy……17
Man—body………….
Deep—well………….
Soft—lady………….19
Eating—man……….. 6
Mountain—hills…….
House—barns………. 2
Black—horse……….
Mutton—sheep……….
Comfort—poison…….19
Hand—man…………. 1
Short—people………. 1
Fruit—trees……….
Butterfly—tree…….
Smooth—people…….. 6
Command—general……
Chair—hands……….16
Sweet—fruit……….
Whistle—man………. 1
Woman—people………. 1
Cold—ice………….
Slow—people………. 6
Wish—dead………….19
River—lakes……….
White—foam………..17

Beautiful—man........ 1
Window—glass.........
Rough—people......... 6
Citizen—man.......... 1
Foot—people.......... 6
Spider—barn..........15
Needle—clothes.......
Red—blood............
Sleep—bed............
Anger—angry..........
Carpet—stores........19
Girl—ladies.......... 2
High—mountain........
Working—people....... 6
Sour—fruit...........
Earth—clay...........
Trouble—bad.......... 1
Soldier—man.......... 1
Cabbage—field........
Hard—case............19
Eagle—bird...........
Stomach—man.......... 1
Stem—pipe............
Lamp—fire............
Dream—bad............ 1
Yellow—chair.........15
Bread—rye............
Justice—right........
Boy—bad.............. 1
Light—ship..........19
Health—pig..........19
Bible—man........... 6
Memory—mind..........
Sheep—mutton.........
Bath—water...........
Cottage—house........
Swift—ship..........15
Blue—lines..........17
Hungry—people........ 6
Priest—man.......... 1
Ocean—deep...........
Head—bad............. 9
Stove—wood...........

- 104 -

Long—trees……….. 2
Religion—form……..19
Whiskey—apples…….17
Child—people………. 1
Bitter—apples……...
Hammer—axe………..
Thirsty—drink……..
City—towns………...
Square—measurement…
Butter—cows………..
Doctor—person…….. 1
Loud—people………. 1
Thief—person………. 1
Lion—animal………..
Joy—person……….. 9
Bed—man………….. 6
Heavy—mountain…….
Tobacco—growing……
Baby—person………. 1
Moon—people………. 6
Scissors—cutting…..
Quiet—mind………..
Green—cloud……….19
Salt—planting……..13
Street—walk……….
King—human………..19
Cheese—milk……….
Blossom—flowers……
Afraid—human………15

CASE No. 01218.—E.M. Repetition of words previously given; non-specific reactions.

Table—tablecloth…..
Dark—dog………….
Music—figure………17
Sickness—drink…….17
Man—people……….. 1
Deep—pull…………19
Soft—light………..
Eating—think………. 1
Mountain—well……..13
House—plumber……..17
Black—horse……….

Mutton—park..........19
Comfort—nice......... 1
Hand—use............. 1
Short—long...........
Fruit—figs...........
Butterfly—cloth......19
Smooth—nice.......... 1
Command—pleasant..... 6
Chair—wash...........19
Sweet—sour...........
Whistle—mug..........19
Woman—pear...........19
Cold—warm............
Slow—quickness.......
Wish—nice............ 1
River—pleasant....... 1
White—use............ 6
Beautiful—comfort....19
Window—looks......... 2
Rough—pleasant....... 6
Citizen—comfort......15
Foot—help............
Spider—wake..........19
Needle—use........... 1
Red—look.............15
Sleep—good........... 1
Anger—no.............12
Carpet—make..........19
Girl—happy........... 9
High—nice............ 6
Working—pleasant..... 1
Sour—bag.............19
Earth—ground.........
Trouble—good......... 6
Soldier—clothes......
Cabbage—eat..........
Hard—good............ 1
Eagle—pleasant....... 6
Stomach—hurt.........
Stem—use............. 1
Lamp—lighted.........
Dream—pleasant....... 1
Yellow—wake..........15

Bread—making.........
Justice—help.........
Boy—pleasant......... 6
Light—big............19
Health—nice.......... 6
Bible—use............ 1
Memory—no............12
Sheep—pleasant....... 1
Bath—good............ 6
Cottage—useful.......
Swift—quick..........
Blue—good............ 1
Hungry—sour..........15
Priest—good.......... 1
Ocean—useful......... 6
Head—nice............ 6
Stove—lighted........ 2
Long—lake............19
Religion—pleasant.... 6
Whiskey—use.......... 6
Child—help........... 6
Bitter—sour..........
Hammer—stick.........19
Thirsty—drink........
City—handy...........19
Square—pleasant...... 6
Butter—useful........ 1
Doctor—help..........
Loud—make............15
Thief—punish......... 2
Lion—bad............. 9
Joy—happy............ 1
Bed—pleasant......... 1
Heavy—light..........
Tobacco—pleasant..... 1
Baby—help............ 6
Moon—sun.............
Scissors—pleasant.... 6
Quiet—sleep..........
Green—beans..........10
Salt—handy...........15
Street—make..........15
King—nice............ 6

Cheese—good.......... 1
Blossom—pleasant..... 1
Afraid—will..........19

CASE No. 4989.—C.H. Repetition of words previously given; non-specific reactions; particles.

Table—work........... 1
Dark—true............19
Music—pleasant....... 1
Sickness—well........
Man—absent...........19
Deep—together........12
Soft—plenty.......... 6
Eating—good.......... 1
Mountain—together....12
House—one............12
Black—America........19
Mutton—vegetable..... 2
Comfort—sleep........
Hand—nothing.........19
Short—never..........12
Fruit—vegetable......
Butterfly—bird.......
Smooth—large......... 9
Command—willing......
Chair—good.......... 6
Sweet—always......... 6
Whistle—music........
Woman—one............12
Cold—medium.......... 6
Slow—quick...........
Wish—hope............
River—lake...........
White—always......... 6
Beautiful—medium..... 6
Window—open..........
Rough—smooth.........
Citizen—American.....
Foot—two.............
Spider—butterfly.....
Needle—steel........
Red—color............
Sleep—plenty.........

Anger—never..........
Carpet—floor.........
Girl—five............12
High—medium..........
Working—always.......
Sour—never........... 6
Earth—cultivate......17
Trouble—none.........
Soldier—willing......15
Cabbage—vegetable....
Hard—seldom..........12
Eagle—American.......
Stomach—no...........12
Stem—one.............12
Lamp—burning.........
Dream—always......... 6
Yellow—sometimes.....12
Bread—soft...........
Justice—always.......
Boy—two..............12
Light—plenty.........
Health—plenty........
Bible—Catholic.......17
Memory—good.......... 1
Sheep—wool...........
Bath—good............ 1
Cottage—plenty....... 6
Swift—medium......... 6
Blue—never........... 6
Hungry—seldom........ 6
Priest—good.......... 1
Ocean—three..........12
Head—good............ 1
Stove—burning........
Long—medium..........
Religion—willing.....15
Whiskey—some.........19
Child—good........... 1
Bitter—never......... 6
Hammer—tool..........
Thirsty—seldom....... 6
City—New York........
Square—always........ 6

Better—good………. 1
Doctor—good………. 1
Loud—medium………. 6
Thief—none………..
Lion—animal……….
Joy—plenty……….. 6
Bed—good…………. 1
Heavy—medium………. 6
Tobacco—yes……….12
Baby—more…………19
Moon—bright……….
Scissors—sharp…….
Quiet—plenty………. 6
Green—good……….. 6
Salt—little……….19
Street—lots……….18
King—none………….
Cheese—seldom…….. 6
Blossom—always……. 6
Afraid—sometimes…..15

CASE No. 4847.—C.C. Distraction

Table—eat………….
Dark—lock………….10
Music—fiddle……….
Sickness—doctors….. 2
Man—woman…………. 1
Deep—water………..
Soft—snow…………
Eating—oats……….17
Mountain—spray…….19
House—building…….
Black—red…………15
Mutton—meat………. 9
Comfort—red……….15
Hand—people………. 9
Short—world……….19
Fruit—age…………18
Butterfly—bird…….
Smooth—eggs……….18
Command—cake………19
Chair—world……….15
Sweet—cherries…….

- 110 -

Whistle—peaches......18
Woman—children.......
Cold—summer..........17
Slow—brother.........19
Wish—pear............19
River—orange.........18
White—black..........
Beautiful—red........13
Window—door..........
Rough—table..........
Citizen—couch........19
Foot—arm.............
Spider—fly...........
Needle—scissors......17
Red—blue.............
Sleep—pink...........13
Anger—box............19
Carpet—rug...........
Girl—boy.............
High—play............
Working—cup..........19
Sour—bread...........17
Earth—picture........19
Trouble—soap.........19
Soldier—towel........18
Cabbage—turnip.......
Hard—tree............
Eagle—clock..........19
Stomach—eat..........
Stem—soap............15
Lamp—oil.............
Dream—glass..........13

Yellow—bottle........18
Bread—soap...........15
Justice—pencil.......19
Boy—picture..........15
Light—darkness.......
Health—washstand.....19
Bible—book...........
Memory—saucer........19
Sheep—chair..........19
Bath—bureau..........14

- 111 -

Cottage—pan..........19
Swift—towel.........15
Blue—wash............ 2
Hungry—eat...........
Priest—church........
Ocean—beans..........19
Head—prunes..........18
Stove—cook...........
Long—fig............19
Religion—church......
Whiskey—tea..........17
Child—people......... 1
Bitter—stomach.......19
Hammer—tack..........
Thirsty—peach........15
City—box.............15
Square—soap..........15
Butter—lard..........
Doctor—sick..........
Loud—head............19
Thief—cup............15
Lion—bottle..........15
Joy—pitcher..........19
Bed—sheet............
Heavy—blanket........13
Tobacco—mustard......19
Baby—pepper..........18
Moon—heater..........19
Scissors—string......
Quiet—lace...........19
Green—red............
Salt—soda............17
Street—soldier.......19
King—box.............15
Cheese—cake..........
Blossom—shell........19
Afraid—blotter.......19

CASE No. 3597.—L.T. Some neologisms, all possessing obvious meaning.

Table—stand..........
Dark—light...........
Music—instrument.....
Sickness—health......

Man—female………..
Deep—detableness….. 4
Soft—hard…………
Eating—starving……
Mountain—isthmus…..17
House—building…….
Black—white……….
Mutton—beef……….
Comfort—patient……
Hand—leg………….
Short—long………..
Fruit—vegetable……
Butterfly—spider…..
Smooth—coarse……..
Command—thought…… 1
Chair—utensil……..19
Sweet—sour………..
Whistle—trumpet……
Woman—man…………. 1
Cold—warm…………
Slow—quick………..
Wish—command………
River—lake………..
White—black……….
Beautiful—pretty….. 1
Window—door……….
Rough—straight…….
Citizen—tramp……..19
Foot—arm………….
Spider—fly………..
Needle—pin………..
Red—blue………….
Sleep—awake……….
Anger—patient…….. 2
Carpet—rug………..
Girl—servant………
High—low………….
Working—laziness…..
Sour—sweet………..
Earth—hemisphere…..
Trouble—goodness….. 9
Soldier—merchant…..17
Cabbage—pumpkin……17

- 113 -

Hard—tight………..
Eagle—hawk………..
Stomach—abdomen……
Stem—leaf…………
Lamp—lantern………
Dream—nightmare……
Yellow—lavender……17
Bread—pastry………
Justice—badness…… 2
Boy—child…………
Light—darkness…….
Health—sickness……
Bible—testament……
Memory—remember……
Sheep—lamb………..
Bath—dirtiness……. 2
Cottage—building…..
Swift—quickly……..
Blue—redness……… 2
Hungry—starving……
Priest—minister……
Ocean—sea…………
Head—topness……… 4
Stove—cooking……..
Long—shorter……… 2
Religion—wickedness..
Whiskey—medicine…..
Child—daughter…….
Bitter—sweetness….. 2
Hammer—pickaxe…….17
Thirsty—drinkness…. 4
City—village………
Square—strightness… 2
Butter—syrup………17
Doctor—queen………19
Loud—low………….
Thief—burglar……..
Lion—tiger………..
Joy—enjoyable…….. 2
Bed—bedstead………
Heavy—lightness……
Tobacco—sweetness…. 2
Baby—infant……….

- 114 -

Moon—sun………….
Scissors—shears……
Quite—noiseness…… 4
Green—greenbill…… 3
Salt—sugar………..
Street—island……..19
King—nephew……….19
Cheese—curdness…… 4
Blossom—bud……….
Afraid—knowledgeable. 4

GENERAL PARESIS.

Cases presenting no considerable dementia or confusion and cases in a state of remission are apt to give normal test records. As we proceed from the records of such cases to those of cases showing mental deterioration we observe a gradual reduction in the values of reactions, contraction of the mental horizon,[1] and the appearance of the phenomenon of perseveration. We submit the following test records for illustration:

[Footnote 1: What we mean by contraction of the mental horizon has already been described in connection with epilepsy, page 47.]

CASE No. 4047.—C.A.F. Almost complete remission of all mental symptoms. Normal record.

Table—dish………..
Dark—light………..
Music—sound……….
Sickness—disease…..
Man—woman…………. 1
Deep—fathomless……
Soft—sweet………..
Eating—food……….
Mountain—high……..
House—barn………..
Black—color……….
Mutton—meat……….
Comfort—ease………
Hand—foot…………
Short—long………..
Fruit—sweet……….
Butterfly—moth…….
Smooth—rough………

Command—order……..
Chair—leg………….
Sweet—pleasant……. 1
Whistle—sound……..
Woman—female……….
Cold—ice………….
Slow—languid………17
Wish—desire……….
River—long………..
White—color……….
Beautiful—fair…….
Window—glass……….
Rough—smooth……….
Citizen—voter……..
Foot—toe………….
Spider—fly………..
Needle—sharp……….
Red—color…………
Sleep—slumber……..
Anger—rage………..
Carpet—sweep……….
Girl—maiden……….
High—lofty………..
Working—toiling……
Sour—distasteful…..
Earth—ground……….
Trouble—sorrow…….
Soldier—fighter……
Cabbage—leaf………
Hard—easy…………
Eagle—fly…………
Stomach—food……….
Stem—petal………..
Lamp—light………..
Dream—slumber……..
Yellow—color……….
Bread—eat…………
Justice—judgment…..
Boy—youth…………
Light—lamp………..
Health—nature……..17
Bible—holy………..
Memory—remember……

Sheep—lamb………..
Bath—water………..
Cottage—house……..
Swift—fast………..
Blue—color………..
Hungry—famished……
Priest—holy………..
Ocean—sea…………
Head—top………….
Stove—fire………..
Long—short………..
Religion—holy……..
Whiskey—drink……..
Child—infant………
Bitter—sour………..
Hammer—knock………
Thirsty—drink……..
City—town…………
Square—round………
Butter—eat………..
Doctor—physician…..
Loud—knock………..
Thief—steal………..
Lion—tiger………..
Joy—happiness…….. 1
Bed—sleep………….
Heavy—weigh………..
Tobacco—smoke……..
Baby—child………..
Moon—stars………..
Scissors—cut………
Quiet—soft………..
Green—color………..
Salt—food…………
Street—lane………..
King—queen………..
Cheese—eat………..
Blossom—flower…….
Afraid—fear……….

CASE No. 6660.—F.F. Repetition of words previously given; non-specific reactions; unclassified reactions some of which are "circumstantial" (see page 25).

Table—bureau………19
Dark—boats……….. 2
Music—piano……….
Sickness—doctor……
Man—sober…………19
Deep—cellar……….
Soft—easy………….
Eating—chewing…….
Mountain—climb…….
House—tenants…….. 2
Black—color……….
Mutton—meat……….
Comfort—easy……….
Hand—use…………. 1
Short—stump………. 2
Fruit—nice……….. 1
Butterfly—like……. 6
Smooth—clean……….
Command—faithful…..17
Chair—easy………..
Sweet—like……….. 6
Whistle—good……… 6
Woman—like……….. 6
Cold—medicine……..
Slow—I……………12
Wish—like…………
River—boats……….
White—sheet……….
Beautiful—flowers….
Window—red………..14
Rough—streets…….. 2
Citizen—honest…….
Foot—walking………
Spider—kill……….10
Needle—sew………..
Red—nice…………. 6
Sleep—rest………..
Anger—cross……….
Carpet—good………. 6
Girl—nice………… 1
High—good………… 1
Working—well………19
Sour—bitter……….

Earth—property.......19
Trouble—fighting.....
Soldier—good......... 1
Cabbage—eat..........
Hard—sorry...........19
Eagle—good........... 6
Stomach—good......... 1
Stem—fair............19
Lamp—use............. 1
Dream—now............12
Yellow—color.........
Bread—good........... 1
Justice—fine......... 1
Boy—good............. 1
Light—good........... 1
Health—right.........19
Bible—home...........
Memory—good.......... 1
Sheep—like........... 6
Bath—good............ 1
Cottage—fine......... 1
Swift—go.............
Blue—nice............ 6
Hungry—bad........... 1
Priest—Father........
Ocean—boats..........
Head—brains..........
Stove—heat...........
Long—streets.........
Religion—Catholic....
Whiskey—bad.......... 1
Child—good........... 1
Bitter—sorrow........
Hammer—use........... 1
Thirsty—drink........
City—Brooklyn........
Squares—park......... 2
Butter—ice...........19
Doctor—cure..........
Loud—holler..........
Thief—no............. 2
Lion—no.............. 6
Joy—hope.............

Bed—rest………..
Heavy—loud………..
Tobacco—good……… 1
Baby—good………… 1
Moon—light………..
Scissors—use……… 1
Quiet—good……….. 1
Green—nice……….. 6
Salt—use…………. 1
Street—nice………. 1
King—right………..19
Cheese—nice………. 1
Blossom—grow………
Afraid—no…………

CASE No. 618.—R.N. Numerous particles of speech; some unclassified reaction, chiefly "circumstantial" (see page 25).

Table—eat…………
Dark—cloudy……….
Music—fond………..19
Sickness—well……..
Man—human…………
Deep—ocean………..
Soft—fine………… 1
Eating—yes……….. 6
Mountain—yes……… 5
House—yes………… 5
Black—yes………… 5
Mutton—yes……….. 5
Comfort—yes……… 5
Hand—finger……….
Short—yes………… 6
Fruit—yes………… 5
Butterfly—yes…….. 5
Smooth—even……….
Command—obey………
Chair—settle………17
Sweet—bitter………
Whistle—can't……..19
Woman—lady………..
Cold—ice………….
Slow—fast…………
Wish—give…………

River—enjoyment......19
White—black..........
Beautiful—yes........ 6
Window—pane..........
Rough—smooth.........
Citizen—yes.......... 6
Foot—one.............12
Spider—yes........... 6
Needle—sewing........
Red—blue.............
Sleep—nap............17
Anger—willing........19
Carpet—yes........... 6
Girl—nature..........19
High—low.............
Working—artist.......17
Sour—sweet...........
Earth—world..........
Trouble—peaceful.....

Soldier—no...........12
Cabbage—vegetable....
Hard—soft............
Eagle—American.......
Stomach—condition....
Stem—post............17
Lamp—light...........
Dream—thinking....... 1
Yellow—green.........
Bread—loaf...........
Justice—yes..........
Boy—human............
Light—heaven.........
Health—wealth........
Bible—yes............ 6
Memory—yes........... 5
Sheep—animal.........
Bath—yes............. 6
Cottage—yes.......... 5
Swift—fast...........
Blue—gray............
Hungry—no............
Priest—yes........... 6
Ocean—water..........

Head—human………..
Stove—coal………..
Long—short………..
Religion—yes……… 6
Whiskey—no………..12
Child—baby………..
Bitter—sweet………
Hammer—pincher…….17
Thirsty—drinking…..
City—population……
Square—circle……..
Butter—lard………..
Doctor—physician…..
Loud—low………….
Thief—penalty……..17
Lion—liar…………10
Joy—welcome……….17
Bed—sleep………..
Heavy—light………..
Tobacco—yes……….6
Baby—human………..
Moon—natural………15
Scissors—no………12
Quiet—yes…………6
Green—shade……….
Salt—eat………….
Street—town……….
King—ruler………..
Cheese—eat………..
Blossom—blooming…..
Afraid—scared……..

CASE No. 6518.—C.Z. Perseveration shown by numerous instances of association to preceding reaction.

Table—horse……….19
Dark—wren…………10
Music—lark………..18
Sickness—cold……..
Man—woman………… 1
Deep—sea………….
Soft—hard…………
Eating—drinking……
Mountain—fountain….

House—barn………..
Black—stable………13
Mutton—cow………..
Comfort—horse……..18
Hand—lamb…………
Short—calf………..
Fruit—apples………
Butterfly—oranges…. 2
Smooth—peaches…….18
Command—plums……..18
Chair—bench………..
sweet—sugar………..
Whistle—drum………17
Woman—man………… 1
Cold—hot…………..
Slow—fast…………
Wish—who………….12
River—water………..
White—blue………..
Beautiful—splendid…
Window—sashes…….. 2
Rough—ready……….
Citizen—Brooklyn…..
Foot—shoe…………
Spider—web………..
Needle—pin………..
Red—blue………….
Sleep—awake……….
Anger—bad………… 1
Carpet—sweeper…….
Girl—boy………….
High—low………….
Working—playing……
Sour—sweet………..
Earth—ground………
Trouble—wheelbarrow..19
Soldier—Mexican……17
Cabbage—potatoes…..
Hard—beets………..18
Eagle—carrots……..18
Stomach—peas………18
Stem—peas………… 5
Lamp—burning………

Dream—happy.......... 1
Yellow—blue..........
Bread—green..........12
Justice—freedom......
Boy—girl.............
Light—burning........
Health—strength......
Bible—prayerbook.....
Memory—thoughts...... 1
Sheep—lamb...........
Bath—water...........
Cottage—house........
Swift—whist..........10
Blue—red.............
Hungry—eating........
Priest—Father........
Ocean—mother.........18
Head—brother.........18
Stove—sister.........18
Long—freedom.........15
Religion—smart.......19
Whiskey—wine.........
Child—lamb...........19
Bitter—goat..........18
Hammer—nails.........
Thirsty—dry..........
City—talking.........19
Square—inches........
Butter—cheese........
Doctor—bread.........13
Loud—oranges.........15
Thief—almonds........18
Lion—apples..........18
Joy—grapes...........18
Bed—peaches..........18
Heavy—cranberries....18
Tobacco—grapes.......18
Baby—watermelon......18
Moon—muskmelons......18
Scissors—citrons.....10
Quiet—squashes.......18
Green—pumpkins.......18
Salt—cucumbers.......18

Street—tomatoes......18
Kings—pears..........18
Cheese—apples........18
Blossom—cherries.....
Afraid—gooseberries..18

CASE No. 5329.—B.W. Perseveration; record almost entirely made up of instances of association to preceding reaction.

Table—San Francisco...19
Dark—comprehensible...19
Music—sinking.........
Sickness—Brooklyn.....19
Man—woman............. 1
Deep—amazing..........19
Soft—pleasant......... 9
Eating—digesting......
Mountain—gulf.........17
House—peninsula.......18
Black—Constantinople..18
Mutton—Bermuda........18
Comfort—Los Angeles...18
Hand—Cuba.............18
Short—cities..........18
Fruit—Iowa............18
Butterfly—England.....18
Smooth—Russia.........18
Command—Turkey........18
Chair—Manila..........18
Sweet—Porto Rico......18
Whistle—Washington....18
Woman—Cincinnati......18
Cold—Pittsburg........18
Slow—Philadelphia.....
Wish—Milwaukee........18
River—St. Louis.......18
White—Japan...........18
Beautiful—China.......18
Window—Berlin.........18
Rough—Glasgow.........18
Citizen—London........18
Foot—Dublin...........18
Spider—Sacramento.....18
Needle—Texas..........18

Red—North Carolina....18
Sleep—Florida.........18
Anger—Seattle.........18
Carpet—Nevada.........18
Girl—Iowa.............15
High—Virginia.........18
Working—Louisiana.....18
Sour—Hawaii...........18
Earth—Connecticut.....18
Trouble—Rhode Island..18
Soldier—Vermont.......18
Cabbage—Massachusetts.18
Hard—Hudson...........18
Eagle—East River......18
Stomach—Staten Island.18
Stem—Kings Park.......18
Lamp—Fort Lee.........18
Dream—Long Island.....18
Yellow—Greenport......18
Bread—Southold........18
Justice—Northport.....18
Boy—New Jersey........18
Light—Rome............18
Health—Italy..........18
Bible—Episcopal.......17
Memory—Methodist......18
Sheep—Congregational..18
Bath—Baptist..........18
Cottage—minister......18
Swift—physician.......18
Blue—horse............18
Hungry—cow............18
Priest—Catholics.......
Ocean—lake.............
Head—bay..............13
Stove—sound...........18
Long—Island............
Religion—Boston........18
Whiskey—Harvard........18
Child—Yale.............18
Bitter—Columbia........18
Hammer—library.........18
Thirsty—Carnegie.......18

City—Rockefeller.......18
Square—Harriman........18
Butter—Leggitt.........18
Doctor—Lincoln.........18
Loud—Roosevelt.........18
Thief—Taft.............18
Lion—Gaynor............18
Joy—Slocum.............18
Bed—Grant..............18
Heavy—McClellan........18
Tobacco—Spain..........19
Baby—New London........18
Moon—Newburgh..........18
Scissors—Troy..........18
Quiet—Schenectady......18
Green—Lake George......18
Salt—Vienna............18
Street—Alsace Lorraine.18
King—Garfield..........17
Cheese—McKinley........18
Blossom—Bryan..........18
Afraid—Blaine..........18

MANIC-DEPRESSIVE INSANITY.

In this disorder the departures from the normal seem to be less pronounced than in the psychoses considered above. The number of individual reactions is in most cases not greatly above the normal average; and, so far as their character is concerned, we find that many of them are classed as normal, in accordance with the appendix to the frequency tables; among the unclassified reactions, which are quite frequent here, we find mostly either obviously normal ones, or some of the type to which we have already referred as "far-fetched," while others among them are "circumstantial" (see p. 25); further we find that most of the remaining individual reactions fall into the general group of partial dissociation: non-specific reactions, sound reactions, word complements, and particles.

In some cases the only abnormality that is found is that of an undue tendency to respond by non-specific reactions, most of them being common and there being no excessive number of individual reactions. It would seem legitimate to assume that this tendency is here to be regarded as a manifestation of the phenomenon which is clinically described as *dearth of ideas*. It is significant that this tendency is observed not only in depressive phases of the psychosis, but also in manic phases and even in the normal intervals of recurrent cases or after apparent recovery in acute cases; this will be seen from some of the test records which are here reproduced.

Occasionally cases are met with which give a large number of unclassified reactions, seemingly incoherent. There can be no doubt that at least some of these cases are clinically perfectly typical ones of manic-depressive insanity, yet the test records strongly resemble, in some respects, those of dementia præcox.

Since clinically the distinction between typical cases of these psychoses can be so clearly made on the basis of the disorders of the flow of thought respectively characterizing them, it could hardly be assumed that the associational disturbances in these two groups of cases are truly related, although there may be an apparent resemblance; it must be acknowledged that we are here confronted with one of the most serious shortcomings of the association test, or at least of the present method of applying it.

CASE No. 5236.—M.B. Depressive attack. Normal record.

Table—eat............
Dark—night………..
Music—play………..
Sickness—death…….
Man—health………..13
Deep—depth………..
Soft—hard............
Eating—chewing…….
Mountain—high……..
House—living………
Black—color………..
Mutton—sheep………
Comfort—kind……… 2
Hand—body…………
Short—small………. 1
Fruit—garden………
Butterfly—spring…..
Smooth—rough………
Command—obey………
Chair—sit............
Sweet—apple……….
Whistle—music……..
Woman—land………..
Cold—chilly……….
Slow—easy…………

Wish—want…………
River—water………..
White—color………..
Beautiful—grand……
Window—light……….
Rough—smooth……….
Citizen—man……….. 1
Foot—body………….
Spider—animal……..
Needle—sew………..
Red—color………….
Sleep—rest………..
Anger—badness…….. 2
Carpet—floor……….
Girl—young………..
High—low………….
Working—busy……….
Sour—sweet………..
Earth—live………..
Trouble—grief……..
Soldier—army……….
Cabbage—garden…….
Hard—stone………..
Eagle—bird………..
Stomach—body……….
Stem—plant………..
Lamp—light………..
Dream—sleep………..
Yellow—color……….
Bread—eat………….
Justice—kind………. 2
Boy—young………….
Light—day………….
Health—strength……
Bible—Christ……….
Memory—think………. 1
Sheep—mutton……….
Bath—clean………..
Cottage—live……….
Swift—run………….
Blue—color………..
Hungry—food……….
Priest—clergy……..

Ocean—water..........
Head—body............
Stove—fire...........
Long—tall............
Religion—teaching....
Whiskey—drink........
Child—young..........
Bitter—sweet.........
Hammer—nail..........
Thirsty—drink........
City—town............
Square—four..........
Butter—eat...........
Doctor—medicine......
Loud—noise...........
Thief—steal..........
Lion—beast...........
Joy—kind............. 6
Bed—sleep............
Heavy—weight.........
Tobacco—smoke........
Baby—mother..........
Moon—light...........
Scissors—cut.........
Quiet—kind........... 6
Green—grass..........
Salt—table...........
Street—walk..........
King—government......
Cheese—eat...........
Blossom—tree.........
Afraid—coward........

CASE No. 6120.—M.L. Maniacal attack. Fifteen individual reactions, of which 11 are classed as normal in accordance with the appendix to the frequency tables.

Table—chair............
Dark—light.............
Music—chorus...........17
Sickness—health........
Man—woman.............. 1
Deep—around............
Soft—light.............

Eating—food............
Mountain—valley........
House—flat.............17
Black—white............
Mutton—beef............
Comfort—disease........
Hand—legs..............
Short—tall.............
Fruit—grapes...........
Butterfly—birds........
Smooth—rough...........

Command—president......17
Chair—assemblyman......18
Sweet—bitter...........
Whistle—birds..........
Woman—man.............. 1
Cold—warm..............
Slow—fast..............
Wish—well..............
River—mountain.........
White—red..............
Beautiful—heaven.......
Window—door............
Rough—smooth...........
Citizen—naturalization.
Foot—hand..............
Spider—bug.............
Needle—doctor..........19
Red—white..............
Sleep—well.............
Anger—passion..........
Carpet—cloth...........
Girl—boy...............
High—low...............
Working—pleasure....... 1
Sour—sweet.............
Earth—heaven...........
Trouble—anger..........
Soldier—mine...........12
Cabbage—steak..........17

Hard—soft..............
Eagle—parrot...........

Stomach—pelvis.........17
Stem—flowers...........
Lamp—light.............
Dream—empty............17
Yellow—black...........
Bread—brown............
Justice—done...........
Boy—baby...............
Light—heaven...........
Health—wealth..........
Bible—love.............
Memory—remembrance.....
Sheep—goat.............
Bath—water.............
Cottage—house..........
Swift—slow.............
Blue—green.............
Hungry—I...............
Priest—minister........
Ocean—sea..............
Head—neck..............
Stove—electricity......17
Long—broad.............
Religion—Presbyterian..
Whiskey—medicinal...... 2
Child—boy..............
Bitter—sweet...........
Hammer—saw.............
Thirsty—water..........
City—Middletown........17
Square—Madison.........
Butter—bread...........
Doctor—love............15
Loud—soft..............
Thief—burglar..........
Lion—animal............
Joy—ecstasy............
Bed—couch..............
Heavy—lead.............
Tobacco—smoke..........
Baby—boy...............
Moon—stars.............
Scissors—cotton........17

Quiet—noisy............
Green—yellow...........
Salt—pepper............
Street—Dean............17
King—God...............17
Cheese—Roquefort.......
Blossom—apple..........
Afraid—never...........

CASE No. 6367.—J.N. Depressive attack. Only two individual reactions, both classed as normal; undue tendency to give non-specific reactions.

Table—cup............17
Dark—light...........
Music—song...........
Sickness—pain........
Man—child............
Deep—high............
Soft—hard............
Eating—tasting.......
Mountain—valley......
House—room...........
Black—white..........
Mutton—lamb..........
Comfort—peace........
Hand—foot............
Short—long...........
Fruit—apple..........
Butterfly—moth.......
Smooth—rough.........
Command—obey.........
Chair—table..........
Sweet—sour...........
Whistle—song.........
Woman—love...........
Cold—warm............
Slow—fast............
Wish—well............
River—water..........
White—black..........
Beautiful—grand......
Window—glass.........
Rough—smooth.........
Citizen—man.......... 1

Foot—hand............
Spider—fly...........
Needle—thread........
Red—blue.............
Sleep—rest...........
Anger—passion........
Carpet—rug...........
Girl—child...........
High—low.............
Working—labor........
Sour—sweet...........
Earth—ground.........
Trouble—overcome.....17
Soldier—brave........
Cabbage—lettuce......
Hard—soft............
Eagle—bird...........
Stomach—heart........
Stem—tree............
Lamp—light...........
Dream—sleep..........
Yellow—red...........
Bread—roll...........
Justice—peace........
Boy—child............
Light—sun............
Health—wealth........
Bible—good........... 1
Memory—good.......... 1
Sheep—lamb...........
Bath—water...........
Cottage—house........
Swift—fast...........
Blue—white...........
Hungry—eat...........
Priest—man........... 1
Ocean—water..........
Head—arm.............
Stove—warm...........
Long—short...........
Religion—good........ 1
Whiskey—none.........
Child—good........... 1

Bitter—sour..........
Hammer—noise.........
Thirsty—water……..
City—country.........
Square—round.........
Butter—salt..........
Doctor—good.......... 1
Loud—noise………..
Thief—man............ 1
Lion—beast………..
Joy—good............. 1
Bed—good............. 1
Heavy—weight.........
Tobacco—smoke……..
Baby—child………..
Moon—sun.............
Scissors—knife.......
Quiet—rest………..
Green—red............
Salt—water………..
Street—city..........
King—man............. 1
Cheese—butter……...
Blossom—flower.......
Afraid—fear..........

CASE No. 5162.—W.H. Recurrent attacks, mixed in character; at time of test patient was in a normal interval. 5 individual reactions, of which 1 is classed as normal, 1 as a derivative, 2 as non-specific, and 1 as a sound reaction; undue tendency to give non-specific (common) reactions.

Table—comfort……...
Dark—darknew......... 8
Music—pleasure....... 1
Sickness—sorrow......
Map—manners..........10
Deep—thought......... 1
Soft—comfort.........
Eating—pleasure...... 1
Mountain—height......
House—comfort……...
Black—darkness.......
Mutton—eating……...
Comfort—pleasure….. 1

Hand—useful………. 1
Short—stumpy………
Fruit—eating……….
Butterfly—handsome…
Smooth—plane……….
Command—ordering…..
Chair—easy………..
Sweet—candy……….
Whistle—noise……..
Woman—love………..
Cold—freezing……..
Slow—laziness……..
Wish—good…………. 1
River—water……….
White—clearness…… 2
Beautiful—handsome…
Window—scene……….
Rough—harshness……
Citizen—voting…….
Foot—stepping……..
Spider—poison……..
Needle—sharpness…..
Red—blood…………
Sleep—comfort……..
Anger—passion……..
Carpet—walking…….
Girl—lovely……….
High—height……….
Working—business…..
Sour—tart…………
Earth—planting…….
Trouble—Sorrow…….
Soldier—fighting…..
Cabbage—eating…….
Hard—harshness……. 2
Eagle—flying………
Stomach—eating…….
Stem—vine…………
Lamp—lighting…….. 2
Dream—pleasure……. 1
Yellow—color………
Bread—eating………
Justice—suing……..17

- 136 -

Boy—children.........
Light—seeing.........
Health—pleasure...... 1
Bible—thinking....... 9
Memory—recollections.
Sheep—wool...........
Bath—pleasure........ 1
Cottage—living.......
Swift—quickness......
Blue—sky............

Hungry—pleasure...... 9
Priest—holiness......
Ocean—sailing........
Head—thinking........ 1
Stove—warmth.........
Long—length..........
Religion—holiness....
Whiskey—badness...... 2
Child—pleasure....... 1
Bitter—sourness......
Hammer—pounding......
Thirsty—drinking.....
City—town...........
Square—measure.......
Butter—greasy........
Doctor—medicine......
Loud—hearing......... 2
Thief—stealing.......
Lion—fierceness......
Joy—pleasure......... 1
Bed—sleeping.........
Heavy—solid..........
Tobacco—pleasure..... 1
Baby—loveliness......
Moon—bright..........
Scissors—sharpness....
Quiet—pleasure....... 1
Green—color..........
Salt—taste...........
Street—walking.......
King—majestic........
Cheese—eating........

Blossom—handsome…..
Afraid—fear……….

CASE No. 6279.—A.F. Maniacal attack; at time of test patient had improved, though not recovered. Non-specific reactions; particles. (Patient does not speak English with perfect fluency.)

Table—board……….
Dark—night………..
Music—piano……….
Sickness—appendicitis
Man—husband……….
Deep—hole…………
Soft—hard…………
Eating—vegetable…..
Mountain—country…..
House—comfort……..
Black—cotton………17
Mutton—lamb……….
Comfort—rest………
Hand—arm………….
Short—Journey……..
Fruit—apples………
Butterfly—love…….13
Smooth—nice……….1
Command—order……..
Chair—down………..12
Sweet—sugar……….
Whistle—blow………
Woman—good………..1
Cold—ice………….
Slow—lazy…………
Wish—home…………
River—boat………..
White—milk………..
Beautiful—flowers….
Window—corner……..
Rough—man…………1
Citizen—not……….12
Foot—short………..
Spider—don't………12
Needle—steel………
Red—rose………….
Sleep—well………..

Anger—not............
Carpet—beauty…….. 1
Girl—love............
High—reason..........19
Working—dress……..19
Sour—vinegar.........
Earth—ground.........
Trouble—much.........
Soldier—blue.........
Cabbage—sour.........
Hard—no…………..12
Eagle—paper..........
Stomach—well.........17
Stem—flower..........
Lamp—light...........
Dream—awful..........19
Yellow—flower……..
Bread—rye............
Justice—court……..
Boy—little...........
Light—room...........
Health—love..........15
Bible—no.............
Memory—good.......... 1
Sheep—lot............19
Bath—cold............
Cottage—little…….
swift—kick………..17
Blue—no…………..12
Hungry—no............
Priest—love..........15
Ocean—Grove..........
Head—black...........
Stove—shine..........19
Long—square..........
Religion—no..........
Whiskey—champagne….17
Child—my............. 2
Bitter—pepper……..
Hammer—knock.........
Thirsty—no………..12
City—New York……..
Square—table.........

Butter—good.......... 1
Doctor—S.............17
Loud—talk............
Thief—night..........
Lion—yes.............12
Joy—good............. 1
Bed—comfort..........
Heavy—Iron...........
Tobacco—strong.......
Baby—love............
Moon—shine...........
Scissors—cut........
Quiet—well..........
Green—bow............17
Salt—hitter..........
Street—Hinsdale......17
King—Franz Joseph....17
Cheese—Swiss.........
Blossom—nice......... 1
Afraid—no............

CASE No. 4578.—E.M. Circular insanity of over twenty years' standing; at time of test patient was in a manic phase. Non-specific reactions; doubtful reactions; neologisms, all possessing obvious meaning.

Table—using.......... 1
Dark—unbright........ 4
Music—songs..........
Sickness—catching....17
Man—masculine........
Deep—high............
Soft—chew............19
Eating—sometimes.....12
Mountain—highlands...
House—live..........
Black—color.........
Mutton—meat..........
Comfort—easy........
Hand—body............
Short—unlongly....... 4
Fruit—plants.........
Butterfly—insects....
Smooth—feeling.......
Command—do..........

Chair—use............ 1
Sweet—taste..........
Whistle—act..........
Woman—female.........
Cold—acting.......... 2
Slow—gradually.......17
Wish—desire..........
River—water..........
White—color..........
Beautiful—niceness... 2
Window—built.........19
Rough—treatment......17
Citizen—country......
Foot—body............
Spider—insect........
Needle—article....... 1
Red—color............
Sleep—tiredness...... 4
Anger—scolding.......
Carpet—article....... 1
Girl—female..........
High—low.............
Working—do...........
Sour—tasting.........
Earth—surface........
Trouble—worriment....
Soldier—man.......... 1
Cabbage—vegetable....
Hard—difficult.......
Eagle—bird...........
Stomach—body.........
Stem—article......... 6
Lamp—article......... 1
Dream—untruly........ 4
Yellow—color.........
Bread—food...........
Justice—unfairly..... 2
Boy—masculine........
Light—easy...........
Health—sickness......
Bible—commandments...
Memory—remember......
Sheep—animal.........

Bath—cleanness.......
Cottage—country......
Swift—quickly........
Blue—color...........
Hungry—food..........
Priest—masculine.....15
Ocean—water..........
Head—body............
Stove—article........ 1
Long—shortly......... 2
Religion—Bible.......
Whiskey—drinking.....
Child—disremembering. 4
Bitter—taste.........
Hammer—using......... 1
Thirsty—drinking.....
City—acting..........15
Square—measuring..... 2
Butter—food..........
Doctor—helping....... 2
Loud—hearing......... 2
Thief—untrue.........15
Lion—animal..........
Joy—gladness.........
Bed—lying............
Heavy—unlightly...... 4
Tobacco—using........ 1
Baby—borning......... 4
Moon—sending.........19
Scissors—using....... 1
Quiet—acting......... 2
Green—color..........
Salt—food............
Street—walking.......
King—person.......... 1
Cheese—food..........
Blossom—plant........
Afraid—frightened....

CASE No. 5878.—A.B. Maniacal attack. 48 individual reactions, of which 18 are classed as normal, 10 are sound reactions (2 sound neologisms), 1 word complement, 8 particles, and 11 unclassified reactions most of which are either obviously normal or "far fetched" but not strictly incoherent.

Table—mahogany.......
Dark—green...........
Music—masonic........10
Sickness—seasickness.10
Man—maternity........10
Deep—well............
Soft—silk............
Eating—cleanliness...19
Mountain—Gibraltar...17
House—bungalow.......
Black—light..........
Mutton—lamb..........
Comfort—linen........17
Hand—left............17
Short—shorthand......10
Fruit—pears..........
Butterfly—canary.....17
Smooth—linen.........17
Command—pilot........17
Chair—round..........
Sweet—sugar..........
Whistle—mother.......19
Woman—twenty-one.....12
Cold—ice.............
Slow—music...........
Wish—girl............
River—Hudson.........
White—plaster........17
Beautiful—nature.....
Window—St. Patrick's.17
Rough—blankets.......19
Citizen—twenty-one...12
Foot—six.............12
Spider—fly...........
Needle—tailor........
Red—Herald...........19
Sleep—seven..........12
Anger—Angoria........ 3
Carpet—green.........
Girl—eighteen........12
High—school..........11
Working—ten..........12
Sour—kraut...........

- 143 -

Earth—round………..
Trouble—son………..19
Soldier—navy………
Cabbage—curly……..19
Hard—stone………..
Eagle—almanac……..17
Stomach—stomjack….. 3
Stem—maple………..17
Lamp—New…..York….19
Dream—husband……..19
Yellow—cards………17
Bread—rye…………
Justice—liberty……
Boy—Joe…………..
Light—white………..
Health—death………10
Bible—holy………..
Memory—seven………12
Sheep—lamb………..
Bath—cleanliness…..
Cottage—gray………17
Swift—ball………..
Blue—balloon………10
Hungry—yes………..12
Priest—doctor……..
Ocean—Niagara……..17
Head—rest…………
Stove—stationary…..10
Long—poems………..19
Religion—Catholic….
Whiskey—Hunter…….
Child—Jesus……….17
Bitter—gall……….
Hammer—steel………
Thirsty—water……..
City—New York……..
Square—Union………
Butter—sweet………
Doctor—S………….17
Loud—discreet……..19
Thief—night……….
Lion—Bostock……… 2
Joy—Joy Line………10

- 144 -

Bed—Ostermoor........17
Heavy—iron...........
Tobacco—Durham.......
Baby—Rose............17
Moon—half............
Scissors—steel.......
Quiet—nursing........19
Green—grass..........
Salt—rock............
Street—Liberty.......17
King—Alphonso........
Cheese—Swiss.........
Blossom—apple........
Afraid—dark..........

CASE No. 6511.—U.B. Maniacal attack. Persistent use of particles *oh, me, I, none*, etc.

Table—none........... 6
Dark—red.............
Music—stock..........19
Sickness—rose........19
Man—Frank............17
Deep—blue............
Soft—pillow..........
Eating—no............12
Mountain—oyster......11
House—mercy..........19
Black—mother.........19
Mutton—me............ 6
Comfort—home.........
Hand—mother..........15
Short—me............. 6
Fruit—me............. 5
Butterfly—it........12
Smooth—oh............12
Command—none......... 6
Chair—none........... 5
Sweet—for............12
Whistle—bird.........
Woman—I.............. 6
Cold—I............... 5
Slow—me..............
Wish—none............ 2

- 145 -

River—are…………12
White—wife………..10
Beautiful—Alma…….17
Window—Stephen…….19
Rough—Rudolphia……10
Citizen—father…….17
Foot—Anthon……….19
Spider—reverend……19
Needle—pine……….17

Red—brother……….19
Sleep—Adam………..19
Anger—I………….. 6
Carpet—home……….
Girl—Agatha……….17
High—niece………..13
Working—I………… 6
Sour—I……………. 5
Earth—I………….. 5
Trouble—I………… 5
Soldier—father…….15
Cabbage—hail………19
Hard—me…………..12
Eagle—I………….. 6
Stomach—I………… 5
Stem—life…………
Lamp—Lambert………10
Dream—I………….. 6
Yellow—I………….. 5
Bread—I………….. 5
Justice—I………… 5
Boy—just………….13
Light—picture……..19
Health—cook……….19
Bible—beads……….17
Memory—Dick……….19
Sheep—to………….12
Bath—none…………
Cottage—home………
Swift—lazy………..
Blue—Nell…………19
Hungry—I………….
Priest—I………….. 5
Ocean—I………….. 5

Head—home............ 6
Stove—home............
Long—short............
Religion—none..........
Whiskey—none..........
Child—Sylvester......17
Bitter—I............. 6
Hammer—my............12
Thirsty—no............ 6
City—no.............. 5
Square—Ben...........19
Butter—I............. 6
Doctor—I............. 5
Loud—bell............
Thief—iron...........19
Lion—I............... 6
Joy—I................ 5
Bed—I................ 5
Heavy—I.............. 5
Tobacco—I............ 5
Baby—I............... 5
Moon—will............12
Scissors—beads.......15
Quiet—nerves.........19
Green—I.............. 6
Salt—I............... 5
Street—Peter.........17
King—I............... 6
Cheese—I............. 5
Blossom—I............ 5
Afraid—no............

CASE No. 4427.—A.R. Maniacal attack. Unusual number of doubtful reactions; 46 individual reactions of which 9 are classed as normal; 29 are unclassified, some seemingly incoherent.

Table—Chicago........19
Dark—Montreal........18
Music—Mississippi....18
Sickness—flowers.....19
Man—ocean............19
Deep—medicines.......19
Soft—accidental......19
Eating—vaccination...19

Mountain—evergreens..17
House—caves..........19
Black—station……..19
Mutton—operations….19
Comfort—money……..
Hand—bandages……..10
Short—soldiers…….19
Fruit—dictionary…..19
Butterfly—storehouse.19
Smooth—vegetables….18
Command—Bible……..
Chair—histories……14
Sweet—farewells……19
Whistle—ammunition…19
Woman—foreign……..19
Cold—armory..........19
Slow—St. Petersburg..19
Wish—wealth..........
River—revenue……..10
White—purity………
Beautiful—colonial…19
Window—shutters……
Rough—planes……… 2
Citizen—naturalization
Foot—carriage……..19
Spider—remedies……19
Needle—canoe………19
Red—refreshments…..10
Sleep—restfulness…. 2
Anger—usefulness….. 9
Carpet—coach………19
Girl—finery..........19
High—fortifications..19
Working—materials….19
Sour—pickles………
Earth—gravitation…. 2
Trouble—graphophone..19
Soldier—guns………
Cabbage—children…..19
Hard—inheritance…..19
Eagle—feathers…….
Stomach—envelope…..19
Stem—roots………..

- 148 -

Lamp—oil………….
Dream—fairies……..17
Yellow—lemons…….. 2
Bread—jams………..17
Justice—repentance…17
Boy—clothes……….
Light—lanterns…….17
Health—joys……….. 2
Bible—heaven……….
Memory—head……….
Sheep—pastures…….
Bath—cleanliness…..
Cottage—home……….
Swift—rapids………. 2
Blue—truth………...
Hungry—appetite……
Priest—saintliness…17
Ocean—ships………..
Head—intelligence….
Stove—woods……….. 2
Long—trains……….. 2
Religion—godliness… 2
Whiskey—drunkenness..
Child—joyfulness….. 2
Bitter—olives……..
Hammer—nuts……….
Thirsty—water……..
City—shopping……..
Square—monuments….. 2
Butter—crackers……17
Doctor—medicines…..
Loud—music………..
Thief—detectives….. 2
Lion—cages……….. 2
Joy—home………….
Bed—restfulness…… 2
Heavy—expressage…..17
Tobacco—cigars…….
Baby—carriage……..
Moon—light………..
Scissors—goods…….
Quiet—peacefulness…
Green—vegetables…..

Salt—water………..
Street—stones……..
King—crown………..
Cheese—knife………
Blossom—plants……. 2
Afraid—enemies…….17

CASE No. 6457.—C.G. Depressive attack. 36 individual reactions of which 9 are classed as normal and 20 as unclassified; among the latter several seem to be incoherent

Table—fish………..17
Dark—boat…………
Music—water……….18
Sickness—tank……..18
Man—horse…………
Deep—ocean………..
Soft—egg………….
Eating—beans………17
Mountain—grass…….
House—roof………..
Black—bath………..10
Mutton—butcher…….
Comfort—cigar……..17
Hand—shoes………..19
Short—baseball…….19
Fruit—orange………
Butterfly—elephant…19
Smooth—glass………
Command—general……
Chair—kitchen……..17
Sweet—cake………..17
Whistle—bird………
Woman—door………..19
Cold—ice………….
Slow—cat………….19
Wish—bed………….19
River—trout……….17
White—paint……….
Beautiful—monkey…..19
Window—bars……….
Rough—rowdy……….
Citizen—policeman….
Foot—fine………… 9

Spider—insect……..
Needle—sewing……..
Red—man………….. 9
Sleep—pond………..19
Anger—hatred………
Carpet—tacks………
Girl—floor………..13
High—mountain……..
Working—dog………..19
Sour—milk…………
Earth—mud…………
Trouble—radiator…..19
Soldier—cannon…….
Cabbage—vegetable….
Hard—wood…………
Eagle—quick………..19
Stomach—flesh……..
Stem—pipe…………
Lamp—burn…………
Dream—thinking……. 1
Yellow—mice………..19
Bread—baker……….
Justice—equality…..
Boy—young………….
Light—green………..17
Health—art………..19
Bible—preacher…….
Memory—return……..19
Sheep—fold………..
Bath—water………..
Cottage—house……..
Swift—fleeting……. 2
Blue—dark…………
Hungry—thirst……..
Priest—elephant……15
Ocean—briny………..19
Head—hard…………
Stove—black………..
Long—grass………..
Religion—thinking…. 1
Whiskey—Kentucky…..
Child—carriage…….
Bitter—pickles…….

- 151 -

Hammer—nails.........
Thirsty—wanting......
City—New York........
Square—base..........17
Butter—cow...........
Doctor—carriage......
Loud—hall............19
Thief—prison.........
Lion—cage............
Joy—automobile.......
Bed—iron.............
Heavy—lead...........
Tobacco—weed.........
Baby—rocker..........
Moon—sky.............
Scissors—laundry.....19
Quiet—peaceful.......
Green—engine.........19
Salt—grocer..........19
Street—Lincoln.......17
King—Spain...........
Cheese—baker.........19
Blossom—flower.......
Afraid—going......... 2

INVOLUTIONAL MELANCHOLIA; ALCOHOLIC DEMENTIA; SENILE DEMENTIA.

There are so few cases of these psychoses in our series that we can say but little concerning their associational disorders.

In Table V. we show all the types of reactions given by each subject.

We have not observed in our cases of *involutional melancholia* any undue tendency to give individual reactions. The records are either perfectly normal or slightly abnormal in that they show an increase of the non-specific (common) reactions. In this respect they resemble strongly the records obtained from some cases of manic-depressive insanity. This similarity is of interest in connection with other evidence, recently brought to light, [1] showing that involutional melancholia is closely related to manic-depressive insanity, if not identical with it.

[Footnote 1: G. L. Dreyfus. Die Melancholic ein Zustandsbild des manisch-depressiven Irreseins. 1907.]

TABLE V.

	Involutional Melancholia						Alcoholic Dementia						Senile Dementia					
Case No.	6207	4818	5719	6480	6368	6607	4812	5535	5298	6369	5967	6469	1009	6018	6717	5837	6338	5788

TYPES OF REACTION

Common reactions:
Specific reactions............ | 86 | 92 | 79 | 92 | 83 | 86 | 83 | 78 | 90 | 79 | 75 | 77 | 80 | 46 | 72 | 71 | 82 | 77 |
Non-specific reactions...... | 13 | 2 | 12 | 1 | 9 | 4 | 6 | 6 | 3 | 11 | 10 | 8 | 3 | 8 | 16 | 8 | .. | 3 |

Doubtful reactions............ | 1 | 2 | 4 | 1 | 1 | 2 | 2 | 3 | 1 | 2 | 5 | 3 | 3 | 7 | .. | 6 | .. | .. |

Individual reactions:
Normal reactions............. | .. | 2 | 1 | 4 | .. | 3 | 1 | 6 | 5 | 4 | 3 | 4 | 3 | 14 | 2 | 4 | 8 | 3 |
Derivatives of stimulus words..... | .. | .. | .. | .. | .. | .. | .. | .. | .. | .. | .. | .. | .. | .. | .. | 1 | 1 | .. |
Non-specific Reactions....... | .. | .. | .. | .. | .. | .. | 1 | .. | .. | .. | .. | .. | .. | .. | 1 | 2 | .. | .. |
Sound reactions (words)....... | .. | .. | .. | 1 | .. | 1 | .. | .. | .. | .. | .. | .. | .. | .. | .. | .. | .. | .. |
Sound reactions (neologisms)...... | .. | .. | .. | .. | .. | .. | .. | .. | .. | .. | .. | .. | .. | .. | .. | .. | .. | .. |
Word complements........... | .. | .. | .. | .. | .. | .. | .. | 1 | .. | .. | .. | .. | .. | .. | .. | .. | .. | .. |
Particles of speech............ | .. | .. | .. | .. | .. | .. | 1 | 1 | .. | .. | .. | .. | .. | 5 | 1 | 2 | .. | 1 |

- 153 -

Association to preceding stimulus.|..|..|..|..| 1|..| 1|..|..|..| 2|..|..|..|..| 1|..|..|
Association to preceding reaction.|..|..|..|..|..|..|..|..|..|..|..|..|..|..|..|..| 3|
Repetition of preceding stimulus..|..|..|..|..|..|..|..|..|..|..|..|..|..|..|..|..| 1|
Repetition of previous stimulus…|..|..|..|..|..|..| 1|..|..|..|..|..| 1|..|..|..|..|..|
Repetition of preceding reaction..|..|..|..| 1|..|..|..|..|..|..|..|..| 1|..|..|..| 2|
Repetition of previous reaction…|..|..|..|..| 1|..| 1|..| 1|..|..|..| 2| 1| 2| 3| 1| 2|
Reaction repeated five times……|..|..|..|..| 4|..|..|..|..| 2| 2| 4|..| 4|..|..|..| 3|
Neologisms without sound relation.|..|..|..|..|..| 1| 1|..|..|..|..|..|..|..|..|..|..|
Unclassified………………….|..| 2| 4|..| 1| 3| 1| 6|..| 2| 3| 4| 8|14| 6| 2| 8| 5|
+—+—+—+—+—+—+—+—+—+—+—+—+—+—+—+—+—+
Total individual reactions 0 4 5 6 7 8 9 13 6 8 10 12 14 39 12 15 18 20

CASE No. 4818.—S.M. Normal record.

Table—wood………….
Dark—black………….
Music—noise…………
Sickness—illness…….
Man—being…………..
Deep—depth………….
Soft—mushy………….
Eating—devouring…….
Mountain—hill……….
House—residence……..
Black—color………….
Mutton—meat………….
Comfort—luxury……….
Hand—body…………..
Short—abrupt………..19
Fruit—oranges……….
Butterfly—insect…….
Smooth—even………….
Command—order……….
Chair—article………. 1

Sweet—taste............
Whistle—noise..........
Woman—sex..............
Cold—temperature.......
Slow—dull..............
Wish—desire............
River—water............
White—color............
Beautiful—sky..........
Window—glass...........
Rough—uneven...........
Citizen—representative.17
Foot—end...............19
Spider—insect..........
Needle—instrument......
Red—color..............
Sleep—repose...........
Anger—temper...........
Carpet—rug.............
Girl—sex...............
High—elevation.........
Working—employment.....
Sour—bitter............
Earth—clay.............
Trouble—anxiety........
Soldier—military.......
Cabbage—vegetable......
Hard—substance.........
Eagle—bird.............
Stomach—body...........
Stem—flower............
Lamp—light.............
Dream—imagination......
Yellow—color...........
Bread—wheat............
Justice—credit.........17
Boy—child..............
Light—sun..............
Health—condition.......
Bible—book.............
Memory—remembrance.....
Sheep—lamb.............
Bath—bathing...........

Cottage—house……….
Swift—rapid…………
Blue—color………….
Hungry—desire……….
Priest—minister……..
Ocean—water………..
Head—body…………..
Stove—fire………….
Long—distance……….
Religion—creed………
Whiskey—liquor………
Child—infant………..
Bitter—sour…………
Hammer—tool…………
Thirsty—dry…………
City—town…………..
Square—block………..
Butter—food…………
Doctor—physician…….
Loud—noisy………….
Thief—burglar……….
Lion—animal…………
Joy—happiness………. 1
Bed—cot…………….
Heavy—weight………..
Tobacco—weed………..
Baby—infant…………
Moon—light………….
Scissors—instrument….
Quiet—noiseless……..
Green—color…………
Salt—seasoning………
Street—block………..
King—ruler………….
Cheese—food…………
Blossom—flower………
Afraid—fear…………

CASE No. 6207.—T.S. No individual reactions; 13 non-specific reactions.

Table—furniture……
Dark—color………..
Music—fiddle………
Sickness—bed………

Man—person………. 1
Deep—water………..
Soft—pliable………
Eating—cake……….
Mountain—high……..
House—bricks………
Black—color……….
Mutton—meat……….
Comfort—easy………
Hand—limb………….
Short—small………. 1
Fruit—vegetable……
Butterfly—insect…..
Smooth—level………
Command—control……
Chair—sit………….
Sweet—nice……….. 1
Whistle—noise……..
Woman—person………. 1
Cold—atmosphere……
Slow—easy………….
Wish—something…….
River—stream………
White—color……….
Beautiful—nice……. 1
Window—glass………
Rough—unpleasant….. 1
Citizen—person……. 1
Foot—limb………….
Spider—insect……..
Needle—instrument….
Red—color………….
Sleep—bed………….
Anger—irritable……
Carpet—rug………..
Girl—person……….. 1
High—elevation…….
Working—try………. 2
Sour—bitter……….
Earth—sand………..
Trouble—anxiety……
Soldier—person……. 1
Cabbage—plant……..

- 157 -

Hard—stone………..
Eagle—bird………..
Stomach—person……. 1
Stem—apple………..
Lamp—light………..
Dream—sleep……….
Yellow—color………
Bread—flour……….
Justice—Equal……..
Boy—child………….
Light—gas………….
Health—doctor……..
Bible—Scripture……
Memory—thought……. 1
Sheep—animal………
Bath—water………..
Cottage—house……..
Swift—quick……….
Blue—color………..
Hungry—want……….
Priest—preach……..
Ocean—water……….
Head—person………. 1
Stove—heat………..
Long—length……….
Religion—belief……
Whiskey—drink……..
Child—person………. 1
Bitter—sour……….
Hammer—tool………..
Thirsty—dry……….
City—place………..
Square—shape………
Butter—eat………..
Doctor—physician…..
Loud—hear………….
Thief—steal……….
Lion—animal……….
Joy—glad………….
Bed—sleep………….
Heavy—weight………
Tobacco—plant……..
Baby—child………..

Moon—light………..
Scissors—tool……..
Quiet—rest………..
Green—color……….
Salt—spice………..
Street—place………
King—ruler………..
Cheese—eat………..
Blossom—flower…….
Afraid—hide……….

CASE No. 5719.—A.W.S. 5 individual reactions; 12 non-specific reactions.

Table—stand……….
Dark—color………..
Music—happy………. 1
Sickness—ill……….
Man—human………….
Deep—thought……… 1
Soft—touch………..
Eating—appetite……
Mountain—ground……
House—shelter……..
Black—color……….
Mutton—lamb……….
Comfort—warm………
Hand—touch………..
Short—small………. 1
Fruit—taste……….
Butterfly—beauty….. 1
Smooth—level………
Command—obey………
Chair—rest………..
Sweet—good………..
Whistle—noise……..
Woman—female………
Cold—chilled……… 2
Slow—move…………
Wish—think……….. 1
River—water……….
White—color……….
Beautiful—nice……. 1
Window—glass………
Rough—push………..

Citizen—man.......... 1
Foot—body............
Spider—insect........
Needle—pointed.......
Red—blood............
Sleep—rest...........
Anger—riled..........
Carpet—covering......
Girl—child...........
High—air.............
Working—ambitious....
Sour—taste...........
Earth—ground.........
Trouble—thought...... 1
Soldier—command......
Cabbage—vegetable....
Hard—blow............17
Eagle—bird...........
Stomach—body.........
Stem—pipe............
Lamp—light...........
Dream—thought........ 1
Yellow—purple........
Bread—food...........
Justice—law..........
Boy—male.............
Light—lamp...........
Health—soul..........19
Bible—Scriptures.....
Memory—thought....... 1
Sheep—lamb...........
Bath—cleanness.......
Cottage—house........
Swift—quick..........
Blue—color...........
Hungry—appetite......
Priest—scholar....... 2
Ocean—water..........
Head—brains..........
Stove—heat...........
Long—measurement..... 2
Religion—good........ 1
Whiskey—alcohol......

Child—baby………..
Bitter—taste………
Hammer—knock………
Thirsty—water……..
City—New York……..
Square—box………..
Butter—milk……….
Doctor—help……….
Loud—noise………..
Thief—burglar……..
Lion—animal……….
Joy—well………….19
Bed—rest………….
Heavy—load………..
Tobacco—nicotine…..
Baby—joy………….
Moon—light………..
Scissors—cutting…..
Quiet—rest………..
Green—color……….
Salt—sand………..19
Street—crossing…... 2
King—ruler………..
Cheese—luxury……..19
Blossom—flower…….
Afraid—fright……..

CASE No. 5635. J.D. 13 individual reactions, of which 6 are classed as normal, 1 particle, 6 unclassified, mostly obviously normal.

Table—eating………
Dark—night………..
Music—amusement……
Sickness—distress….
Man—working……….
Deep—sorrow……….
Soft—easy…………
Eating—supper……..17
Mountain—pleasure…. 1
House—home………..
Black—grief……….19
Mutton—butchers…… 2
Comfort—home………
Hand—shake………..

Short—baseball…….19
Fruit—eating………
Butterfly—field……
Smooth—soft……….
Command—oblige…….17
Chair—seat………..
Sweet—flowers……..
Whistle—fire………
Woman—home………..
Cold—winter……….
Slow—easy…………
Wish—home…………
River—dock………..17
Whiter—day………..
Beautiful—handsome…
Window—glass………
Rough—wagon………..19
Citizen—voter……..
Foot—walking………
Spider—web………..
Needle—sticking……19
Red—danger………..
Sleep—rest………..
Anger—right……….19
Carpet—house………
Girl—out………….12
High—air………….
Working—labor……..
Sour—bitter……….
Earth—ground………
Trouble—worry……..
Soldier—man……….1
Cabbage—farmer…….2
Hard—bath…………19
Eagle—birds……….
Stomach—body………
Stem—pipe…………
Lamp—burn…………
Dream—thinking…….1
Yellow—color………
Bread—eating………
Justice—peace……..
Boy—soldier……….17

Light—day............
Health—happy......... 1
Bible—books..........
Memory—good.......... 1
Sheep—lamb...........
Bath—washing.........
Cottage—house........
Swift—quick..........
Blue—color...........
Hungry—eating........
Priest—church........
Ocean—bathing........
Head—mind............
Stove—fire...........
Long—hours...........
Religion—church......
Whiskey—drinking.....
Child—home...........
Bitter—sour..........
Hammer—working.......
Thirsty—dry..........
City—New York........
Square—block.........
Butter—cow...........
Doctor—hospital......
Loud—speaking........ 2
Thief—sentence.......17
Lion—animal..........
Joy—pleasure......... 1
Bed—sleeping.........
Heavy—weight.........
Tobacco—smoking......
Baby—home............
Moon—night...........
Scissors—cutting.....
Quiet—alone..........
Green—color..........
Salt—eating..........
Street—walking.......
King—William.........17
Cheese—milk..........
Blossom—flower.......
Afraid—fright........

Our cases of *alcoholic* dementia are clinically without evidences of disturbance of flow of thought. The dementia consists mainly in impairment or loss of the power of retention, with resulting amnesia for recent occurrences, and temporal disorientation. The records are either normal or show but slight departures from normal.

CASE No. 6369.—J.S. Slight deterioration.

Table—eat…………
Dark—night………..
Music—enjoyment……
Sickness—sadness…..
Man—work…………. 1
Deep—hole…………
Soft—feathers……..
Eating—appetite……
Mountain—hill……..
House—live………..
Black—dark………..
Mutton—eat………..
Comfort—pleasant….. 1
Hand—work…………. 1
Short—story……….
Fruit—eat…………
Butterfly—annoyance.. 6
Smooth—iron……….
Command—officer……
Chair—sit…………
Sweet—nice……….. 1
Whistle—pleasure….. 1
Woman—pleasure……. 1
Cold—annoyance……. 6
Slow—car………….
Wish—like…………
River—water……….
White—sack………..17
Beautiful—house……17
Window—look……….
Rough—unpleasant….. 1
Citizen—man……….. 1
Foot—walk…………
Spider—annoyance…..
Needle—sticking……19
Red—color…………

- 164 -

Sleep—happy.......... 1
Anger—annoyance......
Carpet—walk..........
Girl—school..........
High—skies...........
Working—labor........
Sour—lemon...........
Earth—walk...........
Trouble—annoyance....
Soldier—army.........
Cabbage—eat..........
Hard—stone...........
Eagle—fly............
Stomach—victuals.....17
Stem—pipe............
Lamp—burn............
Dream—sleep..........
Yellow—orange........
Bread—eat............
Justice—person....... 1
Boy—school...........
Light—see............
Health—comfort.......
Bible—read...........
Memory—recollection..
Sheep—eat............
Bath—cleanness.......
Cottage—live.........
Swift—go.............
Blue—color...........
Hungry—eat...........
Priest—confession....
Ocean—vessels........ 2
Head—knowledge.......
Stove—burn...........
Long—time............
Religion—faith.......
Whiskey—drink........
Child—infant.........
Bitter—unkind........17
Hammer—nail..........
Thirsty—dry..........
City—inhabitants.....

- 165 -

Square—brick………
Butter—eat………..
Doctor—cure……….
Loud—noise………..
Thief—steal……….
Lion—animal……….
Joy—happiness…….. 1
Bed—lay…………..
Heavy—feeling…….. 2
Tobacco—chew……….
Baby—nurse………..
Moon—bright……….
Scissors—cut……….
Quiet—ease………..
Green—flower……….
Salt—taste………..
Street—walking…….
King—control………19
Cheese—eat………..
Blossom—flower…….
Afraid—nervousness…

CASE No. 6418.—J.R. Marked deterioration.

Table—mahogany…….
Dark—dawn…………17
Music—harp………..17
Sickness—none…….. 6
Man—white…………19
Deep—unfathomable…. 2
Soft—silken………. 2
Eating—good……….. 1
Mountain—high……..
House—place……….
Black—color……….
Mutton—cooked……..17
Comfort—rest……….
Hand—clasp………..19
Short—small……….. 1
Fruit—apples……….
Butterfly—buttercups. 2
Smooth—iron………..
Command—home………19
Chair—ebony……….19

Sweet—potatoes.......17
Whistle—song.........
Woman—pretty......... 1
Cold—depressed.......19
Slow—process.........17
Wish—home............
River—Mississippi....
White—wings..........17
Beautiful—palace.....19
Window—clear.........
Rough—no.............12
Citizen—patriot......
Foot—heath...........19
Spider—none.......... 5
Needle—darning.......
Red—apples...........
Sleep—plenty.........
Anger—mistake........17
Carpet—floor.........
Girl—pretty.......... 1
High—ordinary........19
Working—eight........12
Sour—nonsense........19
Earth—fruits......... 2
Trouble—little.......
Soldier—patriot......
Cabbage—garden.......
Hard—wood............
Eagle—high...........

Stomach—leave........19
Stem—stalk...........
Lamp—kerosene........
Dream—happy.......... 1
Yellow—aster.........17
Bread—white..........
Justice—right........
Boy—white............15
Light—white..........
Health—good.......... 1
Bible—puzzled........19
Memory—bad........... 1
Sheep—cheviot........17
Bath—marble..........17

Cottage—story……..17
Swift—fast………..
Blue—waist………..17
Hungry—not……….. 2
Priest—confessor…..
Ocean—Pacific……..17
Head—oval…………19
Stove—polish………
Long—forever……….12
Religion—Protestant..
Whiskey—none………
Child—none……….. 5
Bitter—sweet………
Hammer—no…………12
Thirsty—no……….. 5
City—New York……..
Square—compass…….
Butter—sweet………
Doctor—cure……….
Loud—quietly………. 2
Thief—jail………..
Lion—brave,……….
Joy—peacefulness….. 2
Bed—good…………. 1
Heavy—no………….
Tobacco—yes……….12
Baby—none…………. 6
Moon—shines……….
Scissors—uncut……. 2
Quiet—peaceful…….
Green—grass……….
Salt—water………..
Street—Queen………17
King—unknown………19
Cheese—Stilton…….17
Blossom—cherry…….
Afraid—not………..

We reproduce in full the record obtained from one of our cases of *senile dementia*.

CASE No. 5788.—E.S.

Table—cat………… 6
Dark—night………..

Music—cat............ 2
Sickness—cat......... 6
Man—mouse............18
Deep—well............
Soft—sack............19
Eating—well..........
Mountain—hill........
House—castle.........
Black—dog............
Mutton—sheep.........
Comfort—lamb.........13
Hand—chicken.........18
Short—light..........19
Fruit—apple..........
Butterfly—fly........
Smooth—iron..........
Command—obey.........
Chair—stool..........
Sweet—sugar..........
Whistle—lump.........18
Woman—man............ 1
Cold—shiver..........
Slow—cold............ 7
Wish—push............19
River—pond...........
White—cat............
Beautiful—cat........ 6
Window—glass.........
Rough—fight..........19
Citizen—tough........
Foot—shoe............
Spider—clock.........19
Needle—pin...........
Red—white............
Sleep—eyes...........
Anger—mad............
Carpet—cloth.........
Girl—boy.............
High—low.............
Working—sewing.......
Sour—sweet...........
Earth—clay...........
Trouble—child........13

Soldier—man………. 1
Cabbage—spinach……
Hard—cat…………. 6
Eagle—bird………..
Stomach—belly……..
Stem—pike…………17
Lamp—globe………..
Dream—eyes………..
Yellow—flower……..
Bread—flour……….
Justice—fight……..
Boy—cat………….. 6
Light—lamp………..
Health—cough………17
Bible—book………..
Memory—mind………..
Sheep—lamb………..
Bath—water………..
Cottage—house……..
Swift—quick………..
Blue—color………..
Hungry—eat………..
Priest—clergyman…..
Ocean—river……….
Head—life………….
Stove—fire………..
Long—short………..
Religion—Catholic….
Whiskey—drink……..
Child—boy…………
Bitter—sweet………
Hammer—noise………
Thirsty—drink……..
City—New York……..
Square—Marion……..17
Butter—cow………..
Doctor—W………….17
Loud—noise………..
Thief—steals………
Lion—heart………..
Joy—happy………… 1
Bed—mattress………
Heavy—lead………..

Tobacco—smoke……..
Baby—boy………….
Moon—shine………..
Scissors—cut……….
Quiet—noisy………..
Green—color………..
Salt—bitter………..
Street—place……….
King—rule………….
Cheese—taste……….
Blossom—flower…….
Afraid—trouble…….

§8. PATHOLOGICAL REACTIONS FROM NORMAL SUBJECTS.

Mental disorders do not always so manifest themselves as to incapacitate the subject for his work or to necessitate his sequestration in a hospital for the insane. It is, therefore, not surprising that in applying the association test to over a thousand subjects selected at random we have obtained a small number of test records which show various types of abnormal reactions. Among the subjects who furnished such records some are described as eccentric, taciturn, or dull, while others are apparently normal but come of neuropathic stock. A few of them are persons wholly unknown to us.

We reproduce in full from the normal series, containing abnormal reactions.

CONSECUTIVE No. 746.—State hospital attendant Efficient in his work but is generally regarded to have married very foolishly. Sound reactions; numerous unclassified reactions.

Table—brought……..19
Dark—some………..19
Music—leaf………..19
Sickness—water…….19
Man—book………….19
Deep—desk………….19
Soft—ground………..
Eating—bark………..19
Mountain—tree……..
House—paper………..19
Black—light………..
Mutton—horse………13
Comfort—hat………..19
Hand—sick………….13

Short—swallow........19
Fruit—mass..........19
Butterfly—leaf.......15
Smooth—wing..........13
Command—man.......... 1
Chair—left..........19
Sweet—sick.......... 2
Whistle—whirl........10
Woman—where..........12
Cold—coal............
Slow—some............15
Wish—whirl..........15
River—rice..........19
White—waist..........
Beautiful—brought....15
Window—women.........10
Rough—row............19
Citizen—sir..........10
Foot—fall............19
Spider—spice.........10
Needle—knee..........10
Red—roam.............19
Sleep—sorrow.........19
Anger—August.........19
Carpet—covered....... 2
Girl—great.......... 9
High—his.............12
Working—map..........19
Sour—slur............10
Earth—eat............19
Trouble—through......12
Soldier—solder.......10
Cabbage—cart.........19
Hard—him.............12
Eagle—earth..........13
Stomach—stall........10
Stem—stair...........10
Lamp—left............19
Dream—dread..........
Yellow—waist.........15
Bread—book..........15
Justice—gem..........19
Boy—bird.............19

- 172 -

Light—left..........10
Health—heart.........17
Bible—base...........19
Memory—moth..........19
Sheep—shrill.........19
Bath—bend............19

Cottage—cart.........10
Swift—swell..........10
Blue—beard...........11
Hungry—heart.........15
Priest—path..........19
Ocean—oar............10
Head—him.............12
Stove—still..........10
Long—left............15
Religion—rest........19
Whiskey—whirl........15
Child—charge.........19
Bitter—bought........10
Hammer—hemp..........10
Thirsty—Thursday.....10
City—salt............10
Square—squirrel......10
Butter—bread.........
Doctor—daisy.........19
Loud—lark............19
Thief—twist..........19
Lion—lesson..........10
Joy—jar..............19
Bed—beard............10
Heavy—health.........10
Tobacco—toboggan.....10
Baby—bird............15
Moon—mill............19
Scissors—setters.....10
Quiet—quart..........10
Green—great.......... 9
Salt—sorrow..........10
Street—stem..........10
King—cart............15
Cheese—chart.........19
Blossom—bed..........19
Afraid—frill.........10

CONSECUTIVE No. 220—Laundryman in State hospital. Nothing abnormal has ever been observed in his case. Numerous perseverations.

Table—house..........
Dark—range...........19
Music—eats..........
Sickness—dog.........18
Man—barn.............19
Deep—hollow..........
Soft—apple...........
Eating—cranberry.....17
Mountain—water.......17
House—pig............19
Black—rats..........18
Mutton—mice.......... 2
Comfort—sheep........13
Hand—lamb............14
Short—birds..........19
Fruit—peach..........
Butterfly—pears......18
Smooth—grapes........18
Command—nut..........18
Chair—bureau.........
Sweet—broom..........19
Whistle—violin.......19
Woman—man............ 1
Cold—child..........10
Slow—infant..........14
Wish—night...........19
River—dark..........14
White—steamboat......17
Beautiful—tugboat....18
Window—yacht.........18
Rough—ferry..........18
Citizen—water........13
Foot—egg.............19
Spider—fly..........
Needle—thread........
Red—spool............18
Sleep—machine........18
Anger—picture........19
Carpet—bed..........17
Girl—bureau..........18
High—oilcloth........18

Working—pen..........19
Sour—ink.............18
Earth—paper..........18
Trouble—chair........19
Soldier—table........14
Cabbage—beet.........
Hard—cauliflower.....13
Eagle—potatoes.......18
Stomach—beans........17
Stem—plum............17
Lamp—wick............
Dream—oil............13
Yellow—stick.........19
Bread—stone..........18
Justice—dirt.........18
Boy—street...........
Light—match..........
Health—sickness......
Bible—book...........
Memory—leaf..........13
Sheep—wool...........
Bath—water...........
Cottage—people....... 1
Swift—fast...........
Blue—residence.......19
Hungry—beef..........17
Priest—clergyman.....
Ocean—rice...........19
Head—eyes............
Stove—nose...........18
Long—mouth...........18
Religion—legs........18
Whiskey—arms.........18
Child—elbows.........18
Bitter—day...........19
Hammer—nails.........
Thirsty—saw..........13
City—plane...........18
Square—chisel........18
Butter—file..........18
Doctor—duck..........10
Loud—goose...........18
Thief—robber.........

- 175 -

Lion—tiger………..
Joy—bear…………13
Bed—leopard……...18
Heavy—tiger……...15
Tobacco—smoke……..
Baby—pipe…………13
Moon—star…………
Scissors—sharp…….
Quiet—noisy……….
Green—blue………..
Salt—yellow……….13
Street—green………14
King—purple……...14
Cheese—axe………..19
Blossom—handle…….19
Afraid—barn……….19

CONSECUTIVE No. 255.—State hospital attendant. Efficient, but unusually taciturn and seclusive. Sound reactions.

Table—linen……….
Dark—sunshine……..17
Music—song………..
Sickness—Saturday….19
Man—manager………10
Deep—dark…………
Soft—sorrowful…….10
Eating—eighty……..10
Mountain—miner…….19
House—heart……….19
Black—blue………..
Mutton—mountain……10
Comfort—company……17
Hand—happy………..10
Short—slow………..17
Fruit—froth……….10
Butterfly—butter…..10
Smooth—smoke………10
Command—company……
Chair—chap………..10
Sweet—slow………..15
Whistle—whip………10
Woman—worried……..19
Cold—cow………….10

Slow—slap............10
Wish—water...........
River—rubbed.........19
White—wash...........
Beautiful—bounty.....10
Window—light.........
Rough—roguish........19
Citizen—sight-seeing.19
Foot—fool............10
Spider—span..........10
Needle—work.......... 1
Red—robe.............19
Sleep—soap...........10
Anger—angel..........19
Carpet—carriage......19
Girl—guide...........19
High—heart...........10
Working—worthy.......10
Sour—satchel.........19
Earth—early..........10
Trouble—trout........19
Soldier—socket.......19
Cabbage—currant......17
Hard—harmful.........10
Eagle—early..........15
Stomach—stable.......19
Stem—stand...........10
Lamp—light...........
Dream—drunk..........10
Yellow—lustre........19
Bread—brand..........10
Justice—judgment.....
Boy—butter...........15
Light—love...........19
Health—help..........10
Bible—book...........
Memory—mental........
Sheep—shop...........10
Bath—bandage.........10
Cottage—cot..........10
Swift—swan...........10
Blue—black...........10
Hungry—height........19

Priest—house………
Ocean—apple……….19
Head—heart………..
Stove—strap……….10
Long—love…………15
Religion—belief……
Whiskey—whisk broom..10
Child—chap………..10
Bitter—butter……..10
Hammer—habit………19
Thirsty—thirty…….10
City—soap…………15
Square—squirrel……10
Butter—bank……….19
Doctor—dentist…….
Loud—laugh………..
Thief—thump……….19
Lion—lump…………19
Joy—jump………….19
Bed—bank………….15
Heavy—happy……….10
Tobacco—tub……….19
Baby—bundle……….
Moon—mantle……….10
Scissors—Saturday….15
Quiet—quarter……..10
Green—drought……..19
Salt—Saturday……..10
Street—straight……
King—cattle……….19
Cheese—captain…….19
Blossom—bandage……15
Afraid—flattered…..10

CONSECUTIVE No. 442.—Nothing abnormal has ever been suspected in the case of this subject; mother eccentric; sister insane. Sound reactions.

Table—stable………
Dark—dreary……….
Music—joy…………
Sickness—silliness…10
Man—manner………..10
Deep—dreary……….15
Soft—sooth………..19

Eating—evening.......10
Mountain—morning.....18
House—help...........19
Black—dark...........
Mutton—mitten........10
Comfort—come.........10
Hand—handsome........10
Short—small.......... 1
Fruit—first..........10
Butterfly—butter.....10
Smooth—sooth.........10
Command—come.........
Chair—air............10
Sweet—good........... 1
Whistle—music........
Woman—wonder.........19
Cold—freezing........
Slow—snow............10
Wish—wind............10
River—riffle......... 3
White—wait...........10
Beautiful—handsome...
Window—light.........
Rough—harsh..........
Citizen—city.........
Foot—walk............
Spider—creep.........
Needle—needless......10
Red—color............
Sleep—sleet..........10
Anger—rough..........
Carpet—carpenter.....10
Girl—going...........19
High—air.............
Working—toiling......
Sour—shower..........10
Earth—eating.........19
Trouble—loneliness...17
Soldier—solid........10
Cabbage—carrying.....19
Hard—hardly.......... 8
Eagle—eating.........10
Stomach—starch.......10

Stem—step………… 2
Lamp—glass………..
Dream—dreary………
Yellow—yonder……..12
Bread—bed…………10
Justice—juice……..10
Boy—ball…………..
Light—likeness…….10
Health—help……….10
Bible—book………..
Memory—memorial…… 2
Sheep—sleep………..
Bath—battle……….10
Cottage—cotton…….10
Swift—fast………..
Blue—blind………..10
Hungry—hurry………10
Priest—prince……..10
Ocean—over………..12
Head—large……….. 1
Stove—stone……….10
Long—heavy………..19
Religion—goodness…. 1
Whiskey—strong…….
Child—small………. 1
Bitter—butter……..10
Hammer—hard……….
Thirsty—thrifty……10
City—seeing……….10
Square—squirrel……10
Butter—bitter……..10
Doctor—dark……….10
Loud—noisy………..
Thief—stealing…….
Lion—eating……….
Joy—joyous……….. 8
Bed—sleep………….
Heavy—weightful…… 4
Tobacco—cocoa……..10
Baby—boys…………. 2
Moon—moo…………. 3
Scissors—successors..10
Quiet—easy………..

Green—grass..........
Salt—simmer..........19
Street—steep.........10
King—kingdom.........
Cheese—squeeze.......10
Blossom—blooming.....
Afraid—Africa........10

CONSECUTIVE No. 314.—School teacher. Efficient; described as very silent. Unclassified reactions, due mostly to distraction.

Table—cat............19
Dark—no..............12
Music—will..........19
Sickness—chair......19
Man—table............ 6
Deep—floor..........14
Soft—paper.......... 6
Eating—wood..........19
Mountain—chair.......15
House—Window.........
Black—wall..........
Mutton—sky..........19
Comfort—air..........18
Hand—table..........
Short—paper.......... 6
Fruit—sweeping.......19
Butterfly—room.......18
Smooth—working....... 2
Command—stone........19
Chair—machine........19
Sweet—radiator.......19
Whistle—clock........19
Woman—cane...........19
Cold—flower..........19
Slow—cord............19
Wish—marriage........ 2
River—chimney........19
White—wheel..........19
Beautiful—cane.......15
Window—pot...........19
Rough—grass..........19
Citizen—paper........
Foot—closet..........19

Spider—awning........19
Needle—good..........9
Red—bad..............9
Sleep—hinge..........19
Anger—will...........15
Carpet—paper.........6
Girl—chair...........15
High—table...........6
Working—cane.........15
Sour—floor...........15
Earth—ceiling........18
Trouble—chain........19
Soldier—desk.........19
Cabbage—paper........
Hard—table...........
Eagle—flower.........15
Stomach—match........19
Stem—match...........
Lamp—table...........
Dream—chair..........14
Yellow—cane..........18
Bread—flour..........
Justice—peace........
Boy—window...........15
Light—wall...........18
Health—floor.........18
Bible—house..........18
Memory—paper.........6
Sheep—dress..........19
Bath—clothes.........18
Cottage—earth........19
Swift—sky............18
Blue—trees...........19
Hungry—leaves........18
Priest—bark..........18
Ocean—boat...........
Head—hat.............
Stove—ashes..........17
Long—short...........
Religion—peace.......
Whiskey—bottle.......
Child—dress..........
Bitter—sour..........

Hammer—teeth.........19
Thirsty—dry..........
City—good............ 1
Square—wood..........
Butter—best..........10
Doctor—shoes.........19
Loud—music...........
Thief—notes.......... 2
Lion—strings.........19
Joy—happy............ 1
Bed—wish.............13
Heavy—lead...........
Tobacco—plant........
Baby—good............ 1
Moon—paper........... 6
Scissors—straw.......19
Quiet—hoop...........19
Green—rope...........19
Salt—dish............
Street—dirt..........
King—bucket..........19
Cheese—plate.........
Blossom—plant........
Afraid—sweeping......15

CONSECUTIVE No. 216.—State hospital attendant. Incompetent, dull. Numerous non-specific reactions.

Table—rolling........19
Dark—swim............19
Music—playing........
Sickness—riding......19
Man—walk.............
Deep—singing.........19
Soft—light...........
Eating—sleep.........
Mountain—low.........
House—small.......... 1
Black—dark...........
Mutton—lean..........19
Comfort—good......... 1
Hand—small........... 1
Short—small.......... 1
Fruit—taste..........

Butterfly—beautiful.. 1
Smooth—long………. 6
Command—immediate…. 2
Chair—small………. 6
Sweet—clear……….19
Whistle—long………
Woman—small………. 1
Cold—long………… 6
Slow—write……….. 2
Wish—quick………..10
River—long………..
White—clean……….
Beautiful—nice……. 1
Window—big………..19
Rough—bad………… 1
Citizen—short……..19
Foot—small……….. 1
Spider—small……… 1
Needle—small……… 1
Red—dark………….
Sleep—easy………..
Anger—bad………… 1
Carpet—small……… 1
Girl—short………..15
High—long…………
Working—good……… 1
Sour—bad…………. 1
Earth—large………. 1
Trouble—bad………. 1
Soldier—good……… 1
Cabbage—small…….. 6
Hard—apples……….
Eagle—small………. 6
Stomach—good……… 1
Stem—short………..
Lamp—bright……….
Dream—good……….. 1
Yellow—light………
Bread—good……….. 1
Justice—good……… 1
Boy—small………… 1
Light—clear……….
Health—good………. 1

Bible—true………..
Memory—good………. 1
Sheep—many………..
Bath—good………… 1
Cottage—large…….. 1
Swift—fast………..
Blue—dark…………
Hungry—long………. 6
Priest—true……….19
Ocean—wide………..
Head—large……….. 1
Stove—black……….
Long—wide…………
Religion—good…….. 1
Whiskey—strong…….
Child—small……….. 1
Bitter—bad……….. 1
Hammer—small……… 1
Thirsty—bad………. 1
City—big………….
Square—long………..
Butter—good………. 1
Doctor—good………. 1
Loud—hearty……….19
Thief—bad…………. 1
Lion—bad…………. 5
Joy—happy………… 1
Bed—easy………….
Heavy—stone……….
Tobacco—strong…….
Baby—small……….. 1
Moon—large……….. 1
Scissors—sharp…….
Quiet—baby………..
Green—dark………..
Salt—strong……….10
Street—wide……….
King—high…………
Cheese—good………. 1
Blossom—apples…….
Afraid—he…………12

CONSECUTIVE No. 318.—School boy. Non-specific reactions.

Table—board..........
Dark—night............
Music—sound..........
Sickness—pleasantness 9
Man—people............ 1
Deep—river............
Soft—cat.............. 2
Eating—pleasantness.. 1
Mountain—high........
House—home...........
Black—dark...........
Mutton—good.......... 1
Comfort—pleasure..... 1
Hand—foot............
Short—little.........
Fruit—good........... 1
Butterfly—pretty..... 1
Smooth—soft..........
Command—go............
Chair—sit............
Sweet—good........... 1
Whistle—noise........
Woman—pretty......... 1
Cold—bad............. 1
Slow—quick...........
Wish—good............ 1
River—deep...........
White—snow...........
Beautiful—pretty..... 1
Window—look..........
Rough—even...........
Citizen—good......... 1
Foot—hand............
Spider—bite..........
Needle—sharp.........
Red—crimson..........
Sleep—wake...........
Anger—mad............
Carpet—floor.........

Girl—good............ 1
High—tall............
Working—sleep........
Sour—bad............. 1

Earth—ground………
Trouble—bad………. 1
Soldier—good……… 1
Cabbage—bad………. 6
Hard—soft…………
Eagle—bird………..
Stomach—ache………
Stem—slender………
Lamp—light………..
Dream—good………… 1
Yellow—pretty…….. 1
Bread—good……….. 1
Justice—good……… 1
Boy—fun…………..
Light—see…………
Health—happiness….. 1
Bible—good……….. 1
Memory—good……….. 1
Sheep—pretty………. 1
Bath—good…………. 1
Cottage—pretty……. 1
Swift—quick……….
Blue—yellow……….
Hungry—eat………..
Priest—good……….
Ocean—big…………
Head—little……….15
Stove—hot…………
Long—distance……..
Religion—good…….. 1
Whiskey—bad………. 1
Child—cute………..
Bitter—good………. 1
Hammer—hard……….
Thirsty—hard……… 5
City—good………… 6
Square—round………
Butter—soft……….
Doctor—good………. 1
Loud—noisy………..
Thief—good……….. 6
Lion—big………….
Joy—good…………. 1

- 187 -

Bed—comfortable……
Heavy—light………..
Tobacco—bad………. 1
Baby—pretty………. 1
Moon—cute…………13
Scissors—sharp…….
Quiet—loud………..
Green—pretty……… 1
Salt—good…………. 1
Street—narrow……..
King—good………… 6
Cheese—good………. 1
Blossom—pretty……. 1
Afraid—scared……..

CONSECUTIVE NO. 234.—School boy. Non-specific reactions.

Table—chair………..
Dark—cold…………
Music—sweet………..
Sickness—hard……..
Man—wise………….19
Deep—dark…………
Soft—sweet………..
Eating—drinking……
Mountain—snow……..
House—great………. 9
Black—horse………..
Mutton—good……….. 1
Comfort—health…….
Hand—foot…………
Short—fat…………
Fruit—good……….. 1
Butterfly—pretty…..
Smooth—hard……….
Command—general……
Chair—soft………..
Sweet—good……….. 1
Whistle—loud………
Woman—large………. 1
Cold—dreary……….
Slow—hard…………
Wish—fairy………..
River—large………. 1

White—snow………..
Beautiful—woman…… 1
Window—large……… 1
Rough—hard………..
Citizen—good……… 1
Foot—small……….. 1
Spider—ugly………..
Needle—thick………
Red—cow…………..17
Sleep—dreams………
Anger—very………..12
Carpet—pretty…….. 1
Girl—small……….. 1
High—tree…………
Working—hard………
Sour—bitter………..
Earth—great……….. 1
Trouble—hard………
Soldier—brave……..
Cabbage—good……… 1
Hard—stone………..
Eagle—great……….. 9
Stomach—weak………
Stem—watch………..
Lamp—pretty……….. 9
Dream—sweet………..
Yellow—buttercup…..
Bread—flour………..
Justice—man……….. 1
Boy—gun…………..
Light—bright………
Health—care……….. 2
Bible—holy………..
Memory—poor………..
Sheep—pretty……… 1
Bath—nice…………. 1
Cottage—low………..
Swift—stream………
Blue—bluebird…….. 2
Hungry—tired………
Priest—church……..
Ocean—water………..
Head—large……….. 1

Stove—fire...........
Long—snake...........
Religion—Jesus........
Whiskey—temperance...
Child—healthy........19
Bitter—apple.........
Hammer—nail..........
Thirsty—water........
City—houses..........
Square—desk..........
Butter—yellow........
Doctor—medicine......
Loud—harse...........
Thief—wicked.........
Lion—fierce..........
Joy—happiness........ 1
Bed—rest.............
Heavy—stone..........
Tobacco—dirty........
Baby—small........... 1
Moon—sky.............
Scissors—sharp.......
Quiet—lonely.........
Green—sour...........
Salt—cows............19
Street—people........ 1
King—rich............19
Cheese—yellow........
Blossom—pretty....... 1
Afraid—fear..........

CONSECUTIVE No. 809.—Lawyer. 28 individual reactions, of which 14 are classed as normal; 10 are unclassified, most of which are also obviously normal.

Table—chair.............
Dark—candle............ 17
Music—girl..............
Sickness—doctor.........
Man—woman............... 1
Deep—swimming...........19
Soft—hand...............
Eating—Reisenweber......17
Mountain—Kipling........19

House—mortgage..........17
Black—spectrum..........19
Mutton—pig…………..
Comfort—chair………..
Hand—ring……………
Short—tall…………...
Fruit—banana…………
Butterfly—color………
Smooth—sphere………..17
Command—soldier………
Chair—teacher………..10
Sweet—apple………….
Whistle—policeman…….
Woman—hat……………
Cold—thermometer……..19
Slow—invalid…………
Wish—million…………
River—Hudson…………
White—Broadway………..19
Beautiful—girl……….
Window—school………..
Rough—ball…………..19
Citizen—justice………
Foot—shoe……………
Spider—insect………..
Needle—tailor………..17
Red—flannel………….
Sleep—potassium bromide.17
Anger—teacher………..
Carpet—tack………….
Girl—belt……………17
High—pole……………
Working—laborer………
Sour—apple…………..
Earth—Columbus……….
Trouble—lawyer……….19
Soldier—gun………….
Cabbage—plantation…… 2
Hard—brick…………..
Eagle—feathers……….
Stomach—juice………..17
Stem—leaf……………
Lamp—light…………..

Dream—pillow............17
Yellow—lemon............
Bread—crust.............
Justice—judge...........
Boy—pants..............
Light—gas..............
Health—medicine.........
Bible—Jacob.............17
Memory—brain............
Sheep—wool..............
Bath—soap..............
Cottage—rod.............19
Swift—ball.............
Blue—sky...............
Hungry—I...............
Priest—surplice.........
Ocean—ship.............
Head—hair..............
Stove—shovel............17
Long—pole..............
Religion—Abraham........19
Whiskey—Kentucky........17
Child—baby.............
Bitter—pepper..........
Hammer—nail.............
Thirsty—lemonade........
City—Manhattan..........17
Square—Washington.......
Butter—salt............
Doctor—nurse...........
Loud—hammer............
Thief—jewelry..........
Lion—Androcles..........18
Joy—automobile.........
Bed—shoes..............15
Heavy—Flannigan.........19
Tobacco—pipe...........
Baby—wife..............
Moon—man................ 1
Scissors—cut...........
Quiet—demure...........
Green—eyes.............
Salt—cellar............

Street—Wall............17
King—Edward.............
Cheese—Roquefort........
Blossom—field...........
Afraid—burglar..........

§ 9. NUMBER OF DIFFERENT WORDS GIVEN AS REACTIONS.

It has been suggested by Fuhrmann [1] that the number of different words given in response to one hundred selected stimulus words may be used as "a fairly reliable measure of the intelligence and degree of education of a patient." The test according to Fuhrmann is applied twice in every case, the interval between the two sittings being at least four weeks. "In very intelligent and well educated persons every 100 stimulus words almost always evokes in the first test 95-100 different associations; in the less intelligent and in the feeble-minded the same associations are more frequently repeated. In the second test with the same stimulus words— which is really much more important than the first, since even persons or inferior intelligence may reach higher numbers in the first test—the difference in the wealth of the stock of representations becomes plainly evident: the man of intelligence will not need to draw on the associations which he gave in the first test, but will produce new ones; the feeble-minded subject will, on the contrary, repeat to a greater or lesser extent the associations of the first test." "In general the associational capacity of an adult person may be taken to be from 80 per cent to 90 per cent. Should the number sink below 70 per cent the suspicion of a pathological condition must then arise; and the higher the subject's degree of education the stronger is this suspicion. In the case of an associational capacity of 60 per cent or less no doubt of its pathological significance can remain any longer."

[Footnote 1: Diagnostik und Prognostik der Geisteskrankheiten, p. 93. Leipzig, 1903.]

Our results are not strictly comparable with Fuhrmann's, because we have obtained but one test record from each subject; it may be said, however, that the results of a single test in each case do not show any considerable differences, corresponding to education or age, in the variety of responses. Further, dementing psychoses, with the exception of epilepsy, show on the whole no diminution in the number of different reactions, although in individual cases this number falls considerably below the general average; and in such cases the diminution may be dependent upon stereotypy or perseveration, and not necessarily upon reduction in the stock of representations.

It would appear from our results that pathological mental states are apt to manifest themselves by a tendency to give reactions belonging to types of inferior values rather than by diminished variety of responses.

We show in Table VI. the numbers of different responses given by our groups of normal and insane subjects, expressed in figures giving for each group the median and the average.

TABLE VI.

Med. Av. 86 normal subjects, common school education; records containing not over 10 individual reactions…….. 85 84.5 66 normal subjects, collegiate education; records containing not over 10 individual reactions…….. 87 86.5 48 normal subjects, school children; records containing not over 10 individual reactions…….. 87 84.9 53 normal subjects; records containing not under 15 individual reactions………………………. 90 88.7 108 cases of dementia præcox……………………….. 87 84.8 33 cases of paranoic conditions…………………… 89 86.5 24 cases of epilepsy………………………………. 781/2 75.8 32 cases of general paresis……………………….. 841/2 82.4 32 cases of manic-depressive insanity……………… 87 85.4

§ 10. CO-OPERATION OF THE SUBJECT.

In our work with insane subjects we encountered many cases in which we were unable to obtain satisfactory test records owing to lack of proper co-operation. Some subjects seemed to be either too confused or too demented to be capable of understanding and following the instructions given them. Others were for one reason or another unwilling to co-operate. It is important to distinguish inability from unwillingness to co-operate, since the former indicates in itself an abnormal state of the mind, while the latter is quite often shown by normal persons.

A subject may co-operate to the extent of giving a single word in response to each stimulus word, and yet fail to co-operate in some other particulars.

He may, instead of giving the first word suggested to him by the stimulus, suppress the first word more or less systematically, and give some other word which may seem to him more appropriate. This probably occurs very often, but does not seem to render the results less serviceable for our purpose.

Further, a subject may react by words related not to the stimulus words, but to each other, thus simulating perseveration; or he may react by naming objects within reach of the senses, thus appearing to be distracted; or he may give only sound reactions.

There is, in fact, no type of pathological reactions which a normal person may not be able to produce more or less readily at will, though in the case of incoherent reactions considerable mental effort may be required, and the end may be attained only by regularly rejecting the first and some subsequent words which are suggested by the stimulus.

In view of these considerations we are led to conclude that the association test, as applied by our method, could not be relied upon as a means of detecting simulation of insanity in malingerers, criminals, and the like.

§ 11. SUMMARY.

The normal range of reaction in response to any of our stimulus words is largely confined within narrow limits.

The frequency tables compiled from test records given by one thousand normal subjects comprise over ninety per cent of the normal range in the average case.

With the aid of the frequency tables and the appendix normal reactions, with a very few exceptions, can be sharply distinguished from pathological ones.

The separation of pathological reactions from normal ones simplifies the task of their analysis, and makes possible the application of a classification based on objective criteria.

By the application of the association test, according to the method here proposed, no sharp distinction can be drawn between mental health and mental disease; a large collection of material shows a gradual and not an abrupt transition from the normal state to pathological states.

In dementia præcox, some paranoic conditions, manic-depressive insanity, general paresis, and epileptic dementia the test reveals some characteristic, though not pathognomonic, associational tendencies.

ACKNOWLEDGMENTS.

It is with pleasure that we acknowledge our indebtedness to the many persons who have assisted us in collecting the data for this work.

About two hundred tests upon normal subjects were made for us by the following persons: Dr. Frederic Lyman Wells, Dr. Jennie A. Dean, Miss Lillian Rosanoff, and Miss Madeleine Wehle.

Dr. O. M. Dewing, the late superintendent of the Long Island State Hospital, and Dr. Chas. W. Pilgrim, superintendent of the Hudson River

State Hospital, have assisted the work by kindly permitting the test to be made upon employees of these institutions, and we are especially indebted to Dr. F. W. Parsons for personal assistance in securing the co-operation of many subjects.

Professor R. S. Woodworth, of Columbia University, extended to us the courtesy of the Psychological Laboratory during several weeks of the summer session of 1909, and gave us much assistance in obtaining interviews with students; we received assistance also from several of the instructors of Teachers' College, especially Mr. Wm. H. Noyes.

We are indebted to Mr. F.C. Lewis and Mr. W.E. Stark, of the Ethical Culture School, New York, for permitting us to make the test upon the pupils of that school.

In the work of compiling the tables we have been assisted by Dr. N. W. Bartram, Dr. Jennie A. Dean, Mrs. H. M. Kent, and others.

We wish, finally, to express our thanks to Dr. Wm. Austin Macy, superintendent of this hospital, to whom we are indebted for the opportunity of undertaking this work.

THE FREQUENCY TABLES.

1. TABLE

accommodation 1 article 3 articles 1

basket 1 bench 9 board 14 book 7 books 5 boy 1 bread 1 breakfast 2 broad 2 brown 1 butter 1

cards 2 celery 1 center 1 chair 267 chairs 7 chemical 1 cloth 57 cockroaches 1 comfort 1 cover 17 cutlery 1

desk 11 dine 2 dining 4 dinner 26 dish 5 dishes 40 dissection 1 dog 1

eat 63 eatables 1 eating 34

ferns 1 fête 1 flat 5 floor 7 food 29 fork 1 form 1 furniture 75

glass 1

hard 9 hat 1 home 2 house 3

ink 1

kitchen 1

lamp 1 large 4 leaf 1 leaves 1 library 1 leg 13 legs 10 linen 2 long 1 low 2

Mabel 1 mahogany 2 mat 1 meal 6 meals 4 meat 2 mess 1

nails 2 napkin 1 number 1

oak 1 object 1 old 1 operating 1 ornament 2

parlor 1 pitcher 1 plate 4 plates 1 plateau 1 polished 1

refreshments 1 rest 3 room 3 round 10

school 1 serviceable 1 set 2 shiny 1 sit 3 sitting 2 slab 1 smooth 1 soup 1 spiritualism 1 spoon 6 spread 2 square 9 stable 1 stand 36 stool 3 straight 1 strong 1 supper 1

tablecloth 1 tea 1 timber 1 top 2 typewriter 1

use 2 useful 3 utensil 1

victuals 2

wagon 1 whist 1 white 1 wire 1 wood 76 wooden 1 work 2 working 1 write 2 writing 6

2. DARK

afraid 6

baby 1 bad 1 barks 1 black 76 blackness 2 blank 1 blind 2 blindness 2 blue 5 board 1 boat 1 bright 15 brightness 4 brown 4

candle 1 cart 1 cat 2 cell 1 cellar 6 close 1 closet 1 cloud 2 clouds 2 cloudy 3 cold 2 color 28 colored 1 colorless 1 coon 1 curly 1

day 1 daylight 1 dead 1 denseness 1 dim 3 dimness 3 dingy 2 dismal 3 dog 1 door 1 dreary 1 dress 4 dungeon 5 dusk 1 dusky 1

evening 4 eye 1 eyes 2

fair 2 fear 6 fearful 1 fearsome 1 fright 2

ghost 1 ghosts 1 gloom 6 gloomy 11 gray 1 green 1 ground 1

hair 5 hall 1 hell 1 hole 1 horse 3 house 2

illumination 1 invisible 2

lamp 1 lantern 1 light 427 lonely 1 lonesome 1 lonesomeness 1

mahogany 1 man 4 mice 1 midnight 1 moon 6 moonlight 1 mysterious 1

nice 1 night 221

oblivion 1 obscure 1

parlor 1 prison 1

red 5 rest 3 room 22

scare 1 shades 1 shadow 2 shadows 1 sky 1 sleep 1 sleeping 1 space 1 starry 1 stars 2 stillness 1 storm 1 stumbling 1 subject 1 sunlight 1

thunder 1 tree 1 twilight 1

unseen 1

walk 1 weather 3 white 9 woods 1

3. MUSIC

accordion 1 air 3 amuse 1 amusement 10 art 7 attention 1 attraction 1

band 6 bassviol 1 beautiful 7 beauty 2 Beethoven 7 bell 1 bird 1 birds 1 book 1 books 2 box 2 brightness 1

captivating 1 cats 1 charm 1 charms 1 charming 2 cheerful 2 cheerfulness 2 Chopin 1 chord 1 chords 1 clarinette 1 classic 1 classical 2 composer 2 company 1 concert 2 conductor 1 dance 17 dances 1 dancing 15 delight 1 delightful 2 discord 3 drama 1

ear 3 ecstasy 1 elevating 1 enchantment 1 enjoyable 1 enjoyed 1 enjoyment 13 entertaining 5 entertainment 3 entrancing 1

feeling 1 fiddle 1 fine 2 flowers 1 flute 1 fun 1

gaiety 2 gay 1 genius 1 girl 2 gladness 1 Goethe 1 good 3 guitar 1

hall 2 happiness 5 happy 2 harmonious 1 harmony 45 hear 1 heaven 2 hurdygurdy 1 hymn 1

idealism 1 instrument 21 instruments 5 instrumental 1

jolly 1 joy 11 joyful 1

lesson 1 light 1 line 1 liveliness 1 lonely 1 loud 1 love 2

man 1 meditation 1 melody 24 Mendelsohn 1 Merry Widow 1 Mozart 1 Mr. B. 1 Mrs. E. 1 musician 3 mute 1

nice 6 nocturne 1 noise 16 noisy 1 note 2 notes 17

opera 5 orchestra 5 organ 6

paper 2 pastime 1 piano 180 pianola 2 pitch 1 play 7 playing 8 pleasant 10 pleasantness 1 pleasing 5 pleasure 31 poem 1 poetry 4 practice 1 pretty 4 pupils 1

quiet 1

rack 1 racket 1 rhyme 1 roll 2 room 1

sadness 2 scale 1 Schubert 2 score 1 sheet 5 sheets 1 sing 12 singer 1 singing 48 soft 1 softness 1 solemn 1 song 68 songs 6 soothing 2 sound 95 sounds 2 stool 2 strain 1 strains 2 string 1 study 2 sweet 47 sweetness 6 symphony 4

talent 2 teacher 6 teaching 1 thought 1 time 2 tone 3 town 1 tune 2

violin 21 voice 2

Wagner 3 wavy 1 window 1 words 1 worship 1

Yankee Doodle 1

4. SICKNESS

affliction 1 age 1 ailing 3 ailment 2 air 1 anxiety 1 appendicitis 3 aunt 1

baby 3 bad 15 bed 54 Bertha 1 better 1 body 1 business 1

calamity 1 care 1 child 2 cold 1 condition 1 consumption 3 contagious 2 convalescence 1 convalescing 2 cure 3

danger 1 death 115 dietary 1 diphtheria 8 disability 1 disabled 2

discomfort 3 disease 20 distress 4 doctor 62

dread 1 dreariness 1

enjoyed 1 ether 1 exhaustion 1

family 1 father 3 fear 1 feeble 4 feel 1 feeling 1 fever 9 fevers 1 fracture 1 fright 1

gloom 1 gravel 1 grief 3 grunting 1

hard 2 hatefulness 1 headache 5 health 142 healthy 4 home 2 horrible 1 hospital 9

ill 48 illness 71 incompetence 1 inconvenience 1 indisposition 1 infirmary 1 insanity 1 invalid 2

K. 1

low 1 lying 1

malady 2 man 1 measles 3 medication 1 medicine 30 melancholy 1 mine 1 misery 3 misfortune 3 mother 3

nervousness 2 neuralgis 1 nurse 15 nursing 2

operation 1 oranges 1

pain 56 painful 1 pale 2 patient 7 patients 1 people 1 person 1 physician 7 pill 1 pills 1 plague 1 pleasantness 1 pneumonia 5 poverty 1

quiet 1 quietness 1

recovery 2 relapsing 1 rheumatism 1 room 1

sad 7 sadness 9 serious 2 severe 4 sigh 1 sore 1 sorrow 24 sorry 2 stomach 1 strength 2 suffer 1 suffering 12 summer 1 sympathy 2

terror 1 together 1 trouble 20 trying 1 typhoid 6

uncomfortable 2 unhappiness 1 unhappy 1 unhealthy 1 unpleasant 5 unpleasantness 2 unwell 11

want 1 weak 1 weakness 11 weariness 2 weary 1 well 40 white 1 worried 1 worriment 1

5. MAN

adult 2 affection 1 age 1 alive 1 animal 12 animals 1 animate 1 appearance 2

baby 1 bad 2 beard 1 beast 2 being 19 biped 3 blond 1 body 3 boy 44 brain 1 bright 1 brightness 1 brother 8 brotherhood 1 brute 1 bum 1 business 6

cane 3 certain 1 Charles 2 child 10 children 2 Christian 1 clergyman 1 clothes 7 clothing 2 coat 3 comfort 1 companion 1 company 1 coon 1 crank 1 creature 8 cross 1

devil 1 doctor 2 dress 1

educator 1 existence 1

fakir 1 false 1 family 1 father 15 female 3 flesh 2 form 2 fraud 1 Fred 1 friend 2

gentle 1 gentleman 7 girl 6 glacier 1 good 10 greatness 1 grown 1 growth 1

hair 1 hat 7 help 2 home 1 homely 1 horrible 1 horse 4 house 1 human 22 humanity 1 husband 4

individual 1 insane 1 institution 1 intellectual 1 intelligent 1

janitor 1 Joe 1

labor 1 laborer 1 lady 7 large 11 life 4 light 1 limb 1 living 2 lord 1 love 1

machine 1 maiden 1 male 99 mammal 1 manhood 1 mankind 5 manliness 1 manly 2 marriage 1 married 1 masculine 6 mason 1 mind 1 might 1 minister 1 minor 1 misery 1 money 1 monkey 1 Mr. D. 1 Mr. H. 1 Mr. N. 1 Mr. S. 3 muscular 1

N. 1 nature 1 Ned 1 nice 1 noble 3 nuisance 1

out 1

papa 1 passion 1 people 2 person 30 pleasure 1 policeman 2 politician 1 power 5 professor 1 prosperity 1 provider 1

Roosevelt 1 ruler 1

self 1 sex 4 shirt 1 shoes 1 short 1 smoking 1 stern 1 stout 1 street 1 strength 32 strong 8 sweetheart 1

Taft 1 tall 12 thought 1 trousers 6 true 1

unfeminine 1 use 1

V. 1 voter 1

walk 1 wedding 1 whiskers 1 wife 5 wise 1 woman 394 work 17 works 1 worker 1 working 3

young 2

6. DEEP

abyss 3 altitude 1 around 1

below 3 beneath 1 black 1 blue 3 bottom 1 bottomless 1 bowl 1 breath 1 broad 1 brooding 1 brook 1

cave 2 Cayuga 1 chair 1 chasm 2 cellar 1 classic 1 clear 1 cliff 1

danger 3 dangerous 5 dark 28 darkness 4 dense 1 depth 31 depths 1 diameter 1 dig 1 distance 8 ditch 8 doleful 1 down 27 dread 1

earth 1 extension 1

fall 2 falling 3 far 3 fathomless 5 fear 1 full 1

gloomy 1 good 1 gorge 1 great 1 ground 1

heavy 1 height 5 high 37 hole 32 hollow 13

large 8 length 8 level 2 light 4 long 18 low 51

measure 2 mighty 1 mind 1 mine 4

narrow 3

ocean 93 organ 1

philosophy 1 pit 1 pond 1 pool 1 precipice 1 profound 4

ravine 1 reaching 1 river 13 rocks 1

safety 1 scare 1 sea 90 sewer 1 shade 1

shady 1 shallow 180 sharp 1 ship 1 short 1 sincere 1 sink 2 sleep 1 smooth 1 sorrow 1 sound 2 space 6 spacious 2 steep 7 story 1 strong 1 study 1 sunken 1 surface 1 swimming 1

thick 1 thickness 1 thin 1 thinking 2 thought 14 thoughts 2 tranquil 1 trench 1

under 1

valley 1 vast 2

wading 1 water 134 well 44 wet 1 wide 12 width 2

7. SOFT

apple 1

baby 7 ball 2 beautiful 1 bed 12 boiled 1 brain 1 bread 4 breeze 1 butter 12

cake 1 candy 1 care 1 carpet 1 cat 1 cement 1 clay 1 clean 1 cloth 3 clothes 1 coal 2 cold 1 color 2 comfort 2 comfortable 5 comply 1 consistency 1 cotton 28 crabs 1 cream 2 creeping 1 cushion 25

dark 1 dough 1 down 6 dress 1 drink 1

earth 7 ease 1 easy 34 egg 2 eggs 2 eyes 1

feather 2 feathers 24 feathery 1 feel 1 feeling 8 felt 1 fine 5 firm 1 flabby 3 fleece 1 flesh 1 flexible 7 floor 1 fluffy 1 food 2 foolish 1 form 1 fruit 3 fun 1 fur 4

gentle 3 girl 1 glove 1 good 3 grasp 1 grass 1 ground 3 gum 1

hair 3 hand 3 hands 1 hard 365 harsh 1 hazy 1 head 1

idiot 1

jelly 1

kitten 2

large 1 light 8 lightly 1 liquid 2 loose 2 loud 5 low 5

maple 1 marshes 1 medium 1 mellow 11 membrane 1 mild 2 moist 1 moss 2 mud 15 mush 10 mushing 1 mushy 12 music 4

nice 4

palatable 1 peach 2 pear 2 pillow 53 pillows 2 pliable 8 plush 2 pudding 4 putty 4

quality 1 quiet 2

rubber 3

sand 1 satisfactory 1 seat 1 silk 10 skin 1 slow 2 slushy 1 smooth 27 snap 3 snow 7 soap 6 soup 1 sponge 22 sponges 1 spongy 8 squash 1 sticky 1 strong 1 substance 1 sweet 8 sweetness 1

tender 8 texture 1 timid 1 tomatoes 1 touch 4

velvet 15 voice 2

wadding 1 warm 1 water 8 watery 1 wax 1 wet 3 white 3 wool 8 woolen 1

yielding 5

8. EATING

abstain 1 abstinence 1 action 2 appetite 28 apple 4 apples 6 assimilation 1

biting 1 bread 46 breakfast 7 butter 1

cake 4 candy 3 Chacona's 1 chew 1 chewing 27 chicken 3 coffee 1 Commons 1 consuming 4 cooking 3 cream 2

devour 1 devouring 2 diet 2 diets 1 digest 1 digesting 7 digestion 10 dine 2 dining 1 dinner 31 drink 6 drinking 166 dyspepsia 1

enjoyable 1 enjoying 1 enjoyment 2 enough 1 etiquette 1

fast 3 fasting 5 fattening 1 feasting 2 feed 1 feeding 5 filling 2 finishing 1 fish 3 flavor 1 flesh 1 food 170 fork 2 forks 1 fruit 8 full 4

gluttonish 1 good 23 gormandizer 1 gratifying 1

habit 3 health 9 healthful 1 heartily 1 hearty 1 hot 2 house 1 hunger 19 hungry 44

ice-cream 2 indigestion 4

knives 1

lemons 1 life 2 live 4 living 5 lobster 1 lobsters 1 lunch 8

masticate 1 masticating 11 mastication 5 matter 1 meal 4 meals 10 meat 11 meeting 1 mild 1 milk 1 more 1 motion 1 mouth 2 movement 1 much 1 myself 1

necessary 4 necessity 7 nice 3 nourish 1 nourishing 2 nourishment 11

olives 1 oranges 1

palatable 2 people 3 pie 3 pleasant 7 pleasantness 1 pleasure 10 plenty 1 poor 1 potato 1 potatoes 2 provisions 1 pudding 1

quick 1 quickly 1

refreshing 2 refreshment 1 Reisenweber 1 relief 1 relish 2 resting 2 room 1

sandwich 1 satisfaction 12 satisfied 4 satisfy 1 satisfying 5 sick 1 sit 1 sitting 1 sleep 1 sleeping 17 slow 2 slowly 1 soup 2 starving 4 steak 2

stomach 2 strawberries 1 strength 2 substance 1 sufficient 2 sugar 1 surfeiting 1 sustaining 1 sustenance 2 swallow 6 swallowing 5

table 21 talking 1 taste 7 tasting 2 teeth 3 thinking 1 throat 1 tongue 1

use 1 utensils 1

vegetable 2 vegetables 8 victuals 4

want 2 water 1 watermelon 1 well 2 work 1

9. MOUNTAIN

abrasion 1 Adirondacks 4 air 2 Alleghany 3 Alps 6 altitude 2 attractive 1 automobile 1

Bald 1 beautiful 1 beauty 2 big 2 Blanc 1 Bluff 1 Breckenridge 1

camping 1 Catskills 8 cliff 2 cliffs 1 Clifton 1 climb 9 climbing 27 close 1 clouds 3 cone 1 country 5 crevice 1

descend 1 descending 2 desert 1 dirt 1 distance 1 ditch 1

earth 3 elevation 9

fear 1 field 1 Flashman 1 foliage 1 fountain 1

Galeton 1 geography 1 grand 1 grandeur 3 granite 1 grass 1 great 1 green 4 ground 1

heath 1 height 73 heights 2 high 246 highlands 1 highness 2 hill 184 hills 82 hilltop 2 hilltops 1 hilly 2 Himalaya 1 hollow 5 Holyoke 1 home 1

horse 1 Hudson 1 huge 2

impressive 1 incline 1 island 1

Kipling 1 knoll 1

lake 8 land 6 landscape 1 large 4 level 1 lofty 1 low 2 lowland 1

Monodonack 1
mound 1
Mount Ivy 1
Mount Kearsarge 1
Mount McKinley 1
Mount Pleasant 1
Mount Shasta 1
Mount Wilson 1

object 2 Owl's Head 1

peak 16 peaks 1 pictures 1 Pike's Peak 1 pines 1 plain 11 plateaus 1 pleasure 3

pointed 1 railway 1 range 3 ranges 1 river 8

rock 10 Rockies 6 rocks 18 rocky 5 rough 1

scene 1 scenery 3 sea 1 seas 1 seashore 1

shadows 1 shooting 1 size 1 sky 2 slope 1 snow 10 steep 12 steepness 1 stone 2 stones 1 stream 2 summit 4 Switzerland 2

tall 1 Terrace 1 top 5 tree 2 trees 17

up 1

vale 2 valley 90 valleys 5 Vermont 1 view 2 volcano 2

Washington 1 White 5 wood 1 woods 3

10. HOUSE

abode 15 alley 1 apartment 3

background 1 barn 74 Bay Ridge 1 beautiful 2 Belknap 1 big 4 blinds 1 boards 3 boat 2 box 1 brick 23 bricks 5 brown 2 build 2 building 78 bungalow 2

cabin 8 camp 1 carpenter 1 carpet 1 castle 4 cattle 1 cellar 1 chair 2 chamber 1 chicken 1 chimney 5 church 1 city 2 clean 2 closed 1 college 1 comfort 9 comforts 1 comfortable 3 contractor 1 corridor 1 cottage 42 cover 3 covering 1

dark 1 den 1 dog 2 domestic 1 domicile 1 door 16 doors 1 dwell 3 dwelling 68

enclosure 1 erection 1

family 4 fancy 1 farm 2 farmer 1 fence 1 field 1 fire 1 floor 1 form 1 foundation 1 frame 5 friends 1 furnace 1 furnishing 1 furniture 11

garden 10 grandmother 1 great 1 green 2

ground 3 grounds 1

habitable 1 habitation 5

happiness 1 height 2 high 3 hill 3 home 103 homeless 1 hospital 4 hot 1 hotel 4 hovel 1 hut 2

inhabitant 1 inhabited 1 inmates 1 into 1

joy 1

land 10 lake 1

large 24 lawn 3 lemon 1 Leonia 1 life 2 live 33 living 19 lot 18 lots 1 lumber 3 man 2 mansion 14 material 1 mine 1 mortgage 1 Mountain House 1 mouse 2

new 1

object 1 old 1 ours 1

palace 1 painting 1 Pasadena 1 people 11 piazza 2 picture 1 place 6 pleasant 1 pretty 3 property 1 protection 3

red 4 refuge 1 residence 19 resident 2 restful 1 road 1 roof 12 room 9 rooms 8

Sage 1 school 2 sea 1 shanty 1 shed 5 shelter 22 sky 2 small 2 spacious 1 square 4 stable 3 star 1 steps 1 stone 7 stoop 1 store 2 street 7 structure 8

tabernacle 1 table 1 tall 1 telescope 1 tenant 1 tenement 2 tent 3 timber 1 top 5 town 1 tree 2 trees 1 tumbler 1

villa 2 village 1

walls 1 warm 3 wealth 1 well 1 white 9 Whittier 1 wide 1 willow 1 window 9 windows 5 wood 31 wooden 1 workman 1 worship 1

yard 10

11. BLACK

agreeable 1

blue 8 board 3 book 2 bright 2 buggy 1

cat 8 chair 1 charcoal 1 cloth 17 clothes 4 cloud 1 clouds 1 cloudy 2 coal 3 coat 3 color 129 colored 1 colorless 3 crepe 2 curtain 1

dark 172 darkness 36 death 4 dense 1 desolate 1 dirty 2 disagreeable 1 disklike 1 dog 4 domino 1 dress 29 dye 2

earth 1 ebony 1

face 1 fear 2 figure 1 flecked 1 floor 1 funeral 1

gloomy 2 gown 1 gray 2 green 7

hair 2 hat 3 heavy 1 hog 1 horror 1 horse 5

impenetrable 1 ink 14

lack 1 light 12

mammy 1 man 2 Mrs. B. 1 mournful 2 mourning 17 mud 1

negro 7 negroes 1 nigger 6 night 51 nothing 1

obscure 1 orange 1

paint 4 paper 1 pen 1 pink 2 pipe 1 pit 1

radiator 1 red 4 ribbon 1 robe 1

sad 1 sadness 2 sack 1 shady 1 sheep 2 shoe 4 shoes 1 sign 1 skirt 2 sky 1 somber 2 soot 1 sorrow 4 space 1 spectrum 1 stocking 1 stockings 1 suit 1

table 1 tar 1 terror 1 tie 1

umbrella 1

velvet 1

wall 2 water 1 white 339

wonder 1 wood 1

yellow 2

12. MUTTON

animal 9 animals 1 appetite 1 Australia 1

baa 1 beef 97 bony 1 breakfast 1 broth 15 brown 1 butcher 2

calf 2 cattle 1 cheap 3 chop 34 chops 33 cow 2

delicious 1 dinner 6 disagreeable 2

dish 1 dislike 2 disliked 1

eat 14 eatable 7 eating 10

fat 7 field 2 flesh 10 flock 1 food 30 fork 1 fowl 1

goat 1 good 9 grass 1 grease 2 greasy 1

ham 2 hate 1 head 2 horrid 1

indigestion 1

knife 1

lamb 121 lambs 2 leg 5

Mary 1 meat 257 mouse 1 muttonhead 1

nice 2

old 1

pastures 1 peas 1 pig 2 pork 3

rare 1 roast 4

sauce 1 sheep 204 smell 1 soft 1 soup 2 stale 1 steak 3 stew 2 strong 2

table 4 tallow 6 tender 3 thinking 1 tough 6

uncle 1

veal 30 vegetables 1 vegetarian 1

wool 4

13. COMFORT

agony 1 annoyance 1

bad 1 bed 42 blanket 4 book 1 books 1

canoe 1 care 4 chair 31 cheer 1 children 1 cloth 1 comfortable 4 comforter 1 consolation 2 console 1 consoling 1 content 2 contentment 4 convenience 2 cozy 1 couch 9 cover 1 covering 1 cushion 4 cushions 1

davenport 1 death 1 delightful 1 desirable 2 discomfort 24 disease 1 displeasure 1 distress 4 driving 1

ease 165 easiness 11 easy 61 eating 1 enjoying 1 enjoyment 6

feather 1 feeling 1 fireplace 2 fireside 2 friends 1

God 1 good 5 goodness 1 great 1 grief 1

hammock 7 happiness 50 happy 17 hard 2 hardship 7 healing 1 health 15 help 3 home 63 house 4 household 1

I 1 idleness 1 ill 1

joy 9 justice 1

kindness 1

lamp 1 laziness 2 lazy 1 leisure 6 less 1 life 1 like 1 living 2 loneliness 1 lounge 6 luxurious 1 luxury 23

man 1 mansion 1 miserable 1 misery 9 money 9 mother 3

neatness 1 nice 4 none 1 nurse 2

pain 4 palace 2 patient 1 peace 12 people 1 pillow 2 pipe 1 playing 1 pleasant 9 please 1 pleasure 77 plentiness 1 plenty 1 Polly 1 post 1

quiet 6 quietness 1 quilt 7

rain 1 relief 1

rest 53 restful 1 restfulness 1 resting 5 rich 1 rocker 8

safety 1 salary 1 satisfaction 4 satisfied 8 security 1 settled 1 sick 1 sickness 3 sit 1 sitting 4 sleep 10 slippers 1 slumber 1 smoke 1 smoking 1 sofa 5 soft 2 solace 1 solid 11 solitude 8 soothing 2 sorrow 5 speak 1 spirit 1 spread 1 suffering 1 sweet 1 swing 1

table 2 taken 1 tea 1 thankfulness 1 tired 1 trials 1

trouble 1

uncomfort 1 uncomfortable 10 uneasiness 3 uneasy 3 unrest 1 unwell 1

warm 6 warmth 4 wealth 6 well 8 well-being 1 wine 1 wish 1 woman 1 wool 1 work 1

ye 1

14. HAND

anatomy 2 arm 63 arms 2

ball 1 beautiful 3 black 3 bleeding 1 body 48 bone 1 bones 1 busy 1

cards 2 clean 1 clock 1 convenience 1 cradle 1 cunning 1

dexterity 1 diligence 1 dissecting 1 do 1 doing 2 dog 1

ear 1 elbow 1 extremity 6

face 7 fat 1 feel 11 feeling 5 feet 35 fellowship 2 finger 39 fingers 83 fist 1 flesh 19 foot 204 form 1 formation 1 friend 1 friendship 1 fruit 1

give 1 glove 20 gloves 5 good 1 grasp 8 greeting 1 grip 8

handle 1 handy 3 hard 1 head 1 heart 2 help 6 helper 2 helping 1 hold 8 holding 1 human 2

instrument 2

jewel 1

kindness 1 knife 1 knitting 1

labor 1 large 1 leg 4 legs 1 lemon 1 life 2 limb 48 limbs 1 long 1 love 1

machine 2 maid 1 man 3 manipulation 1 member 14 mind 1 mine 1 mouth 4 move 1 muscle 4

nail 2 nails 1 name 1 narrow 3 necessity 2 nice 1 nimble 1 nose 1

object 1 organ 4

palm 5 part 1 paw 2 pencil 1 perfect 1 person 10 piano 1 pen 1 power 8 pretty 8 purity 1 reach 1 rest 1 right 11 ring 28

rings 2

satisfaction 1 servant 1 sew 2 sewing 2 shake 9 shape 1 shapely 1 shop 1 shoulder 1 akin 4 slim 1 small 8 soap 1 soft 8 something 1 sore 1 strength 6 strong 3 support 1 system 1

table 1 thread 1 touch 9 two 2

use 12 useful 24 usefulness 4

watch 1 woman 1 work 49 white 15 wrist 1 write 3 writing 11

you 1

15. SHORT

abbreviated 2 age 1 arm 2

baby 1 beach 1 beam 1 board 1 boy 3 brevity 1 brick 1 brief 7 broad 1 build 1

C. 1 cake 1 chair 1 change 1 child 4 children 1 clock 1 cloth 1 comfort 1 compact 1 cut 1 cylinder 1

dainty 1 day 4 deficient 2 dimension 1 diminiature 1 diminutive 2 disagreeable 1 distance 10 dot 1 down 1 drawn 1 dress 3 dumpy 2 dwarf 11 dwarfs 1

easy 2 elongated 1 extension 1

fat 4 finger 1 flowerpot 1 foot 2 friend 2

girl 11 good 1 grandmother 1 grass 5

hair 2 happiness 1 height 13 high 4 hour 1 hours 3

inch 5

journey 2

Karl 1

lacking 1 lady 4 lake 1 large 2 leg 2 length 18 lesson 1 lessons 1 life 5 little 15 line 1 lived 1 long 279 low 11 lowly 1

man 20 measure 3 measurements 1 medium 2 midget 1 millimeter 1 minus 1 Miss K. 1 money 1 mother 1 myself 6

name 1 narrow 1 near 1 needle 1 not 1

out 1

pencil 6 people 3 person 15 petticoat 1 pin 1 pity 1 plant 1 plants 1 pony 1 post 2 pygmy 2

quick 8 quickly 1

road 1 round 1

session 1 shallow 1 sister 1 size 5 skirt 1 sleek 1 slight 1 slightly 1 small 136 space 1 speech 2 square 1 staccato 1 stature 2 stem 2 stick 8 stop 2 story 1 stout 24 strawberries 1 street 2 string 1 strong 1 stubborn 1 stubby 9 stumpy 4 stunned 1 stunted 1 sufficient 1 sum 1 sweet 1

tall 168 thick 6 thin 1 time 8 tiny 1 Tom Thumb 1 tree 1

unpleasant 1 useless 1

vacation 1

waisted 1 walk 3 want 1 wanting 2 water 1 well 1 wide 1 woman 6 wood 1 worm 1

you 1

16. FRUIT

acid 2 appetite 2 apple 157 apples 102 article 1

bake 1 banana 11 bananas 8 berries 7 berry 1 blackberries 1 bread 2

cake 2 can 1 candies 1 candy 3 cherries 2 cherry 2 country 1 currants 1

dainty 1 delicacy 2 delicious 9 desire 1 digest 1 digestion 1

easy 1 eat 62 eatable 33 eatables 15 eating 35 edible 1 eggs 1 enjoyment 2

figs 1 fish 1 flesh 1 flower 3 flowers 3 fond 1 food 22 fresh 1

garden 2 good 24 grain 2 grape 4 grapes 14 grapefruit 1 green 1 groves 1 grow 1 grows 1 growth 2

health 3 healthy 3 home 1

Italians 1 invigorating 1

jam 1 juice 6 juicy 5

knife 1

lemon 2 liked 1 love 1 luscious 5 luxury 2

meat 4 medicine 1 melon 1 milk 1

nourishing 1 nourishment 2 nice 5 nutritious 2 nuts 2

orange 25 oranges 26 orchard 6 outcome 1

palatable 2 peach 17 peaches 32 pears 11 picking 1 pie 1 pineapple 2 plant 1 plants 1 pleasant 2 pleasure 1 plenty 2 plum 2 produce 2 prune 1

raspberries 1 raspberry 1 red 1 result 1 ripe 9 ripeness 1

salad 1 seed 5 sickness 1 sour 4 south 1 spring 1 stalk 1 stand 1 stems 1 store 1 strawberries 2 strawberry 1 summer 2 swallow 1 sweet 24 sweets 1

table 3 taste 5 tree 25 trees 27

vegetable 75 vegetables 28

watermelon 1 wine 1

17. BUTTERFLY

air 1 airiness 1 airy 2 animal 24 animals 2 ant 2

beast 1 beautiful 24 beauty 20 bee 31 bees 4 beetle 5 bird 64 birds 10 black 2 blossom 1 blue 1 bread 2 bright 1 brilliant 2 brown 1 bush 1 butter 3 buttercup 6 bug 11 bugs 1 bumblebee 1

cabbage 1 caterpillar 37 caterpillars 1 chase 1 chrysalis 3 cocoon 6 cocoons 1 collection 4 color 12 colors 8 colored 3 country 2 cricket 1

daisy 1 dish 1 dove 1 dress 1 dust 1

eagle 1 ease 1 ephemeral 1

fairy 1 field 2 fields 1 firefly 1 flies 6 flight 2 flippant 1 flittering 1 flitting 1 flits 1 flower 13 flowers 12 flutter 2 fluttering 1 fly 44 flying 20

gaudy 1 gauze 1 gay 2 girl 2 gnat 2 golden 3 good 1 grace 2 graceful 1 grass 1 grasshopper 5 grasshoppers 2 grub 5

handsome 1 happy 1 high 1 horse 1 human 1

idler 1 insect 261 insects 2

Japanese 1

kite 1

lady 1 lepidoptera 8 light 5 lightness 2 lilies 1 little 1

meadows 1 metamorphosis 1 miller 4 monarch 1 mosquito 8 motion 1 moth 30 moths 1 mountains 1 mourning cloak 1

nature 2 net 6 nets 1 nice 2

orange 1 outdoors 1

pancake 1 pig 1 pigeon 2 plumage 1 powder 1 pretty 30 red 1

small 2 snakes 1 snare 1 soul 1 sparrow 1 speckled 1 spider 9 spotted 2 spring 5 summer 17 sun 1 sunshine 6 swallow 1 sweet 1 swift 1

temporary 1 tree 1 two 1

useless 1

vanity 2 variegated 1

wasp 11 white 2 wind 1 wing 11 wings 81 word 1 worm 12 worms 2 yellow 37

18. SMOOTH

apple 2

ball 1 basin 1 bed 2 board 9 butter 1

calm 4 carpet 1 character 1 cheek 1 chip 1 circus 1 clean 2 clear 8 cloth 3 clothes 1 coarse 2 coat 1 country 1 course 1 cream 2 cube 1

deceitful 1 deep 1 desk 1 done 1 dry 1

ease 2 easy 12 even 30 evenness 1

face 8 fair 1 feeling 1 fine 8 finished 2 flat 14 flexible 2 floor 15 folded 1 fur 2

glass 56 glassy 4 glazed 1 glide 3 gliding 1 glossy 11 good 2 goods 1 grand 1 grass 8 grease 1 ground 4

hair 3 hand 2 hard 41 harmonious 1 harsh 4

ice 14 iron 13 ironing 1 ivory 1

kind 1

lake 1 lawn 2 lens 1 level 52 lightly 1 lovely 1

machinery 1 mahogany 1 marble 10 mercury 1 mild 1 mirror 1 molasses 1

narrow 1 nice 4 nicely 1

oyster 1

paint 1 paper 9 paste 2 pat 1 path 1 pebble 1 person 1 piano 1 placid 1 plain 17 plane 23 planed 1 pleasant 5 pleasing 1 plum 1 polished 5 pressed 1

quality 1 queer 1

river 1 river 2 road 4 roads 1 roof 2 rough 277 round 2 rubber 1 rugged 1 rule 1 running 1

sailing 1 sandpaper 1 satin 2 sea 1 shape 1 sharp 1 shave 1 shiny 4 silk 4 silken 1 skin 5 sleek 2 slick 3 slippery 4 snail 2 snake 1 soft 70 softness 1 sphere 1 stone 1 straight 2 street 1 stroke 1 surface 25

table 29 thin 1 thought 1 tidy 1 tomato 1 tongue 1 touch 4 tranquil 1

uneven 2

velvet 20 velvety 1 very 1

wall 5 walls 1 water 10 wave 1 window 1

wood 8 work 1 worm 1 wrinkled 1 wrinkles 1

19. COMMAND

ability 1 act 1 acting 1 anger 1 answer 1 anything 1 appeal 1 appearance 1 army 16 arrogance 1 ask 2 asking 2 athletics 1 attention 3 authority 14

baseball 1 Bible 1 bid 1 boss 6 boy 1

captain 7 charge 2 chief 2 church 1 combine 1 combined 1 come 5 commander 5 commandment 2 company 2 compel 1 control 8 cross 1

dare 1 demand 18 demanding 1 desire 2 determined 2 dictate 3 dictatorial 1 dignity 2 direct 2 disability 1 discipline 2 dislike 1 do 27 doing 3 domineer 2 domineering 2 done 2 don't 2 door 1 drill 2 driver 1 duty 5

earnestness 1 easy 1 eat 1 effort 1 employ 1 employees 1 enforce 1 entreat 1 entreaty 7 exclamation 1 exertion 1 experience 1

father 1 firm 1 forbid 1 force 7 forced 1 foreman 1

gain 1 general 43 gentleness 1 gently 1 Germany 1 give 1 go 25 God 1 God's 1 good 2 govern 1 grand 1

halt 4 harsh 4 harshly 1 haughty 1 head 1 him 1 holy 1 honorable 1 horse 1

I 1 immediately 1 imperative 3 imperious 4 independent 1 insist 1 instant 1 institution 1 instruct 2 instruction 1 intelligence 1

judge 1

knowing 1

labor 1 language 1 law 2 laziness 1 lead 2 leader 1 lieutenant 1 listen 2 loud 2 love 1 madam 1 man 9 master 2 masterful 1 military 3 mind 2 mother 1 move 1 must 1

noble 1 nuisance 1

obedience 12 obedient 2 obey 230 obeyed 1 officer 30 only 1 order 171 ordering 2 orders 9

parents 1 peace 1 people 2 peremptory 2 perfect 1 person 1 plead 1 policeman 1 power 10 powerful 2 praise 1 proper 1

question 1 quick 1

refuse 2 regiment 1 reply 1 reprimand 2 request 11 respect 5 respond 1 retreat 1 right 3 rule 2 ruling 1 running 1

say 1 saying 1 school 2 severe 1 shalt 1 ship 1 soldier 16 soldiers 6 something 1 speak 3 spoken 1 stamina 1 statement 1 stern 7 strength 3 strict 1 strong 3 stubborn 1 superintend 1 superior 1 supervisor 1 surly 1 surrender 1

talk 2 teach 1 teacher 14 teachers 1 teaching 1 tell 15 telling 1 temper 3 temperament 1 thee 1 them 1 think 2 thinking 1 thoughtfulness 1 threat 1 told 2

uncomfortable 1 upright 1

voice 6 vow 1

wagon 1 wife 1 will 3 willing 1 words 2 work 2 wrong 1

you 3

20. CHAIR

arm 4 article 4

back 1 beauty 1 bed 1 bench 13 book 1 boy 1 broken 2 brown 4 bureau 1

cane 3 caning 1 careful 1 carpet 1 cart 1 color 1 comfort 21 comfortable 8 convenience 3 couch 5 crooked 1 cushion 12 cushions 1

desk 9

ease 7 easy 6

fatigue 1 floor 10 feet 1 foot 1 footstool 1 form 1 furniture 83

Governor Winthrop 1

hair 1 hard 5 hickory 2 high 4 home 2 house 3

- 216 -

idleness 1 implement 1

joiner 1

large 3 leg 7 legs 11 lounge 3 low 3 lunch 1

mahogany 3 massive 1 mission 1 Morris 5 myself 1

necessity 2

oak 2 object 1 occupy 1 office 1

people 1 person 3 place 1 placed 1 plant 1 platform 1 pleasant 1 pleasure 1 posture 1

reading 1 rest 45 resting 3 rocker 17 rocking 15 room 9 rounds 2 rubber 1 rung 3

seat 127 seated 5 seating 2 settee 3 sit 107 sitting 56 size 1 sofa 6 soft 5 spooning 1 stand 1 stool 38 stoop 1 study 1 support 1

table 191 tables 1 talk 1 teacher 1 timber 1 tool 1

upholstered 1 upholstery 1 use 2 useful 3

white 1 wood 49 wooden 6

21. SWEET

agreeable 5 appetizing 1 apple 11 apples 3

beautiful 3 bitter 50 black 1 breath 1

candies 1 candy 82 cherries 1 child 1 chocolate 3 chocolates 1 clean 2 confectionery 1 cream 1 cunning 1

delicious 7 dessert 1 dinner 1 dog 1 dreams 1

E. 1 eat 2 elegant 1 eyes 1

face 1 flavor 2 flower 2 flowers 3 food 1 fresh 1 fruit 9

gentle 1 girl 6 good 26

harsh 2 honey 12 hunger 1 Huyler's 1

insipidity 1

kiss 2

limited 1 lovely 1 loving 1 low 2

Mary 1 mellow 1 melody 1 milk 2 molasses 1 mouth 1 music 8 musty 1

- 217 -

name 1 nausea 1 nice 33

orange 1 oranges 2

palatable 9 peach 3 peaches 1 perfume 3 pie 2 plausible 1 pleasant 31 pleasing 4 pleasurable 1 pleasure 1 plum 1 preserves 1

quality 1

saccharine 1 salt 3 salty 1 sharp 1 sickish 1 sixteen 2 soft 6 soothing 1 sour 301 stuff 1 sugar 224 syrup 2

taste 57 tasteful 4 tasting 2 tasty 11 tea 1 toothsome 2

ugly 1 unpleasant 1

very 1 voice 1

wholesome 1

22. WHISTLE

act 1 action 1 air 7 alarm 3 annoyance 3 attention 2 automobile 1

bad 1 bell 2 bird 15 birds 3 blast 1 blew 5 blow 95 blowing 6 blows 2 boat 2 boy 56 boys 5 breath 1 bright 1 brother 1 buzzing 1

call 26 calling 2 cars 2 cent 1 chain 8 children 1 clean 1 clear 1 come 1 conductor 1 crow 1 cry 2 cuckoo 1

dance 3 dear 1 disagreeable 1 distant 1 dog 7 drink 1 dumb 1

ear 1 echo 3 effort 1 engine 15

factory 2 fife 3 fingers 1 fire 3 flute 5 fly 1 Franklin 2 fun 2 funny 1

Galton 1 girl 1

habit 1 happiness 3 harmony 1 harsh 1 holler 5 hollow 1 horn 4 humming 1

instrument 6

joy 2

lad 1 laugh 3 letter-carrier 1 lips 5 locomotive 5 long 3 loud 27 low 1

man 1 mash 1 melodious 1 metal 1 mill 2 mine 1 mocking 1 mouth 27 music 44

nice 3 nightingale 1 noise 173 noisy 3 note 1 notes 1

person 1 piercing 1 pipe 7 pleasure 2 police 1 policeman 6 postman 1 postman's 1 pretty 1 pucker 4

quiet 1

racket 2 report 1 running 1

scream 1 screech 1 sharp 5 shout 4 shrieking 1 shrill 26 shrillness 1 signal 3 sang 1 sing 75 singing 4 soft 1 softly 1 song 12 songs 1 sorority 1 sound 108 sounds 1 steam 3 steamboat 1 stick 1

talk 4 telephone 1 throat 1 tin 7 tool 1 top 1 toy 4 train 6 tree 1 trumpet 2 tune 18

umpire 1 unpleasant 1

vibration 1 voice 3

warble 1 warning 1 whisper 1 whispering 1 willow 8 wind 10 wood 1 wooden 1 work 1

yell 1

23. WOMAN

adult 2 affinity 1 aged 1 angel 2 appearance 1 appreciating 1 artificial 1

baby 1 Barnard 1 beautiful 17 beauty 7 being 9 Bible 1 biped 1 body 3 bonnet 1 boy 3 bright 1

capability 1 cat 1 character 1 child 45 children 2 clean 2 clever 1 clothes 6 clothing 1 comfort 2 companion 1 creature 4 cross 1

dear 1 deceit 1 delicate 1 delightful 1 develop 1 dignity 1 dinner 1 domestic 1 dress 28 dresses 4 dressmaker 1

dust 1

Edna 1 endurance 1 Eve 2 eyes 1

fair 9 fashion 3 female 134 feminine 10 flesh 2 figure 1 fine 2 freedom 1 friend 3

genteel 1 gentle 5 gentleness 1 girl 59 girls 3 goddess 1 good 4 goodness 1 gown 1 grace 3 graceful 2 grand 2 grandmother 1 great 2

hair 9 handsome 4 hat 5 hats 1 helper 1 helpmate 3 her 1 home 3 honor 1 house 2 housekeeper 1 housewife 1 human 11 humanity 2

inexplicable 1 individual 1 intellect 1 interesting 1

kind 5 kindness 1

labor 2 lady 41

large 4 leader 1 liar 1 living 1 lovable 1 love 5 loveliness 1 lovely 3 loving 1

Mabel 1 maid 1 majesty 1 man 292 mankind 2 marriage 2 married 2 mate 2 modesty 1 mother 30 Mrs. S. 1 myself 1

nature 1 necessity 1 nice 3 noble 1 nurse 1

old 1

palmist 1 parasol 1 people 1 perfection 1 person 17 petticoats 1 pleasure 3 pretty 10 purity 1

rib 1

sex 5 short 5 sister 4

skirt 3 skirts 3 slender 2 small 1 softness 1 spiritual 1 stout 2 style 2 suffrage 1 sweet 2 sweetness 2 sweetheart 1

talk 1 tall 7 teacher 1 temporary 1 truth 1

uneasy 1 use 1

virtue 2

waist 1 walks 1 weak 1 weakness 2 wife 15 will 1 womanhood 1 work 2

you 5 young 4

24. COLD

activity 1 agreeable 2 air 4 arctic 1 atmosphere 4 autumn 1

bad 2 bitter 4 bracing 1 breezy 1 brisk 1 bum 1

chill 9 chilly 30

clothes 2 clothing 1 coal 1 coat 5 comfort 2 comfortable 1 comfortless 1 cool 5 cough 5 cure 2

damp 2 dark 4 darkness 1 day 5 death 1 degree 1 disagreeable 6 discomfort 8 dreary 3

feel 1 feeling 10 feet 1 Finland 1 fire 6 fold 1 freeze 7 freezing 23 frigid 2 frost 9 frozen 4 fuel 1 furs 2

grippe 1 gloomy 1

ham 1 hands 1 hard 2 head 2 hearted 1 heat 37 hot 151

ice 114 ice-cream 1 irritating 1

January 1

latitude 1 lemonade 1 light 2

man 2 medicine 1 misery 1 mushroom 1

nature 1 naughty 1 near 1 never 1 night 1 numb 1 numbness 1

overcoat 1

pain 1 Peary 1 penetrating 2 pleasant 1 pressure 1

quiet 1

raw 1 refrigerator 1 rhinitis 1 room 1 running 1 rough 1

sensation 1 severe 5 sharp 3 shiver 6 shivering 2 shivers 1 shivery 1 shrivel 1 shudder 1 sick 4 sickness 6 skating 1 sleighing 1 slow 1 sneezing 1 snow 45 snuffles 1 stone 1 storm 1 stove 3

temperate 1 temperature 8 thermometer 1 touch 1

uncomfortable 10 unpleasant 4

warm 166 warmth 6 water 7 weather 49 well 1 white 1 wind 5 windy 1 winter 120 wraps 1

zero 2

25. SLOW

action 1 age 1 anger 1 animal 2 ant 1 anxiety 1 association 1 automobile 1 awful 1

baby 2 backward 3 backwards 1 bad 1 bear 1 beggar 1 behind 1 better 1 Bill 1 boat 3 boring 1 boy 2 breakdown 1

camel 1 canal boat 1 car 6

cars 2 careful 1 carpenter 1 cart 1 catch 1 caterpillar 2 caution 1 child 1 climb 1 clock 5 coach 3 conversation 1 cow 1 crawl 1 creep 1 creeping 2

dead 1 decrease 1 delay 2 deliberate 1 dilatory 2 distance 1 dizzy 1 donkey 1 drag 1 dragging 1 dreary 2 dressing 1 drive 1 driver 1 drone 1 Dr. R. 1 dull 7

ease 2 easy 63 Erie 1

fast 316 feeble 1 fine 1 fire 1 fly 1 foot 1 funeral 1

gait 3 gin 1 going 1

hard 2 haste 3 hasty 2 heavy 1 horse 14 hot 1 hurry 3

impatience 1 inactive 1 inanition 1 incessant 1 indecision 1 insect 1 invalid 2 irritating 1

laggard 1 lagging 1 lassitude 1 late 2 laziness 2 lazy 28 lecture 1 leisure 1 lingering 1 long 6

man 3 march 1 market 1

me 3 medium 1 mice 1 mind 1 mode 1 moderate 1 molasses 20 monotonous 1 moon 1 motion 7 motionless 1 move 1 movement 8 moving 5 Mr. T. 1 mule 3 music 3 myself 3

nasty 1 nature 1

obstacle 1 old 2 ox 2 oxen 1

pace 1 papa 1 person 8 Philadelphia 2 poke 1 poky 2 Poughkeepsie 1 pupil 1

quality 1 quick 55 quickly 2 quickness 1 quiet 12

rain 1 rapid 9 rhythmic 1 river 1 Rose 1 run 2

sharp 1 short 1 sick 1 sickness 1 slack 1

sloth 2 slowly 1 sluggish 7 smart 10 smooth 1 snail 62 snails 1 snake 1 softly 1 speech 2 speed 7 speedless 1 starting 1 step 2 still 3 stop 3 stubborn 1 stupid 7 subway 1 sure 27 swift 8 swing 1

talk 1 tardy 3 team 1 tedious 1

terrapin 1 thought 1 thoughtful 1 tide 1 time 14 tired 5 tiresome 2 tortoise 4 train 18 trains 1 trolley 1 turtle 9

unpleasant 2 unsatisfactory 1

vehicle 1

wagon 7 walk 8 walking 7 walks 1 water 1 waves 1 weak 2 weather 1 wheel 1 white 1 work 1 working 1 world 1 worm 3 writing 1

you 1

26. WISH

accomplish 1 accomplishment 1 achieve 1 Aladdin 1 ambition 2 angel 1 answer 1 anxiety 1 anxious 1 any 1 anything 7 apology 1 ardent 1 ask 8 asking 1 attain 1

baby 1 beg 2 benefit 1 best 1 better 1 bone 19 books 1 boy 1 boys 1 breakfast 1 brightness 1 candy 1 cannot 1 check 1 chicken 2 child 2 Christmas 3 clover 1 clovers 1 cold 1 come 2 comfort 4 command 9 conditions 1 cool 2 craving 1

demand 2 desirable 1 desire 197 desires 1 diamond 1 disappoint 1 disappointed 1 disappointment 3 dish 1 dislike 1 did 1 do 5 dog 1 doll 1 dollars 1 dream 2 dress 1 driving 1

eat 1 entreaty 1 enjoyment 1 examination 1 expectation 1 express 5 expression 1

fairy 11 fancy 2 farm 1 favor 5 feeling 1 finish 1 fish 1 fond 1 foolishness 1 for 5 fortune 2 fulfil 1 fulfilled 2 fulfilment 6 fun 1

gain 2 get 14 gift 4 girl 1 give 3 glad 1 go 4 gold 1 good 19 grant 7 granted 15 gratification 4 gratified 6 gratify 11 greetings 1 guess 2

happiness 18 happy 3 hard 1 hat 2 hate 1 have 18 health 6 hearty 1 heaven 3 heavens 1 help 1 home 12 hope 51 hoping 1 hopeful 2 house 1

idea 2 imagination 1 impossible 1 inclination 1

journey 2 joy 1

know 1

letter 2 like 8 liked 1 lonesome 1 long 10 longing 18 love 2 luck 9

make 1 marry 1 million 2 mind 4 money 32 moon 1 morning 1 music 1 myself 1

news 1 nice 1 no 1

obey 3 object 1 obtain 1 offer 1 one 1 opportunity 1 opposition 1 orange 1 order 1

perhaps 1 person 1 pick 1 picture 1 pie 1 plan 1 play 1 pleasant 1 pleasure 5 plenty 2 position 3 possess 1 possession 1 present 2 promise 2

quiet 1

reality 1 receive 1 remembrance 1 renown 1 repeat 1 request 8 rest 1 rich 1 riches 3 ring 1

sail 1 satisfactory 1 satisfied 2 satisfy 1 satisfying 1 say 2 secret 1 sincere 1 sleep 1 some 1 something 15 sorrow 1 sorry 1 speak 1 special 1 star 9 stars 2 strong 1 success 4 suggest 1 summer 2 sweetheart 1 swim 1

think 18 thinking 6 thought 47 toy 1 trip 1 trouble 1 true 6 try 1

unattainable 1 uncertain 1 unfulfilled 1 unlawful 1 unsatisfied 1

vacation 2

want 66 wants 1 wanted 1 wanting 9 waste 1 watch 1 water 1 wealth 2 well 6 will 3 wisdom 2 wise 1 wishbone 14 wonder 2 would 2 wouldn't 1

yes 1 you 1

27. RIVER

Amazon 1
Androscoggin 1

bank 1 banks 2 barrow 1 bathing 3 bay 1 beautiful 1 beauty 1 bend 1 blue 6 boat 20 boats 3 boating 1 body 1 bridge 2 broad 5 brook 20 bubbling 1

Calumet 1 camping 1 canal 1 canoe 3 canoeing 1 Chignagnette 1 cliffs 1 commerce 1 Connecticut 1 creek 10 current 8

dangerous 1 deep 35 Delaware 1 depth 1 drowned 1

East 4

fish 1 flow 24 flows 5 flowing 17 Freiberg 1 front 1

God 1 Grand 1 green 1

Hudson 33

island 1

Jordan 1

lake 65 lakes 1 land 5 large 7 launch 1 length 1 life 1 liquid 1 long 8

meadow 1 Mississippi 8 Mississquoi 1 Missouri 1 Mohawk 1 motion 1 mountain 10 moving 2

ocean 17
Ohio 2
Ottanqueehee 1
Owasco 1

Pacific 1 peace 2 Piscatague 1 plain 1 pleasure 1 pond 5

rain 1 Rappahannock 1 rapid 2 Rhine 1 rill 1 rivulet 2 rivulets 1 row 1 rowing 1 run 3 runs 3 running 11 rushing 1

Saco 1 sailing 4 salt 1

sea 14 shallow 2 Shannon 1 shining 1 ship 4 ships 1 side 1 sky 1 slow 2 small 1 smooth 7 spring 1 St. Lawrence 1 stream 117 streams 1 streamlet 1 strong 1 sunset 1 Susquehanna 2 swift 3 swim 4 swimming 4

Tay 1 tide 1 tree 1 tug 1 turbulence 1

- 224 -

valley 5

Ware 1 water 303 well 3 wet 2 white 3 wide 5 winding 2 winds 1

28. WHITE

almost 1 apron 2

baby 1 beach 1 beautiful 1 beauty 1 bird 1 black 308 bleached 1 blue 9 boat 1 Bob 1 body 1 bride 1 bright 4 brightness 1 Broadway 1 brown 2

cat 2 cerement 1 chair 1 chalk 3 cheerful 1 cherries 1 clean 10 cleanliness 2 cleanness 1 clear 2 cloth 17 clothing 1 cloud 4 clouds 2 coat 1 color 170 colored 1 colorless 11 cotton 3 cream 1 curtain 2 curtains 1

dark 35 darkness 1 day 1 daylight 1 dazzling 2 delicate 1 dove 2 dress 34 dresses 1

easy 2 evening 1

face 1 feathers 2 flag 2 flower 2

garment 2 ghost 1 glare 1 good 1 gray 2 green 6

hall 1 handkerchief 2 hands 1 hard 1 horse 2 house 4

innocence 1

lady 1 lawn 1 lead 1 lemon 1 lie 1 light 51 linen 3 lovely 1

man 2 marble 1 milk 9 Mountain 1 Mountains 1 muslin 8

napkin 1 nearly 1 nice 2

paint 5 pale 2 paper 17 pencil 1 person 2 pigeon 1 pink 2 pleasing 1 powder 1 pretty 1 pure 20 purity 19

race 1 red 7 restful 1 retired 1 ribbon 1 rightness 1 rose 2

sand 1 Sarah 1 shade 1 sheet 6 shoes 1 shroud 1 silvery 1 simple 1 skirt 1 sky 2 snow 91 snowflake 1 snowy 1 soft 1 soul 1 space 1 spread 1 still 2 summer 1 sunlight 1 swan 1

tablecloth 4 tent 1 tile 1 trees 1 trousers 1

waist 2 wall 6 wash 1 wedding 2

yellow 7

29. BEAUTIFUL

admirable 1 admiring 1 aesthetic 1 all 1 ancient 1 appearance 2 art 6 article 1 artistic 1 attractive 1

baby 1 bird 1 birds 1 brilliant 1 building 1 butterfly 2

carpet 1 carving 1 charming 7 child 6 city 1 classic 1 clear 1 clouds 1 color 1 colors 1 comely 3 common 1 complexion 3 conceited 1 country 3 curtain 1

dainty 1 day 7 delicious 1 delightful 5 description 1 desire 1 divine 1 dress 2

earth 1 elegant 5 enjoyed 1 ethereal 1 Eunice 2 Evelyn 1 everything 1 exquisite 4 eye 1 eyes 2

face 3 fair 5 falls 1 fancy 2 fascinating 1 fine 8 flower 13 flowers 42 foliage 1 forest 1 Formosa 1 fragrant 1 friend 2

gift 1 girl 24 glorious 2 God 2 good 4 gorgeous 2 graceful 1 grand 40 grandeur 2 grass 1 grounds 1

hand 1 handsome 86 happy 1 hard 1 hateful 1 heaven 2 heavens 1 hideous 1 hills 2 homely 27 horrible 1

joy 1

kind 1

lady 5 lake 1 landscape 7 lightness 1 long 1 look 1 looks 1 looking 1 lovable 2 lovely 64 luxurious 1

magnificent 10 maiden 2 man 2 mansion 1 money 1 morning 1 mountain 2 mountains 6 music 4 myself 1

nature 16 Niagara 1 nice 73 nicely 1 night 1 noble 1

object 1 ocean 3

Palisades 2 pansies 1 park 1 peacock 3 perception 1 perfect 3 perfection 1 person 2 picture 19 pictures 4 place 1 plain 2 pleasant 14 pleasing 16 pleasure 2 pretty 113

queen 1

rainbow 1 religion 1 resplendent 1 ribbon 1 rich 1 robin 1 rose 6 roses 2

sad 1 satisfaction 1 scarce 1 scene 1 scenery 23 school 1 sculpture 1 sensitive 1 shapely 1 sight 1 sky 16 soft 1 sometimes 1 soothing 1 sorrowful 1 splendid 8 statue 1 straw 1 summer 2 sun 1 sunset 8 sunshine 1 superb 1 supreme 1 sweet 4 symphony 1

things 2 tree 4 trees 10

ugliness 2 ugly 66

vanity 1 verdure 1 violets 1

weather 4 wife 1 woman 29 women 1 wonderful 1 world 2

you 1

30. WINDOW

air 12 airing 1 airy 1 aperture 2 awning 1

bars 1 blind 4 breeze 1 bright 3 broken 2

cage 1 casing 3 children 1 church 1 clean 6 cleaner 1 clear 7 colored 1 cool 1 curtain 13 curtains 4

danger 1 dirty 2 door 57 doors 1 doorway 1 draught 1

eyes 1

few 1 frame 5

garden 1 glass 316 glasses 1

hole 4 home 1 house 22

joyful 1

landscape 2 large 11 lattice 2 ledge 1 light 186 look 15 looking 5 low 1

Newcastle 1

object 1 open 19 opened 1 opening 16 outdoors 1 outlook 5

pane 82 panes 6 picture 1 porch 1

rain 1 rock 1 room 3

sash 20 scene 2 scenery 3 school 2 screen 1 screens 1 seat 1 see 9 shade 8 shades 2 shed 1 shining 1 sight 7 sightly 1 sill 13 sky 1 skylight 3 small 1 square 1 stained 2 stop 1 street 1 structure 1 sun 3 sunshine 2

thing 1 translucent 1 transom 1 transparent 24 trees 2

useful 2

vast 1 ventilation 5 ventilator 2 view 15 viewing 1 visible 1 vision 1

wall 4 wash 1 wide 2 winter 2 wood 1

31. ROUGH

bad 4 bag 1 ball 1 basket 1 bear 1 blisters 1 blow 1 board 10 boards 1 boisterous 4 bold 2 boy 4 boys 4 bristle 1 brush 2 brutal 3 brutality 1 bumpy 1

calm 2 careless 1 carpet 2 chaps 1 cloth 4 coarse 29 coarseness 1 cobblestones 1 cold 1 country 2 crooked 2 cross 1 cruel 1

desert 1 difficult 1 dirt 1 disagreeable 8 discomfort 1 discouraging 1 dog 1 dress 1 dry 3 dull 1

earth 2 easy 2 even 2 land 1 face 1 fast 1 file 7 fine 2 floor 6 football 2 forest 1

gambler 1 genteel 1 gentle 8 girl 1 granite 1 granular 1 grater 1 grating 1 gravel 1 ground 8

hairy 1 hall 1 hand 2 hard 38 hardness 1 harsh 10 harshness 1 haste 1 hill 2 hills 2 hilly 5 horrid 1 house 1 porcupine 1 ice 3 impertinent 1 injurious 1 iron 2 irregular 2

jagged 1

knife 1

late 1

level 3 lurk 1 lump 1

man 8 manner 1 manners 1 material 1 me 1 mean 1 mild 3 mountain 6 mountains 1

nice 1 noisy 1

obstetricians 1 ocean 27 orange 1

paper 1 pavement 1 peasant 1 pebbles 1 person 2 picture 1 pineapple 1 plane 2 plank 1 play 1 poor 1 stern 1 push 1 stone 12 quality 1 quiet 1 quite 1

radiator 1 ragged 5 railway 1 rasp 1 ready 5 refined 1 rider 1 riders 1 river 1 road 21 roads 5 rock 10 rocks 10 rocky 12 rowdy 1 ruddy 1 rude 7 rudeness 1 rug 1 rugged 22 ruggedness 1 Russian 1 rut 1

sand 5 sandpaper 13 savage 1 sea 15 sedate 1 scratch 1 shock 1 sliver 1 slow 1 smooth 346 smoothness 2 soft 4 sponge 1 west 1 sticky 1 wind 2 stones 3 stony 7 storm 5 stormy 1 straight 1 street 3 surface 6

table 4 tempestuous 1 tongue 2 touch 2 tough 2 towel 1 tramp 4 trouble 1 tumble 1 turbulent 1 ugly 4 uncomfortable 4 uncouth 4 uneasy 1 uneven 38 unfairness 1 unfinished 1 unpleasant 7 unsatisfactory 1 untaught 1

voices 1 voyage 2 vulgar 5

walk 2 wall 1 washing 1 water 21 waves 5 weary 1 weather 4

wild 2

winds 1 wood 7 woodsman 1 work 1 world 1 wrong 1

32. CITIZEN

alien 14 America 5 American 35 Americans 3 army 1 arrived 1

belong 4 belonging 1 beloved 1 beneficial 1 bird 1 born 3 Brooklyn 1 brother 1 business 1

C. 1 candidate 1 capital 1 cat 1 cistern 1 citizeness 1 city 27 civies 4 civilian 2 civilized 4 clothes 1 club 1 commander 1 community 3 comrade 1 conspirators 1 constitution 1 cosmopolitan 1 countrified 1 country 17 countryman 7 criticise 1

democrat 1 duties 2 duty 3 dweller 1 dwelling 1

ear 1 election 1 eligible 1 emigrant 2 emigration 1

F. 1 faithful 1 farm 1 farmer 3

fellow 3 fellowship 2 fine 1 five 2 fool 1 foreign 1 foreigner 12 free 1 freeman 2 friend 1 friendship 1

gardener 1 gentleman 8 German 3 good 26 government 6 green 1

helper 1 home 3 honest 3 honor 1 honorable 2 human 3

I 1 immigrant 1 independence 1 indian 1 individual 4 inhabit 1 inhabitant 23 invader 1 Italian 1

justice 2

K. 1 king 1

large 1

law 11 laws 1 lawyer 3 leader 1 leading 1 legislature 1 Lincoln 1 little 1 live 1 lives 1 loyal 3

male 7 man 278 manhood 1 mayor 5 me 1 member 5 men 2 merry 1 moral 1 Mr. A. 1 Mr. C. 1 Mr. S. 1 municipal 1 myself 1 name 1 nationality 1 native 25 natural 1 naturalization 1 naturalized 5 navy 1 near 1 neighbor 3 newspaper 1 New York 4 noble 1 nobleman 2 nonsense 1

obedient 1 obey 1 occupant 1 office 2 officer 1 old 1 orderly 1 outlaw 1

paper 2 papers 2 patrician 1 patriot 2 patriotic 2 peasant 1 people 41 person 64 plebeian 1 policeman 2 politician 4 politicians 1 politics 8 poor 1 president 4 proud 1

relative 1 republic 3 republican 1 residence 2 resident 20 respectable 1 revolution 1 righteousness 1 Roman 2 Roosevelt 2 ruler 1

season 1 ship 1 soldier 5 state 10 statesman 5 stationed 1 straight 1 subject 5 suburban 1 suffrage 3 suffragette 2

Taft 3 Tammany 1 taxes 1 Teddy 1 thoughtful 1 tough 1 town 5 townsman 5

undesirable 2 unit 1 United States 19 useful 2

village 2 vote 13 voting 4 Voter 35

Washington 1 woman 2 work 2

years 1

33. FOOT

anatomy 2 animal 2 ankle 11 appendage 2 arm 11

baby's 1 base 1 bicycle 1 big 2 black 3 body 34 bone 4 bones 5 boot 6 bottom 1 broken 1 brown 1

careful 1 comfort 3 corn 3 corns 2

dainty 1 difficult 1 distance 1

expansive 1 extremity 9

finger 1 firm 1 flat 1 flesh 6 football 1 foundation 3

gear 1 girls 1 going 1 good 1 ground 2

hand 185 hands 5 head 7 heel 3 help 1 helper 1 horse 1 house 1 human 1 humility 1 hurt 1

inch 3 inches 2

kick 4 knee 2

labor 1 lame 1 large 14 leg 54 legs 1 length 2 limb 58 long 2 man 5 measure 3 member 10 mine 1 Miss F. 1 movement 2 music 1

nail 1 naked 1 necessity 2 needful 1

organ 1

pain 1 painful 1 part 2 pavement 1 pedal 3 pedant 1 pedestal 1 pedestrian 1 person 5 plaster 1

quadruped 2

rheumatism 1 right 1 rubber 1 rule 4 ruler 1 run 2

shape 1 shoe 146 shoes 17 short 4 size 1 skin 1 slipper 2 small 22 sole 1 sore 8 speed 1 stability 1 stand 6 standing 1 standard 1 step 6 stepping 1 stocking 2 stone 1 strength 1 strong 1 stumps 1 support 1 swiftness 1

three 1 tired 5 toe 30 toes 41 travel 2 trod 1 twelve 1 two 1

useful 5

velocity 1

walk 106 walking 38 warm 1

yard 1

34. SPIDER

abhorrence 1 afraid 1 animal 38 annoyance 1 ant 3 arachnida 2 arachnoid 1 awful 1

bee 3 bees 2 beetle 4 big 1 bird 2 bite 20 black 8 breakfast 1 bug 58 bugs 2 butterfly 5

camp 1 caterpillar 3 centipede 1 chills 1 climb 1 cobweb 12 cobwebs 2 country 1 crawl 14 crawls 1 crawling 11 crawly 1 creature 2 creep 6 creeps 1 creeping 7 creepiness 1 creepy 5 cricket 2 cringe 1 cross 1 crow 1 cunning 1

daddy-long-legs 1 danger 1 dangerous 4 dark 2 dirty 1 disagreeable 3 displeasure 1 dread 1

evil 1

fear 3 fish 1 flies 4 fly 136 fright 1 fry 1 frying 1

grass 1

harlequin 1 harmful 1 horrible 1 horrid 4 horror 3

industry 1 insect 276

jumping 1

- 231 -

large 5 leg 3 legs 27 loathsome 1 long 1

Miss Muffet 1 mosquito 1 moth 1 movements 1

nasty 3 nest 1 net 2 nuisance 1

objectionable 1 obnoxious 1 octopus 1

pain 1 pan 1 pest 1 poison 10 poisonous 1 pretty 1

rats 1 Robert Bruce 2 roach 1 room 1

shivers 1 shudder 1 sinister 1 small 2 snake 1 snakes 1 sparrow 1 sting 7 stings 1 stung 1 study 1

tarantula 3 thing 1 thread 2 tortoise 1 treachery 1 tree 1

ugly 6 undesirable 1 unpleasant 1

venomous 2 vermin 1

walk 1 wall 1 wasp 6 watching 1 weaves 2 weaving 1 web 188 webs 3 wiggly 1 worm 4

young 1

35. NEEDLE

article 3

blood 1 book 2 broken 1 button 1 buttons 1

camel 1 cloth 4 clothes 2 coat 2 cotton 7 crocheting 1 cut 1

darning 4 diligence 1 dressmaker 2

embroidery 1 eye 17

fine 3

handy 1 help 1 hole 1 home 1 housewife 1 hurt 2 hypodermic 2

implement 5 industry 2 instrument 26 knitting 4

labor 1 long 1

magnetic 1 material 1 mending 1 metal 3

nail 1

ornament 1

patching 1 pin 147 pins 11 pincushion 1 point 50 pointed 9 prick 10 pricks 1 pricking 2

- 232 -

sew 134 sews 1 sewing 107

sharp 152 sharpness 4 shiny 1 slippers 1 small 2 steel 53 sting 2 stitching 1 surgeon 1

tailor 1 thick 2 thimble 15 thin 2 thread 100 tool 5

use 1 using 1 useful 12

weapon 1 wire 1 woman 1 work 6

36. RED

aggravating 1 anarchist 1 anger 2 apple 13 apples 3

ball 1 banner 1 barn 2 beauty 2 becoming 1 black 61 blood 71 bloody 1 blossom 1 blue 99 book 8 bravery 1 brick 3 bricks 2 bright 40 brightness 2 brilliant 3 brook 1 brown 7 building 1 bull 2

cap 1 cape 1 carpet 1 ceiling 1 cheeks 1 cheer 1 cherries 1 closet 1 cloth 8 clouds 1 coat 2 color 254 colors 1 colored 1 coloring 1 comfortable 1 Cornell 1 cow 1 crimson 2 curtain 2

danger 14 dark 6 dashy 1 dislike 1 dress 18

eat 1 Ed 1

fiery 2 fire 81 flag 16 flannel 3 flashy 1 fright 1 flower 2 flowers 1 flushing 1

garment 1 garnet 3 gaudy 1 glaring 2 glass 1 globe 1 glow 1 grass 1 green 30

hair 6 handsome 1 hat 1 head 2 healthy 1 heat 4 Hereford 1 holly 1 hood 1 horse 1 hot 5 house 2

Indian 2 ink 4 iron 1

jacket 1

lavender 1 light 1 lips 1

maroon 1 Mars 1 mixture 1 moon 1

object 1 objectionable 1 offensive 1 orange 1

paint 5 paper 4 passion 1 pencil 1 pink 1 plush 1 poinsettia 1 pretty 2 purple 6

ribbon 3 riding 1 robin 3 rose 15 rosy 3 rug 2

scarlet 3 shoe 1 sky 2 smooth 1 soldier 1 spots 1 story 1 sun 5 sunset 3 sweater 1

tablecloth 1 thread 4 tie 1 tomatoes 1 turkey 2

vivid 1

war 1 warm 6 warmth 3 whiskey 1 white 97 wool 1 world 1 yarn 1 yellow 15

37. SLEEP

awake 94 awaking 1 awaken 3 awakening 1

baby 2 beautiful 1 bed 75 bedstead 1

calm 2 chance 1 child 2 children 1 coma 1 comfort 30

dead 2 death 7 deep 5 desire 1 desperate 1 dope 1 dormitory 2 dose 1 doze 4 dream 28 dreams 10 drowsy 6 drowsiness 3 dullness 1

ease 3 easy 4 eat 4 enjoyable 1 enjoyment 1 enough 1 experiment 1 eyes 10

fast 1 fatigue 2 fine 1 forgetfulness 2

gentle 1 girl 1 go 1 good 5

habit 1 happiness 1 health 3 heavy 1 home 1

insomnia 2

lady 1 leisure 1 lain 1 lie 3 living 1 luxurious 1 luxury 1

mesmerism 1 midnight 1 myself 1

natural 1 necessary 4

need 1 needful 1

nice 1 night 40

peace 1 peaceful 1 peacefulness 2 perfect 1 pillow 5 pleasant 3 plenty 1 poorly 1 potassium 1 profound 2

quiet 8 quietness 2 quietude 1

rage 1 recline 2 reclining 1 refreshing 7 refreshment 2 relax 1 repose 31 rest 300 resting 14 restful 9 restless 4 restore 1 restorer 2 retiring 1 rise 1 rising 1

senses 1 Shakespeare 1 sheet 1 shut 1 silence 1 sleeplessness 1 sleepy 1 slumber 20 slumbering 2 snore 4 soft 1 solace 1 song 1 soothing 2 sound 16 soundly 3 still 2 sweet 3

thinking 1 tired 26 tiresome 1

unconscious 12 unconsciousness 7

wake 60 wakefulness 4 wakened 1 wakening 1 waking 4

walk 2 wanting 1 watchful 1 weariness 3 weary 1 well 1 woman 1

38. ANGER

abuse 1 aggravated 1 aggravation 2 agony 1 amiability 2 amiable 1 angry 6 anguish 2 annoyance 1 annoyed 3 appearance 1 aroused 1 awful 1

bad 13 bitter 2 bitterness 3 blow 1 blows 1 blush 1 boy 3 breathing 1

calm 7 calmness 1 cat 2 catching 1 cause 2 character 1 cheer 1 child 1 children 1 choler 1 cold 1 command 3 compose 1 control 5 cool 1 cranky 1 crazy 1 cross 44 crossness 2 covetous 1 cruel 1 cry 1

danger 1 deliberation 1 despise 1 devil 1 disagreeable 4 disappointed 1 disappointment 2 discomfort 3 dishonor 1 dislike 1 disobedience 1 disobedient 1 displeased 2 displeasure 2 disturbance 3 disturbed 5 dog 4 downhearted 1 duel 1

emotion 3 enemy 2 energy 1 enmity 1 excitability 1 excited 3 excitement 4 exclamation 1

face 1 father 1 fear 9 feeling 4 ferocity 1 fierce 1 fiery 1 fight 8 fighting 1 fist 1 flush 1 foolish 1 foolishness 3 force 1 forgive 1 forgiveness 3 frenzy 1 fret 1 fright 1 frown 1 frowning 1 fun 1 furious 2 fury 4

gentle 2 gentleness 3 giant 1 girl 1 glad 4 gladness 2 good 2 great 1 grief 3 grieve 1 grouchy 2

happiness 4 happy 2 harsh 3 haste 2 hasty 3 hate 9 hateful 1 hatred 26 headache 1 horrid 1 horror 1 hot 3 hot-headed 1 house 1 humor 1 hunger 1 hysteria 1

ill 1 impatience 4 impatient 3 Indian 1 indignant 1 indignation 2 insanity 1 insult 1 insulted 1 intense 1 intensity 1 intoxication 1 ire 2 irritable 1

jealousy 1 Jimmy 1 joy 4 joyful 1 judgement 1

kind 2 kindness 2

laughter 1 light 1 lion 2 little 1 loud 3 love 5 low 1

mad 121 maddest 1 madness 19 malice 2 man 6 mean 1 meekness 4 mild 1 mind 4 mirth 2 myself 2

name 1 nature 1 nerves 1 nervous 1 never 1 nice 1 noise 2 noisy 1 none 1 nonsense 1 not 1 noticeable 1

obey 1 out 1 outrage 1

pain 1 passion 51 passionate 1 patience 3 peace 6 peaceful 1 peevish 1 person 2 placid 1 pleasant 5 pleasure 4 provocation 2 provoke 1 provoked 1 provoking 2 quarrel 3 quarreling 2 quarrelsome 1 quick 4 quickness 1 quiet 6 quietness 1 quite 1

rage 16 rarely 1 rashly 1 rashness 1 raving 1 reason 1 red 3 remorse 1 resentment 2 resistive 1 rest 1 restless 1 revenge 8 riled 2 rough 3 roughness 1 rude 1

sad 1 scold 2 scolding 2 scowl 1 sedative 1 selfishness 1 sharp 1 shorn 1 sick 1 sin 1 slow 1 smooth 2 sober 1 soft 1 soldier 1 sometimes 1 soothing 1 sorrow 10 spite 1 spiteful 1 storm 1 strike 1 strong 1 suffering 1 sulky 1 swear 1 sweetness 1 sword 1

talking 1 teacher 2 tears 1 temper 149 temperament 1 terrible 1 terror 1 thought 3 torment 1 trouble 6 turbulent 1 turmoil 1

ugliness 1 ugly 4 unbecoming 1 uncomfortable 1 unhealthy 1 unpleasant 4

very 1 vexation 3 vexed 13 vicious 1 violence 1 violent 2 voice 1

war 1 wicked 5 wickedness 1 wish 1 woman 4 words 1 wrath 52 wrathful 1 wroth 2 wrong 4

yelling 1

39. CARPET

appearance 1 article 1

beat 1 beating 2 beater 1 beautiful 2 beautifying 1 beauty 2 bedroom 1 blue 2 bright 2 broom 1 brown 2 brush 1 brushes 1 Brussels 14

chair 1 chairs 1 clean 3 cleaning 2 cleaner 1 cloth 20 color 6 colors 1 comfort 15 comfortable 8 cotton 2 cover 27 covering 76 curtains 1

dark 1 design 6 designer 1 dirt 2 down 1 drag 1 dullness 1 dust 4 duster 1

ease 3 electric 1 expense 1

fancy 2 figure 3 flat 1 floor 256 flooring 2 foot 2 fur 1 furnishing 1 furniture 4

germs 1 good 2 goods 4 grain 1 gray 1 green 8

hall 1 heavy 3 home 4 house 4

ingrain 2

lay 1 loom 1 lot 1 luxury 3

mat 6 material 3 matting 10 mattress 1 microbes 1 moss 1

nail 1 neatness 1 nice 2 none 1

oilcloth 7 oriental 1 ornament 2

parlor 3 pattern 1 pennant 1 pleasant 1 plush 2 pretty 4 protection 2

quick 1

rag 7 rags 3 ragged 1 red 8 reddish 1 refinement 1 rich 1 room 17 rough 2 rug 163 rugs 14

shoes 1 small 1 smooth 8 soft 78 softness 4 stairs 2 stove 1 straw 1 sweep 7 sweeping 3 sweeper 10

table 1 tack 8 tacks 8 tapestry 2 textile 2 thread 2 tread 2

use 2 useful 1

velvet 9

walk 15 walking 6 wall 1 Wanamaker 1 warm 2 warmth 5 weaver 1 weaving 1 wear 1 white 1 wide 1 wood 1 wool 10 woolen 7 worsted 1 woven 2

40. GIRL

ankles 1 Annie 1 associate 1

baby 1 Beatrice 1 beautiful 8 beauty 6 being 9 belt 1 big 1 biped 1 blonde 1 blooming 1 book 1 boy 350 boys 3 braids 2 bright 1

changeable 1 cheerful 1 child 49 children 2 childhood 2 childish 1 choice 1 class 1 classmate 1 clever 1 clothes 4 clothing 1 Coleen 1 college 1 companion 2 cook 1 cunning 1 curls 2 cute 2

dainty 2 damsel 1 dance 1 dancing 1 daughter 2 delight 1 diabolo 1 domestic 1 Doris 1 Dorothy 1 dream 1 dress 8 dresses 4

Effie 1 Ethel 1 eyes 1

fair 1 fellow 2 female 77 feminine 3 flesh 3 flirtation 1 Frances 1 friend 7 futurity 1

garden 1 gay 1 gentility 1 gentle 1 Gertrude 1 good 6 grace 1

hair 3 hand 1 handsome 5 happiness 1 harmlessness 1 has 1 hat 3 head 1 here 1 hood 1 hoop 1 human 7 humanity 1

immature 1 infant 2 innocence 3 innocent 1 intelligent 1 Irene 1

jealousy 1 jolly 2 joy 2

kid 1

lady 20 large 1 lassie 1 learning 1 little 3 lively 1 Lizzie 1 love 2 loving 1 lovely 4 maid 7 maiden 13 maidenhood 1 malt 1 man 7 men 1 meek 1 mischievious 1 miss 4 Miss S. 1 modesty 1 mother 2 myself 3

neat 2 necessity 2 nice 11 niece 2 noise 1

Pelar 1 person 18 petticoats 1 play 2 pleasure 4 pretty 29 pupil 1

quick 1

rarely 1 running 1

saucy 1 school 19 servant 3 sex 4 shirk 1 silly 4 sister 6 sixteen 2 skirts 1 slender 1 slight 1 slim 1 small 8 smart 1 smartness 1 student 1 studious 1 study 3 stylish 1 summer 1 sweet 4 sweetness 1 sweetheart 2

talks 1 tall 4 thoughtless 1

ugly 1 useful 1

vanity 1 virgin 2

walk 1 water 1 weak 2 white 1 wife 1 woman 61

young 31 youngster 1 youth 24

41. HIGH

above 9 air 5 Alps 1 altitude 14 ascend 1

bank 1 beam 1 beanstalk 1 big 3 bridge 1 building 24 buildings 2

Cathedral 1 ceiling 4 chair 2 church 2 cliff 1 climb 1 climbing 1 clouds 7

deep 5 depth 4 dimension 1 distance 11 distant 3 dizzy 2

elevated 11 elevation 2 erect 1 exalted 2 extended 1

fall 3 falling 2 far 1 fast 1 fear 2 feet 1 fence 3 first 1

giant 2 great 1

hat 1 heaven 1 heavens 3 heavenward 1 height 14 hill 20 hills 4 hot 1 house 24 houses 1

ideal 1 ideas 1 immense 1

jump 2

kite 1

ladder 2 large 5 length 7 lighthouse 1 lofty 20 long 7 low 328

magnificent 1 man 1 mast 2 measure 1 medium 3 Metropolitan 1 mind 1 monument 2 mount 1 mountain 157 mountains 16 myself 1

notion 1

- 238 -

peak 4 pine 1 pinnacle 1 play 1 pole 8 power 1 precipice 3

reach 2 rich 1 rocky 1 roof 3 room 1

see 1 shallow 1 short 3 skies 1 sky 17 skyscraper 2 small 1 soft 1 spire 1 staff 1 stand 1 steep 13 steeple 12 stick 1 stone 1 summit 1 swing 2

tall 57 temperature 1 temple 1 top 5 tower 12 tree 19 trees 4

up 26 upward 1

valley 1 vision 1

wall 5 waves 1 wind 2 woman 1

42. WORKING

accomplish 1 accomplishment 1 active 3 activity 1 always 1 ambition 1 ambitious 5 anxious 1 apron 1 attendant 1

bent 1 book 1 boy 2 broom 2 business 6 busy 51

carpenter 1 class 3 comfort 1 complication 1 content 2 continually 2 continuous 1 cooking 1

day 6 difficult 1 digging 1 diligence 1 discomfort 1 do 2 doing 10 done 1 drawing 1 driving 1 drudge 1 dusting 1 duties 1 duty 2

earning 2 ease 2 easiness 1 easy 4 eating 2 effort 1 employed 10 employers 1 employment 4 energetic 2 energy 3 engaged 2 English 1 essay 1 exercise 15 exercising 1 exertion 3

factory 3 fair 2 faithfully 1 farm 1 fast 1 father 3 fatigue 7 fatigued 2 field 1 flowers 1 foundry 1 function 1

girl 2 good 4

hammer 2 hands 3 happiness 1 hard 105 health 2 healthy 1 hoeing 1 horse 2 hour 1 house 1

idle 44 idleness 10 idling 2 inconvenience 1 indolent 1 industrious 13 industry 8 intelligent 1 interest 1 Italian 2 job 1

keeping 1

labor 147 laboring 20 labors 1 laborer 5 lack 1 ladies 1 late 1 laziness 2 lazy 18 leisure 1 Lillie 1 little 1 live 1 livelihood 2 living 5 loaf 1 loafing 5 loafer 1 lounging 1

machine 2 machinery 1 machinist 1 making 1 man 50 men 6 model 1 money 4 morning 1 motion 3 movement 2 moving 5 mowing 1 myself 2 necessary 4 necessity 1 neighbor 1 never 1 night 1 noble 1 nothing 1 nursing 1

obstetrics 1 occupation 13 occupied 1 occupy 1 order 2

paid 1 patients 1 people 5 person 2 perspiration 1 play 8 playing 22 pleasant 1 pleasure 4 plow 1 plowing 1 policy 1 position 1 possession 1 prosperous 1

quick 1

railroad 1 reading 1 recreation 1 rest 17 resting 24 result 1 rowing 1 running 3

salary 1 satisfaction 1 saving 1 school 6 scrubbing 3 servant 2 setting 1 sewing 7 shirking 2 shop 7 shorthand 1 sickness 1 singing 1 sitting 3 slave 4 slavery 1 slaving 1 sleep 2 sleeping 8 slow 1 smart 1 starving 1 steady 2 stenographer 1 strenuous 2 struggle 1 study 5 studying 5 sweep 1 sweeping 3 swift 1

table 1 task 2 thinking 1 thought 1 time 1 tired 28 tiresome 3 tiring 1 to-day 1 toil 7 toiling 8 tools 2 treadmill 1 trouble 1 trying 2 typewriter 1

unemployed 2 useful 2

wages 4 walking 2 washerwoman 1 washing 5 weariness 1 willing 2 woman 2 work 1 workman 1 world 1 writing 2

43. SOUR

acetic 1 acid 23 acrid 1 anger 1 angry 1 apple 27 apples 10 astringent 1

bad 6 beer 1 bitter 70 bitterness 1

cherries 3 cider 2 cross 1 crowd 1 currants 1

dangerous 1 death 1 delight 1 disagreeable 18 dislike 1 disposition 3 distasteful 4 drink 1

face 1 flavor 1 fruit 3

gall 1 good 4 goodness 1 grape 3 grapes 36 grapefruit 2 green 1

hate 1 hurts 1

juice 1

kraut 2

lemon 78 lemons 17 lime 1

man 1 milk 31

nasty 3 naturally 1 nice 3 no 1 nourishing 1

odor 1 orange 2

painful 1 persimmon 1 pickle 15 pickles 20 pleasant 1 plum 1 plums 1 pucker 3

quince 3

rancid 1 repulsive 1 rhubarb 5 rough 1

salt 2 salty 1 sauerkraut 2 sear 1 sharp 2 soft 1 song 1 spoiled 1 stomach 1 sugar 2 sweet 349

tart 17 taste 55 tasting 2 tasteless 2 teeth 1 turned 1 twinge 1

ugly 4 unhappy 1 unpalatable 3 unpleasant 16 unpleasantness 1 unsweetened 1

vinegar 91

wholesome 1 wine 1

44. EARTH

agriculture 1 air 3 ashes 1

ball 4 beautiful 3 big 2 black 7 body 1 broken 2 brown 17 building 1

cemetery 1 clay 71 climate 1 cloud 1 coffin 1 cold 2 color 1 Columbus 2 continent 1 corn 2 country 2 cover 1 creation 1 crunching 1 crushed 1 crust 5

damp 5 dark 10 delve 1 depth 2 dig 1 digging 2 dirt 115 dirty 4 dogs 1 dry 4 dust 9

farm 3 farming 1 fence 1 fertile 1 fertilized 1 field 4 fields 1 flag 1 floor 3 flower 1 flowers 8 foot 1 foundation 1 fresh 1 fruitful 1 Fuller's 1

garden 8 geranium 1 globe 16 grain 2 grand 1 grass 11 grave 3 gravel 2 gravity 1 great 2 green 3 greenhouse 1 ground 166 growth 1

habitation 2 hard 4 heaven 31 heavens 1 heavy 2 hell 1 hemisphere 1 home 3 house 1 huge 1

inhabitable 1

land 28 large 7 level 1 live 3 living 2 loam 3 lot 1 low 2

man 1 map 2 Mars 3 mass 1 material 1 matter 1 metal 1 mine 1 mineral 1 moist 3 moon 11 mother 6 mould 2 mouldy 1 mountain 4 mountains 2 mud 16

nature 4

object 1 ocean 1 one 1 orange 1

paradise 1 place 1 planet 17 plant 2 plants 5 planting 1 pleasure 1 potential 1 productive 1 put 1

rain 1 rampart 1 rest 1 revolution 1 rich 4 river 1 road 1 rock 2 rocks 2 round 61 roundness 1

sand 5 sky 81 smelly 1 smooth 3 sod 2 soft 5 soil 37 solid 1 solidity 2 space 1 sphere 4 star 1 stone 2 stones 2 street 1 substance 1 sun 4 surface 3

travel 1 tree 4 trees 5

unfertile 1 universe 8

vastness 1 vegetable 1

walk 3 water 10 wide 1 wood 1 world 46 worm 5 worms 2

- 242 -

45. TROUBLE

accident 2 affliction 4 aggravation 3 anger 6 angry 6 anguish 1 annoy 1 annoyed 2 annoyance 5 anxiety 15 avoid 2

bad 11 begins 1 black 1 borrowed 1 borrows 1 bother 4 bothered 2 bothersome 1 brains 1 brewing 1 broke 1 burden 1 burdens 1 business 1 busy 1

calm 1 calmness 1 care 27 cares 3 careless 1 children 4 college 1 comfort 6 comforts 1 comfortable 1 coming 2 consequences 1 contented 2 contentment 1 court 1 cry 1 crying 1

danger 6 darkness 1 day 1 death 16 deep 2 despair 2 difficult 1 difficulties 1 difficulty 1 disagreeable 1 disagreement 2 disappoint 1 disaster 3 discomfort 7 discontent 2 disease 3 dislike 2 disobedience 1 displeased 1 displeasing 1 displeasure 2 dissatisfactory 1 distress 7 disturbed 2 doctor 1 dogs 1

ease 4 easiness 1 easy 1 ended 1 enemies 1 enemy 1 error 1 everywhere 1 exams 1 excited 1 excitement 2

family 3 father 1 fear 3 feeling 1 few 1 fight 5 fighting 2

flunking 1 fret 1 friends 1 fun 1 funeral 1 fuss 3

girl 2 gossip 2 great 2 grief 26

handkerchief 1 happiness 19 happy 8 hard 5 hardship 6 harm 1 health 3 heart 1 heaviness 1 hemorrhage 1 home 2 horror 1 horse 1 hurried 1 husband 1

idea 1 illness 2 imaginary 1 inconvenience 2

joy 9

kindness 1 kinds 1

labor 1 laugh 1 lawyer 1 lessons 1 life 2 little 1 lonesome 1 loss 1 lots 5

mad 2 madness 1 man 5 many 1 marriage 2 me 2 mind 10 minded 1 mischief 8 miserable 1 misery 14 misfortune 6 misunderstanding 1 money 4 monotony 1 mother 1 Mrs. Wiggs 1 much 5

nervousness 1 no 3 noise 2 none 4 nuisance 1

pain 20 patience 2 patient 2 patients 1 peace 15 peaceful 3 people 3 perplexed 1 perplexity 1 person 3

pity 1 pleasure 10 plenty 1 poor 2 poverty 2 psychologist 1

quarrel 3 quarreling 3 quiet 3 quietness 1

release 1 relief 1 remorse 1 rest 1 reverses 2 Romeo 1 ruffled 1

sad 6 sadness 13 school 1 scrape 1 sea 1 seldom 1 sereneness 1 shadow 1 ship 1 shooting 1 sickness 47 simple 1 sin 1 sleep 1 sometimes 1 sorrow 202 sorrows 1 sorrowful 4 sport 1 squabble 1 study 1 suffer 1 suffering 1 sweetener 1 sympathy 2

table 1 task 1 tears 9 teasing 1 temper 1 temptation 1 thought 2 thoughts 1 torment 1 travel 1 trial 1 trials 3 troublesome 5

ugly 1 unavoidable 1 uncertainty 1 uncomfortable 2 uneasiness 6 uneasy 6 unfortunate 2 unhappiness 13 unhappy 8 unlucky 1 unnecessary 2 unpleasant 6 unpleasantness 3 unrest 1 unsafe 1 unsatisfactory 2 unsettled 1 upset 2

want 1 war 2 weak 1 weary 3 weeping 2 welfare 1 woe 1 woman 5 women 1 work 8 worked 1 working 1 worried 3 worries 2 worry 65 worrying 1 worriment 5 wrinkles 2 wrong 2

yesterday 1 youth 1

46. SOLDIER

academy 1 armlet 1 army 137 arms 3 Arnold 1 artillery 2

baseball 1 battle 8 bayonet 1 blood 1 blue 1 boy 23 boys 1 brave 46 braveness 1 bravery 8 Brazilian 1 brother 1 buttons 2

cadet 4 camp 2 cannon 2 cap 1 captain 8 cavalry 3 citizen 14 civilian 3 clothes 1 colonel 1 command 6 commanding 1 commander 3 costume 1 country 4 courage 5

danger 1 defender 2 defense 1 discipline 2 disliked 1

double 1 drill 2 drums 1 duty 4

enemy 1 England 1 English 1 erect 3

fellow 1 fight 17 fights 1 fighter 12 fighting 12 firearm 1 fort 2 fortune 1

general 4 Germany 1 glory 1 good 3 Grant 1 guard 8 guardian 1 guardsman 1 gun 27 guns 2

helmet 1 hero 8 him 1 hobo 1 home 1 hurt 1

infantry 2

jacky 1 Jim 1

king 1

lieutenant 5

male 3 man 189 men 4 manly 1 march 12 marching 5 marine 1 marshal 2 mechanic 2 military 17 militia 3 murder 1 music 1 musket 2

N. 1 nation 1 national 1 navy 2 necessary 1 nobility 1

obedience 1 obey 1 officer 12 officers 1 order 1 orderly 2

patriot 5 patriotic 1 patriotism 1 person 3 Philippines 1 police 1 policeman 6 protection 1 protector 2 proud 1

red 4 redcoat 1 regiment 1 regular 2 respectable 1 Richmond 1 rifle 3

sailor 58 sailors 1 salute 1 sentry 1 servant 1 service 1 show 1 sick 1 single 1 smart 1 sorrow 1 stateliness 1 store 1 straight 3 strength 1 stremious 1 strict 1 strong 4 sword 2

tall 2 tent 1 tin 4 training 1 travel 1 troop 1 troops 1

uniform 39 United States 1 upright 3 uprightness 1

valiant 1 veteran 3 volunteer 3

war 94 warfare 1 warrior 12 West Point 8 widow 2 work 2

47. CABBAGE

away 1

bad 1 beans 2 beef 11 beet 1 beets 2 boiled 1 broth 1 bud 1 bunchy 1

carrot 2 carrots 1 catsup 1 cauliflower 17 cigar 1 cold-slaw 1 cook 1 cooking 4 corn 1 cucumbers 1 cut 1

decayed 1 disagreeable 1 dish 2 dislike 1 dinner 4

eat 30 eating 6 eatable 6 eatables 3

farm 11 farming 1 field 3 fields 2 fine 1 flower 4 fond 22 fruit 7

garden 43 German 1 Germans 1 goat 1 good 13 green 44 greens 2 ground 3 grow 1 grows 1 growing 2 growth 1

ham 1 hard 3 head 30 heads 1 healthy 1 heavy 2 herb 1 home 1 horrid 2

indigestion 8

kale 1 kraut 2

large 3 leaf 2 leaves 11 letters 11 lot 1

meal 2 meat 8 Mrs. Wiggs 2 mustard 1

nice 1 nothing 1

odor 2 onion 2 onions 3

paper 1 parsley 1 patch 16 plant 48 plants 3 plantation 1 planted 1 planting 1 plate 1 pork 5 potato 5 potatoes 18 purple 1

quart 1

rabbit 2 red 3 rose 2 round 4

salad 5 sauerkraut 17 slaw 2 smell 11 soapy 1 solid 2 soup 2 sour 4 spice 1 spinach 1 sprouts 1 stalk 3 stew 1 stinking 1 strong 1 sustenance 1 sweet 3

taste 3 tender 1 tomato 2 tomatoes 2 turnip 20 turnips 6

unnecessary 1 unwholesome 1

Valhalla 1 vegetable 294 vegetables 10 vinegar 4 Virginia 1

white 1

48. HARD

adamant 2 apple 3 apples 1

bad 2 ball 5 baseball 1 bed 1 bench 1 blackboard 1 board 6 boards 2 bone 1 bread 1 break 1 brick 12 brittle 2 bullet 2

cabbage 2 callous 1 candy 2 can't 1 chair 3 character 1 coal 7 coarse 1 cold 1 crystallized 1

dense 1 diamond 3 difficult 5 disagreeable 1 do 1 durability 1

earth 1 earthen 1 easy 17 egg 7 eggs 1 examination 2

fare 1 farmer 1 faery 1 feeling 4 firm 11 firmness 7 fist 1 flint 1 floor 10 formidable 1 fruit 1

glass 2 glittering 1 gold 1 good 2 granite 1 ground 2

hammer 1 harsh 2 heart 2 hearted 2 heavy 2 hickory 1 hurt 1

ice 8 immovable 1 impenetrable 1 indestructible 1 individual 1 indurated 1 inflexible 1 injustice 1 icksome 1 iron 44

kind 1

labor 1 lead 2 lesson 2 lignum-vitae 1 life 2 low 1

hick 3

maple 1 marble 3 mathematics 1 mean 2 medium 2 metal 5 murder 1 mush 1

nail 1 nails 1 natural 1 nut 1 nuts 1

oak 1 opaque 1

pavement 2 perplexing 1 physics 1 piano 1 principle 1 pulpy 1

quality 1 questions 1

raining 1 resistance 4 resistant 1 rigid 1 road 1 rock 38 rocks 4 rocky 1 rough 11

saltpetre 1 severe 1 sidewalk 1 smooth 15 soft 367 solid 15 stale 1 steel 14 stick 1 stingy 1 stone 102 stones 1 stony 1 stove 2 strength 1 strong 4 stuff 1 substance 6

table 5 tack 1 thick 1 tight 1 touch 2 tough 12 tree 2 trouble 1 turnip 1

unbreakable 5 uncomfortable 5 uneasy 1 unimpressionable 1 unpleasant 2 unpliable 1 unripe 1 unyielding 1 uselessness 1

very 1

walnuts 1 water 2 wisdom 1 wood 66 work 19 working 2

49. EAGLE

air 3 altitude 1 America 7 American 12 animal 4 aspiring 1

bald 1 beak 8 beast 2 bill 2 bird 568 birds 6 birdie 1 black 1 butterfly 1 buzzard 2

carnivorous 1 carrion 1 chickens 1 claws 2 clouds 1 contour 1 crag 1 crow 3 cruelty 1

dollar 4 dove 5

eggs 1 emblem 8 eye 12 eyed 1 eyry 1

falcon 1 feathers 7 fierce 1 flag 2 flies 6 flight 22 flint 1 fly 46 flying 23 flyer 2 fowl 3 freedom 3

glare 1 glorious 1 golden 2 graceful 1 gray 1 great 1

hawk 18 height 1 high 21

insect 1 insignium 1

keen 1 king 4

large 9 lark 1 liberty 1 lofty 2

might 2 mountain 14 mountains 8

nest 12

owl 4

paper 3 parrot 1 partridge 1 peacock 1 pigeon 2 power 2 prey 5

quail 1 quarry 1

robin 1 rock 1

scarce 1 sharp 3 sight 1 sky 2 sly 2 soar 5 soars 3 soaring 14 solitude 1 space 1 sparrow 6 sport 1 spread 1 strength 11 strong 3 sun 1 swallow 3 swan 1 swift 4 swiftness 1 sword 1

talon 1 talons 1 tern 1 Times 1 turkey 1

United States 2

vulture 3

wing 8 wings 16

young 1

Zoo 2

50. STOMACH

abdomen 32 ache 31 anatomy 21 animal 2 appetite 5 apples 1 arm 2

back 1 bad 1 bag 7 basket 1 beast 2 beef 1 belly 6 belt 1 biology 1

body 99 bowels 18 brain 1 bread 1 breast 1

cancer 3 care 1 careful 2 cat 1 cavity 1 chart 1 chest 18 coil 1 condition 2 contain 1

delicate 1 diaphragm 1 digest 6 digesting 1 digestion 50 digestive 3 digests 2 dinner 7 disease 1

distress 1 doctor 2 dress 1 duodenum 1 dyspepsia 4

eat 45 eating 27 empty 8 engine 1 excellent 1

face 1 fat 1 feed 1 feeding 1 feet 1 food 102 foot 2 flesh 1 frame 1 front 1 full 7 function 1

gastric 5 Gertrude 1 good 4 grind 1 grinding 2

hand 2 hands 1 head 9 health 5 heart 24 hog 1 hunger 6 hungry 6 hurt 2 hurts 1 hygiene 1 illness 1 indigestion 17 inside 5 interior 2 internal 2 intestine 28 intestines 32

juice 1

large 4 leg 1 limb 1 liver 13 living 1 lung 1 lungs 3

machinery 1 man 5 meal 1 meals 1 member 5 milk 1 mortal 1 mouth 3 muscle 1

nausea 2 necessary 3 necessity 1 neck 1 nuisance 1

object 1 oblong 1 oesophagus 4 organ 81 organs 3 overeating 1 overloaded 1

pain 28 part 3 person 9 physiology 3 picture 1 poor 2 portion 1 pouch 4 psychology 1 pump 3 punch 2

receiver 1 receptacle 3 reservoir 2 rest 1 round 3

self 1 sick 10 sickness 7 skin 1 small 2 soft 4 sore 1 sour 2 specimen 1 strong 1 suffer 1 suffering 1 sustenance 1 system 2

tender 1 tenderness 1 thought 1 throat 1 tongue 2 trouble 25 troubles 1 troublesome 5 trunk 1 tube 3

upset 1 useful 1

vessel 2

want 1 water 1 weak 3 weakness 1 work 1

51. STEM

anything 1 appendage 1 apple 43 apples 1

base 1 beginning 3 blade 1 blossom 3 boat 1 body 1 brain 1 branch 33 branches 1 broad 1 broom 1 bud 4 bush 5 butt 1

cane 2 cherry 2 connection 3 connects 1 cord 2 core 2

end 10 ending 1 evolution 1

fibre 1 fibres 2 finger 1 flower 259 flowers 7 foundation 2 fruit 14

grass 1 green 9 growth 3

handle 20 hard 1 head 1 hold 2 holding 1 holder 4

holes 1

join 1

leaf 96 leaves 4 leg 1 length 3 lettuce 1 life 1 light 2 lily 1 limb 4 living 1 long 18

match 1

necessity 1

object 1 offshoot 1 organ 1

part 4 parts 1 particle 1 peach 2 pear 9 peduncle 1 pencil 3 petal 4 pick 1 piece 3 pipe 70 pit 1 plant 74 plow 1 point 6 poppy 1 projection 1 prop 1

reed 1 river 1 rod 1 root 27 roots 1 rose 21

shank 2 short 6 slender 7 small 1 smoke 1 soft 1 stalk 21 steps 2 stern 6 stick 14 stiff 1 stone 1 stop 1 storm 1 straight 2 support 8

thin 4 thorn 2 tide 2 tobacco 1 top 1 tree 44 trees 2 trunk 3 twig 7

valve 1 violet 1 vine 3

watch 7 water 2 weed 3 wind 3 winding 2 winder 3 wood 4

52. LAMP

Aladdin 1 arc 1 articles 6

black 5 blaze 1 brass 1 bright 12 brightness 3 burn 20 burning 10 burner 3 burns 1

candle 13 chandelier 2 cheer 1 chimney 37 convenience 1 crockery 1

dangers 1 dark 3 darkness 2 daylight 1 distance 1 dull 1

electric 5 evening 1

fire 5 flame 1 full 1 furniture 2

gas 4 glaring 1 glass 8 globe 7

high 3 home 1 hot 1 house 1

illumination 2

kerosene 7

lantern 1 large 2 library 1 light 650 lights 2 lighted 4 lighten 1 lit 2

match 1

nickle 1 night 4

oil 49 ornament 1

petroleum 1 post 5 pretty 1

reading 2 red 1 Rochester 1 room 2

see 2 shade 37 shadow 1 small 1 smoke 4 smokes 1 smoking 1 smoky 1 stand 2 stove 1 student 1

table 8 tall 1

useful 2

vessel 2

warmth 1 wick 23 wisdom 1

53. DREAM

absence 1 angel 1 angels 1 anger 1 anything 1 asleep 6 awake 11 awaking 1 awaken 1 awakening 3

baby 2 bad 16 beautiful 4 bed 11 bliss 3 book 1 boy 1

comfort 1 consciousness 2 conversation 1

dangerous 1 darkness 1 days 1 death 2 delusion 1 delusions 1 disagreeable 1 disappointment 1 discontent 1 disturbance 2 disturbing 1 doze 1 dread 1 dreary 2

easy 1 expectation 1 experiment 1 eyes 1

falling 2 fancy 9 fantasy 1 fear 1 feeling 1 feelings 1 forgotten 1 fortune 1 funny 1

girl 1 good 7 goodness 1 grand 1 grieving 1

hallucination 2 happiness 3 heaven 1 home 3 hope 1 horrible 3

idea 1 illusion 3 image 1 imaginary 2 imagination 12 imagine 5 imaginings 1 impression 2 indigestion 2 insanity 1 inspiration 1

kind 1

land 1 languid 2 lie 2 like 1 love 2

M. 1 man 2 mare 1 meditate 1 melancholy 1 melody 1 mesmeric 1 mind 8 money 1 music 1

nature 2 never 1 nice 3 night 42 nightmare 24 no 1 none 1 nonsense 2

- 251 -

object 1 omen 1 on 1 opium 1

paradise 1 patients 1 peace 1 peaceful 2 phantoms 1 picture 3 pillow 1 play 1 pleasant 38 pleasure 13 presentiment 1 prophesy 1 psychology 1 purple 1

queer 1 quiet 1

realization 1 recollection 1 relax 1 remember 1 repose 2 reposing 1 rest 3 restless 6 restlessness 1 reverie 2

sad 2 sadness 1 scene 1 second 1 semiconscious 1 sensation 1 sense 1 shade 1 shadows 1 short 1 sickness 2 sight 1 sights 1 sleep 339 sleeping 39 sleeper 2 sleeplessness 2 sleepy 2 slept 1 slumber 20 something 1 somnambulist 1 snore 2 soliloquy 1 stale 1 startling 1 story 1 sweet 14

talk 1 terrible 1 things 3 think 29 thinking 8 thought 38 thoughts 22 tiring 1 trouble 1 true 2

uncomfortable 1 unconscious 1 unconsciousness 1 uneasiness 1 uneasy 2 unfortunate 1 unpleasant 5 unpleasantness 1 unreal 2 unrest 2 unstable 1

vacancy 1 vagueness 1 vision 48 visions 6 vivid 1

wake 9 waking 1 wander 1 wandering 4 weird 1 wonder 2 woods 1 work 1

54. YELLOW

alive 1 amber 2 apple 3 autumn 1

banana 5 beautiful 3 beauty 2 becoming 1 bird 8 black 24 blossoms 1 blue 41 bright 23 brightness 2 brilliant 1 brown 13 buff 1 butter 7 buttercup 11 buttercups 2 butterfly 8

canary 4 cat 1 China 2 Chinaman 3 Chinee 3 Chinese 2 chrome 1 chrysanthemum 1 chrysanthemums 1 cloth 3 coarse 1 color 301 coloring 1 common 1 complexity 1 corn 1 cream 2 crocus 1

daffodil 3 daffodils 3 daisy 6 dandelion 7

dark 6 delightful 1 desert 1 disagreeable 1 dog 1 door 1 dream 1 dress 9 dresses 1 dull 1

ecru 1 egg 1

fade 1 fancy 1 fence 1 fever 3 flag 4 flame 1 flower 38 flowers 9 fruit 3

G. 1 garments 1 gay 1 glare 1 gold 13 golden 5 goldenglow 1 goldenrod 5 goods 1 gorgeous 1 grass 1 green 41

hair 2 house 2 hue 1

ink 1

jasmine 2 jaundice 3 jealousy 6 jonquil 1 journal 2

kid 2

leaf 2 leaves 1 lemon 7 light 14 lily 2

maize 1 man 1 marigolds 1 matter 1 mellow 1 melon 1 molasses 1

nature 1 nice 1

obnoxious 1 ochre 1 orange 47

paint 5 pale 2 pansy 3 paper 4 peach 2 pears 1 pillow 1 pink 13 plague 1 poppy 1 pretty 4 primrose 1 pumpkin 2 pumpkins 1 pure 1 purple 5

red 34 ribbon 1 rose 9

satin 1 school 1 sear 1 shade 4 silk 1 sky 2 soft 2 suit 1 sulphur 1 sun 21 sunflower 8 sunlight 7 sunshine 1

table 1 tan 2 tarnish 1 tree 1

ugly 1 unharmonious 1

violet 2

wagon 1 warm 1 warmth 1 wax 1 wheat 1 white 70

55. BREAD

appetite 1

bake 2 baking 4 baker 3 bakery 1 biscuit 14 biscuits 2 blue 4 board 1 box 1 breakfast 2 brown 3 buns 1 butter 151

cake 15 cheese 1 children 1 color 1 common 1 cookies 1 corn 1 crackers 1 crumbs 1 crust 6 cut 1

daily 3 diet 4 dinner 6 dish 1 dough 26 doughnuts 1

earn 1 eat 148 eating 44 eatable 28 eatables 6 edible 1

feed 1 flour 88 food 191 fresh 3 fruit 2

good 21 graham 2 grain 2

ham 1 hand 1 hard 3 heavy 2 holes 1 home 2 hot 1 hunger 7 hungry 4

knife 8

life 23 light 8 living 1 loaf 7 lunch 1

making 1 man 2 meal 1 meat 5 milk 1 mixing 1

necessary 1 necessity 2 needful 1 nourishment 4

oatmeal 1

pantry 1 pastry 1 plate 1 pudding 1

roll 1 rolls 2 rye 6

salt 1 salty 1 satisfaction 1 sister 1 soft 8 sour 1 staff 8 stale 3 strengthen 1 substance 2 substantial 1 sugar 1 sustenance 1 sweet 4

table 3 tea 2 toast 1 tough 1

useful 1

water 9 wheat 21 white 15 wholesome 1 wine 1 winner 1

yeast 8

56. JUSTICE

action 2 administered 2 administration 1 all 2 always 1 ask 1 authority 1

B. 1 bad 1 bed 1 blind 3 blindfolded 1 body 1

caught 1 charity 1 chastise 1 chief 1 clearness 1 comfort 1 command 3 commanding 1 conqueror 1 constable 1 court 64 courts 2 Creator 1 crime 1 criminal 1 cruelty 2

dealing 1 deeds 1 defying 1 delayed 1 demand 1 deserved 1 dispute 2 distribution 1 do 3 doing 2 done 1 Dr. E. 1 duty 5

elusive 1 emblem 1 employer 1 energy 1 equal 8 equality 9 equally 1 equity 3 even 2 exactness 1 execution 1

fair 32 fairness 21 favor 1 fear 1 fine 1 freedom 6 friendship 1

gift 1 give 1 given 3 God 8 godliness 1 good 14 goodness 2 govern 1 government 3 guilty 1

happy 1 harm 1 hasty 1 have 1 heaven 1 help 1 him 1 honest 5 honesty 3 honor 7

impartial 1 iniquity 1 injury 1 injustice 26 innocent 1

J. 1 jail 2 joy 1 judge 91 judged 1 judgment 6 jury 2 just 5 justified 4

kindness 6

lacking 1 large 1 law 74 lawful 2 lawyer 4 lenient 2 liberty 11 lots 1 love 1 magistrate 2 man 13 merciful 1 mercy 23 merit 1 mind 1 moral 1 mother 1

never 1 nobility 1 noble 1 none 1 nonsense 1

obey 1 obtain 1 oppression 1 order 4

pardon 1 partiality 4 peace 143 perfect 1 person 1 picture 1 Plato 1 police 1 policeman 1 politics 1 popular 1 power 1 privilege 1 purity 1

reason 1 reward 3 right 157 righteous 3 righteousness 13 rightly 1 rightness 1 rights 11 ruler 1

satisfaction 4 satisfied 1 satisfying 1 scales 5 severe 2 severity 1 sorrow 1 square 3 squareness 1 squire 1 statue 4 story 1 supreme 3 sure 2

tranquility 1 true 6 truth 14 truthfulness 2

unbias 1 unfairness 1 unhappiness 1 unjust 8 uprightness 1

vengeance 1 virtue 3

well 2 wicked 1 willingness 1 wisdom 2 wise 1 work 2 wrong 8

yes 1 yield 1

57. BOY

action 2 active 2 activity 2 agility 1 animal 3 athletic 3 athletics 2

baby 6 bad 9 ball 10 barefoot 1 baseball 5 beautiful 1 being 6 Ben 1 body 2 boisterous 1 book 1 bright 2 brother 6 busy 2

cap 1 careless 1 Charles 1 chicken 1 child 86 children 1 class 1 clothes 1 clothing 1 companion 2 cousin 1 curls 1

dead 1 development 1 dirty 2 dog 1

Edward 1 eighteen 1 embryonic 1 errand 1

fair 1 female 3 fight 1 flesh 1 foolish 1 football 1 Frank 1 friend 4 frolic 2 fun 4 funny 1

games 1

girl 319 good 7 grown 1 growth 1 gun 2

handsome 1 Harry 1 hat 1 head 1 hearty 1 hero 1 hood 2 hoop 2 human 9 humanity 1

imbecile 1 imperfect 1 incorrigible 1 industrious 1 infant 2 inhabitant 1 innocent 1

jacket 1 James 2 Jimmy 1 Joe 1 joyful 1 jump 1 jumper 1 juvenile 2 kid 4

lad 7 large 2 laugh 1 legs 1 life 2 little 3 lively 3

maid 1 male 63 man 104 manhood 1 mankind 1 manliness 1 manly 1 marbles 1 masculine 3 master 2 meanness 1 Michael 1 mischief 11 mischievous 7 mother 1 muscles 1 myself 1

naughty 1 Ned 2 nephew 1 newspaper 1 nice 3 noise 7 noisy 3 nuisance 1

obedient 1 out 1

pants 6 Paul 1 person 11 play 20 plays 1 playful 1 playfulness 1 pupil 2

rough 6 running 1 runs 1

scallywag 1 scamp 2 scholar 1 school 11 sex 4 sharp 1 shoes 2 small 14 smart 2 smiles 1 son 3 spirit 1 spoiled 1 sport 2 street 1 strength 2 strong 3 suit 2 sweetheart 1 swimming 1

tall 3 terror 1 think 1 Thomas 1 top 2 toys 1 Tracy 1 trait 1 tramp 1 trouble 1

useless 1

water 1 whistle 1 whistles 1 wicked 1 wild 2 wildness 1 woman 2 woods 1 work 1 working 1

young 22 youngster 1 youth 33 youthful 1

58. LIGHT

agreeable 1 air 8 airy 1 arc 1 assistance 1 awake 1

beacon 1 beautiful 2 beautifying 1 beauty 1 biscuit 1 black 3 blue 2 bread 1 bright 47 brightness 21 brilliant 3 brown 1 burn 2 burning 1

candle 8 cheer 1 clear 2 clearness 2 coat 2 color 19 comfort 2 complexion 1 convenient 1 cork 1

dark 231 darkness 93 dawn 2 day 81 daylight 2 daytime 6 dimness 1 distance 1 dress 1 dull 1

early 2 easy 1 education 1 electric 7 electricity 8 element 1 emptiness 1 enjoy 1 evening 1 eyes 1

fair 1 feather 6 feathers 1 fire 6 flame 1 fleshy 1 forward 1 fuel 1

gas 21 glare 1 gleam 1 good 8

hair 2 happiness 4 health 1 healthy 1 hearted 1 heat 8 heaven 1 heavy 5 hills 1

Illuminate 1 illumination 7

joy 1

kerosene 1 knowledge 1

laboratory 1 lamp 82 lamps 1 life 7 long 1 look 1 luminous 1

match 1 moon 10 morning 7

nice 1 night 3 necessity 1

paper 1 pathway 1 peaceful 1 pink 1 pipe 1 placid 1 pleasant 8 pleasure 1 plenty 1

rays 2 red 1 reflection 1 right 1 room 3

see 24 seeing 3 seen 1 shade 8 shadow 2 shadows 1 shine 2 shines 9 shining 2 sight 3 sign 1 sky 8 soft 1 sound 1 space 1 splendor 1 steam 1 sun 85 sunlight 1 sunshine 11 swift 1

transparent 1 truth 1 twilight 1

ventilation 1 Vera 1 vibration 1 vision 2 vivid 1

waist 1 warmth 2 waves 1 weak 1 weight 2 white 8 whiteness 2 window 15 world 1

yellow 6

59. HEALTH

action 1 activity 2 air 9 athletics 1

bad 5 baseball 1 beautiful 1 beauty 10 better 1 blessing 4 blood 1 board 1 body 9 boon 1 boy 2 broad 1 buoyancy 2

care 1 careful 1 cheer 1 circulation 1 cleanliness 1 climate 1 color 1 comfort 26 condition 6 constitution 1 consumption 1 contentment 1 convenience 1 country 2

desirable 3 disease 9 doctor 4

eating 1 enjoyment 5 everything 2 excellent 1 excursion 1 exercise 3 existence 1

face 1 feel 2 feeling 12 fine 1 food 4 form 1 fortune 2 freedom 1 fun 1

gift 3 girl 1 gladness 2 glow 1 golf 1 good 94 goodness 1 grand 2 gymnasium 1 gymnastics 1 happiness 111 happy 7 haste 1 healing 1 healthful 1 healthy 1 heaven 1 holiness 2 hygiene 2

ill 3 illness 13

joy 6

life 5 light 1 live 1 living 3 luck 2 luxury 1

man 4 me 1 medicine 3 merriment 1 mother 1 mountain 1 moving 1

necessary 1 needed 1 needful 1 normal 4

optimism 1

pain 1 perfect 8 person 6 physical 3 physician 1 physiology 1 play 1 pleasant 2 pleasure 14 plenty 1 poor 2 preserve 1 proper 1 prosperity 4

quick 1

red 1 riches 3 robust 9 rose 1 rosy 1 round 1 rugged 2

self 1 sick 9 sickly 2 sickness 153 smiles 1 sound 5 spirit 1 spirits 1 state 1 strength 112 strengths 1 strong 31 sturdy 1 success 1

temper 1 thankful 2 trouble 1

unhealthiness 1 unhealthy 3 useful 2

valuable 1 vigor 11 virility 1

walking 1 want 2 warm 1 water 1 weakness 1 wealth 76 well 63 wholesome 1 woman 1 wonderful 1

youth 1

60. BIBLE

academy 1 all 1 ancient 1

beauty 1 belief 1 beneficial 1 black 2 book 388 books 1

catechism 1 Christ 8 Christian 3 church 50 class 3 clean 1 clergyman 1 comfort 2 command 2 commandment 1 commandments 2 creed 1

devotion 1 directions 1 drama 1 duty 2

encyclopedia 1 excellent 1

fable 1 faith 1 family 2

Genesis 1 glass 1 God 48 good 28 goodness 12 gospel 3 gospels 1 grand 1 guide 1

- 258 -

heaven 2 heavy 1 help 1 history 26 holiness 5 holy 57 home 2 hope 1 hymns 2

instructive 1

Jacob 1
Jesus 4

knowledge 2 Koran 1

large 4 law 3 leaf 1 leaves 1 lectern 1 legend 1 lie 2 life 3 light 2 literature 2 Lord 5 love 2

message 1 mine 1 minister 3 Moses 2 mother 1

necessary 1 noble 1

obey 2 open 1

paper 1 piety 1 pious 2 pray 3 praying 2 prayer 19 prayers 7 prayer-book 13 preacher 2 preaching 1 prophet 1 psalms 4

rarely 1 read 31 reading 19 reformation 1 religion 89 religious 4 reverence 1 righteous 1 rot 3

sacred 3 Saviour 2 school 2 scripture 17 scriptures 3 sermon 1 shelf 1 sour 1 stones 1 stories 2 story 4 strength 1 studies 2 study 6 Sunday 6

table 3 teach 1 teacher 1 teachings 1 Testament 24 text 4 tradition 1 true 2 truth 17 truthfulness 1

unnecessary 1 useful 2

verses 1

weariness 1 word 8 words 1 worship 2 writ 1

61. MEMORY

absent 2 acquire 1 aid 1 analysis 1 ancient 1 association 2 attention 1 aunt 1

back 1 bad 19 beautiful 1 bird 1 blank 3 book 2 books 3 brain 46 brains 5 brightness 1 bucket 1

catechism 1 cause 1 charming 1

childhood 4 clear 1 concentration 2 connection 1 conscience 1 consciousness 2

dancing 1 death 1 debts 1 defect 2 defective 1 desirable 1 deterioration 1 dictionary 1 dim 1 distant 1 dream 1 dreams 3 dull 1 easy 1 educated 1 effort 1 elusive 1 English 1 Europe 1 events 2 everything 1 excellent 2 experiment 1

faces 1 faculty 1 failing 1 fails 1 fair 4 fancy 1 far 1 farther 1 fascination 1 faulty 1 feeling 1 fine 1 fleeting 1 fond 1 fool 1 forget 25 forgetful 5 forgetfulness 37 forgetting 5 forgotten 3 forty 1 friends 1

gone 2 good 68 gravestone 1 great 1 green 2

happiness 1 happy 1 head 9 hearing 1 history 2 home 2 hopefulness 1

idea 2 image 1 imagination 2 impossible 1 increase 1

intellect 7 intelligence 5 interpret 1 invisible 1

joy 1

keep 1 know 1 knowledge 4

lack 2 lacking 2 language 1 lasting 1 learn 1 learning 2 lecture 1 length 1 lessons 2 light 1 long 3 loss 1 love 1

magnificent 1 man 3 marvelous 1 me 1 memorandum 1 memorizing 1 mental 4 mind 138 mindful 1 mnemonics 2 mother 1 mud 1 my 1 myself 1

names 1 necessary 3 necessity 1 needful 1 noble 1 none 1

oblivion 1

painful 1 past 8 patient 1 pen 1 perception 2 person 2 picture 2 pictures 1 pleasantness 1 pleasure 2 poem 3 poems 1 poetry 7 poor 23 power 1 psychology 1

quick 1

reading 1 reason 1 recall 4 recalling 2 recognition 3 recollect 2 recollection 16 recollections 3 reflect 1 remember 27 remembering 4 remembrance 18 remind 2 reminder 1 reminiscence 2 reminiscences 1 reproductive 1 result 1 retain 1 retaining 2 retention 5 retentive 3 retrospect 1

sadness 1 scenes 1 scholar 1 school 6 sensation 1 sense 5 senses 2 short 7 simple 1 song 1 sound 2 splendid 1 stanza 1 storehouse 1 story 1 strengthen 1 strong 1 student 1 study 4 studying 1 sure 1 sweet 7 swift 1 swing 1

teacher 1 tender 1 test 5 thankful 1 things 1 think 58 thinking 38 thinks 1 thought 81 thoughts 28 thoughtful 8 thoughtfulness 3 thoughtlessness 1 time 1 train 1 training 1 tree 1

unconsciousness 1 understand 3 understanding 6 unstable 1 useful 2

verses 2

weak 1 well 1 will 1 wit 1 wonderful 1 work 2

youth 2

62. SHEEP

animal 225 animals 18 astray 1 awkward 1

baa 1 beast 3 bed 1 Bethlehem 1 black 5 blind 1 buffalo 1

calf 1 calm 1 cattle 47 cloth 1 country 3 cow 22 cows 5

death 1 deer 2 dirty 2 dog 6 dogs 2 eat 1

farm 4 feed 1 field 12 fields 6 fleece 3 flesh 1 flock 24 flocks 1 fold 4 follow 1 food 2 foolish 1 fowl 1 fur 1

gentle 1 gentleness 1 goad 1 goat 17 goats 10 good 2 grass 4 graze 1 grazing 5 group 1

hair 1 harmless 1 herd 4 herder 1 hill 1 hillside 2 horn 1 horse 1 humanity 1

innocence 5 innocent 2

jump 1

lamb 151 lambs 36 landscape 1 large 2 lecture 1 lowing 1

many 1 meadows 3 meat 5 meekness 1 mountain 3 mutton 60

nature 1

oxen 1

park 2 pasture 27 pastures 3 peace 1 peaceful 1 pet 1 picture 1 pig 2 plains 1 play 1 pretty 4

quadruped 2

raising 1 ram 1 rocks 1 run 1 running 1

shear 1 shearing 1 shears 1 shepherd 15 simple 1 sleep 1 small 2 soft 1 spring 1 stock 2 stupidity 1

tick 1 trust 1

wander 1 water 1 white 18 wolf 2 wool 143 woolly 10

63. BATH

baby 1 basin 1 bathe 2 bathing 6 beneficial 1 boat 1 boy 1

clean 120 cleaning 1 cleanliness 109 cleanly 2 cleanness 9 cleanse 6 cleansing 8 cold 14 comfort 3 cool 3 Creal Springs 1

- 261 -

delight 1 dirt 4 dirty 5 dry 1

English 1 every 1

filth 1 filthiness 1 fine 1 flowers 1 fluid 1 fresh 2

good 7

health 9 healthful 1 healthiness 1 healthy 4 hot 10 house 4

invigorates 1 invigorating 2

joy 1

large 1 luxury 1

man 1 massage 1 morning 2

nakedness 1 neatness 1 necessary 5 nice 2 none 1

ocean 6 often 1 once 1

pleasant 3 pleasure 2 plenty 2 plunge 3 porcelain 1

refreshed 1 refreshing 6 refreshment 1 river 2 robe 3 room 6

salt 1 sanitary 1 scrub 1 sensation 1 shower 3 sleeping 1 soap 13 soothing 1 sponge 1 spray 4 springs 1 swim 10 swimming 5

take 1 taken 1 toilet 2 towel 6 towels 2 tub 71

vapor 1 vessel 1

want 1 warm 3 wash 102 washing 16 water 339 wet 5 wood 1

yesterday 2

64. COTTAGE

abode 2 agreeable 1 alone 1 apartments 1

barn 2 beach 1 beautiful 1 box 1 brick 3 brook 1 brown 2 building 31 bungalow 13

cabin 3 camp 1 camping 2 Cape Cod 1 castle 2 chair 1 cheese 1 city 3 comfort 15 contentment 2 cottage 1 country 36 couple 2 cozy 2 cute 1

distant 1 door 2 dwelling 23

family 2 far 1 farm 4 fence 1 field 6 fine 2 flowers 4 frame 2

garden 7 green 3

habitable 1 habitation 3 hamlet 1 hammock 1 handsome 1 happiness 5 happy 1 hill 3 home 85 homelike 1 homestead 1 hope 1 hospital 1 house 461 houses 1

innocence 1 ivy 1

lake 5 lane 1 large 1 lawn 4 little 4 live 17 living 5 log 1 lonesomeness 1 love 4 low 2 lumber 1

Maine 1 mansion 15

name 1 neat 3 Newburgh 1 nice 4

one 2 open 1 orchard 1 outing 1

painted 1 palace 2 personage 2 patient 1 patients 1 peace 1 people 1 picturesque 1 place 1 pleasantness 1 pleasure 1 pond 1 porch 4 prettiness 1 pretty 3 pudding 1

reside 1 residence 4 resident 1 resort 1 rest 3 river 1 rod 1 roof 3 roomy 1 roses 2 rustic 1

school 1 sea 10 seashore 5 seaside 2 shelter 6 shingles 2 shore 2 simplicity 1 sleep 1 small 30 snug 1 stands 1 structure 3 summer 9 sweet 1 Switzerland 1

table 1 tent 4 thatched 2 tower 1 trees 1 two 3

unity 1

vacation 2 veranda 1 villa 1 village 3 vine 1 vines 3

white 3 window 2 woman 1 wood 11 wooden 1 woods 3

yard 1

65. SWIFT

active 2 aeroplane 2 ahead 1 antelope 1 arrow 13 automobile 11 autos 1

ball 6 beauty 1 better 1 bicycle 1 bird 16 birds 1 boat 1 brisk 1 brook 1 bullet 3

cat 1 channel 1 child 1 choice 1 clever 1 creek 1 current 7 curve 1 cutting 1

deer 7 degree 1 doctor 1 dog 1

eagle 8 easy 2 engine 3

fast 222 fastness 1 fear 1 fish 1 feet 5 flight 6 fly 3 flying 3 foot 1

girl 1 go 1 going 1 good 1 grand 1 Greek 1

heard 1 hare 1 haste 1 hear 1 high 1 horse 28 hurry 12 hurrying 1

Indian 1

kite 1

launch 1 lazy 1 light 2 lightening 4 lively 3

man 1 Marathon 1 Mercury 1 messenger 1 meteor 1 more 1 morning 1 motion 2 motoring 1 movement 2 moving 1 muscles 1

near 1 Niagara Falls 1

power 1

quick 117 quickly 13 quickness 5 quiet 1

race 6 rapid 27 rapidity 2 rapidly 2 real 1 riding 1 river 18 rivers 1 road 1 rocket 1 run 19 running 20 runner 18 rushing 1

sail 1 sharp 1 shot 1 sleigh 1 slow 100 slowly 4 smart 16 smartness 1 smooth 3 speed 29 speedily 1 speeding 1 speedy 7 spinchiled 1 spy 2 steam 1 sting 1 stone 1 stream 8 strong 2 sure 2 swallow 5 swallows 1

throw 1 tide 2 time 1 train 18 trains 1

walking 1 water 11 wind 8 work 1

66. BLUE

air 1 azure 1

ball 1 beautiful 1 becoming 1 bell 1 binding 1 bird 5 black 38 blood 1 blossom 1 blotter 1 bluebird 1 bluing 2 blusey 1 book 1 bright 5 brown 8

cadet 1 chemical 1 clock 1 cloth 7 clothes 3 clothing 1 cloud 1 could 1 color 256 colors 2 coloring 2

dainty 1 dark 24 deep 5 depth 1 dress 18 dull 1

ether 1 eyes 6

fair 1 feeling 4 fidelity 1 flag 6 flower 3 forget-me-not 1

gentian 1 globe 1 gloominess 2 gloomy 2 glum 1 good 1 grass 2 gray 10 green 54

hat 1 heaven 5 heavens 2 heavenly 1 homesick 1 hopeful 1 horizon 1 house 1 hue 1

indigo 5 ink 6

lake 1 light 8 lily 1 lonesome 1

melancholy 2 Monday 1

navy 1 necktie 1

ocean 12

paint 8 pale 1 paper 1 pencil 1 pink 9 pleasant 2 pleasing 1 policeman 1 pretty 4 purity 1 purple 2

red 54 restful 1 ribbon 3 river 1 room 1

sad 2 sailor 1 sea 7 serge 1 shade 2 skies 1 sky 239 soft 1 somber 1 space 1 stripes 1 suit 1

tie 2 tint 1 true 7 truth 2 turquoise 1

unhappy 1 unrest 1

velvet 1 violet 2 violets 3

washing 2 water 8 white 47 wind 2

Yale 2 yellow 27

67. HUNGRY

aching 1 ambitious 1 angry 1 animal 2 appeasing 1 appetite 57 appetizing 2

baby 2 bad 3 bananas 1 bear 1 beggar 4 biscuit 1 boy 5 bread 26 breakfast 8 butcher 1

candy 1 child 5 children 5 cold 4 college 1 country 1 crackers 1 crave 1 craving 7 cupboard 1

dark 1 desirable 1 desire 11 devil 1 devour 1 dinner 31 disagreeable 1 discomfort 4 displeasure 1 dissatisfaction 1 dissatisfied 1 distress 1 dog 14 dogs 1 dry 1

eat 126 eating 64 eatables 2 emotion 1 emptiness 4 empty 13 exhausted 2

faint 9 fainting 1 famine 5 famish 1 famished 11 famishing 1 fascinating 1 fast 3 fasting 5 fatigue 4 fatigued 1 fed 4 feel 1 feeling 8 fill 1 filled 4 food 136 form 1 fulfilment 1 full 9 fruit 3

gaunt 1 Gertrude 1 girl 1 gnawing 2 good 1 grub 1

hardship 1 Henrietta 1 hog 1 horse 1 hunger 2

I 3 ice-cream 1

kitchen 1

lack 2 lion 1 longing 5 lunch 4

man 5 me 4 meal 1 meat 3 milk 1 miserable 2 misery 1

- 265 -

nausea 1 necessary 1 need 2 needy 1 never 1 nice 1 no 1 noon 1 nothing 1 nourish 1 now 2

ocean 1 often 1

pain 5 painful 1 pallid 1 pang 1 peaches 1 perishing 1 person 2 picnic 2 pie 2 plenty 2 plow 1 poor 6 potatoes 1 poverty 2 present 1

ravenous 1 repletion 1

sad 1 sandwiches 2 satiated 3 satiety 2 satisfied 14 satisfy 2 school 1 sensation 1 sharp 1 ship 1 sick 1 sleepy 1 slow 1 sorrow 2 starvation 10 starve 8 starved 15 starving 29 steak 2 stomach 13 suffering 1 sufficiency 1 sufficient 1 supper 2

table 1 thirst 12 thirsty 61 thought 1 tiger 1 tired 12 tiresome 1 tramp 3 traveling 1

uncomfortable 1 unhappiness 1 unhappy 4 unpleasant 4 unsatisfied 3 very 1 viands 1 victuals 1

walk 1 want 25 wanting 5 weak 5 weakness 3 wish 2 wolf 10

68. PRIEST

altar 3 authority 1

belief 1 Bible 3 bishop 6 black 13 blessing 1 book 1 boy 1 brother 1

cassock 1 cathedral 2 Catholic 36 Catholics 2 Catholicism 4 ceremony 1 chancel 1 chapel 2 childhood 1 church 166 clean 1 clergy 30 clergyman 62 cleric 1 clerical 2 cloister 1 cloth 1 clothes 1 collar 1 comforter 1 command 1 communion 1 confession 5 confessor 2 conscientious 1 console 1 counsellor 1 crucifix 1

dignified 1 discipline 2 discontent 1 dishonor 1 dislike 1 divine 1 divinity 1 doctor 5 doing 1 dominie 1 dress 1 Dr. K. 1 duty 1

exalted 1

faithful 2 fakir 2 fakirs 1 fat 3 father 15 follower 1 forgive 1 forgiveness 1

garb 2 gentleman 1 God 2 good 9 goodness 1 gown 6

heaven 2 high 1 holiness 3 holy 15 honor 2 hood 2 house 1 humble 1 hypocrite 2

inspired 1 instruction 1

Jew 2 just 1 justice 1

- 266 -

kind 1 knowledge 1

layman 2 leader 4 lecture 1 Levi 1 Levite 2 Lord 1

male 5 man 75 mass 5 minister 178 monastery 5 monk 9 moral 1

noble 1 nun 12

office 1

parson 11 pastor 11 people 1 person 3 piety 1 pious 4 Pope 3 power 1 praise 1 pray 3 prays 1 prayer 8 prayers 1 preach 3 preaches 2 preacher 35 prelate 2 priestess 2 profession 1 prophet 3 pulpit 1 purity 2

rabbi 2 religion 57 religious 7 representative 1 repulsive 1 reserved 1 reverend 1 righteous 2 road 1 robe 12 robes 8 ruler 1

sacred 2 sacrifice 1 sanctity 1 school 1 sent 1 serious 1 sermon 3 sermony 1 servant 2 service 2 services 1 shaven 2 shoot 1 sinner 1 sister 1 slim 1 solemnity 1 sometimes 1 spookism 1 stern 1 student 1 Sunday 2 surplice 3

table 1 teacher 2

ugly 1

vest 1 vicar 1

York 1

169. OCEAN

afraid 1 angry 1 Atlantic 11

barge 1 bathing 3 bay 3 beach 5 beautiful 1 big 5 bigness 1 billows 1 blue 25 boat 6 boats 1 body 2 boisterous 1 breadth 3 breeze 1 broad 3 Bryon 1

Cape Cod 1 Coney Island 2 country 1 crossing 1 current 1

dark 1 deep 87 deepness 1 depth 10 depths 1 distance 2

enormous 1 Europe 1 expanse 2 expansive 1

float 1 foam 2

grand 2 grandeur 2 great 3 greatness 1 green 2 Grove 2 gulfs 1

Hudson 1

immense 1 immensity 2 infinity 2

joy 2

lake 12 land 8 large 9 launch 1 liquid 1

Maine 1 Mauretania 1 might 1 mighty 3 motion 2

power 1 pretty 1

quantity 1

river 36 roars 1 rough 12

sail 2 sailing 2 salt 10 sand 2 Sandy Hook 1 sea 75 seas 3 seashore 2 seething 1 shining 1 ship 24 ships 11 shore 2 sky 1 sound 1 storm 1 storms 1 steamboat 1 steamer 14 steamers 1 steamship 1 stream 4 swiftness 1 swim 2 swimming 1

tide 1 terrible 1 traveling 1 trip 1

valley 1 vast 7 vastness 9 vessel 2 voyage 1

waste 1 water 427 waters 1 wave 12 waves 45 wavy 1 wet 2 white 1 wide 15 wonder 1 wonderful 1

70. HEAD

above 1 ache 9 aches 1 anatomy 8 animal 2 appearance 1 arm 2 arms 3 asymmetrical 1

baby's 1 back 2 bald 1 ball 1 beautiful 1 beginning 1 big 5 black 1 body 146 bonehead 1 boss 1 brain 58 brains 32 branch 1 bright 1 brown 1

cabbage 7 captain 3 cattle 1 cavity 2 chess 2 chief 2 chop 1 clear 1 comb 2 combs 1 consciousness 1 cover 1 covered 1 cow 2 cranium 11 crown 1

director 1 donkey 1

ear 1 ears 1 emptiness 1 empty 1 encephalon 1 end 1 extremity 1 eye 2 eyes 10

face 13 father 1 feature 1 features 2 feet 26 figure 1 firm 1 first 2 food 1 foot 64 forehead 1 front 1

girl 1 glasses 1 good 3 govern 1 great 1

hair 159 hand 11 hands 2 handsome 1 hard 2 hat 17 headless 1 heart 8 heels 2 high 3 highest 2 hot 2 house 1 human 4

individual 1 intellect 2 intelligence 3

king 1 knee 1 knowledge 17

large 19 leadership 1 leading 1 life 1 light 2 limb 8 limbs 1 little 1 long 1 louse 1 man 14 man's 1 masterpiece 1 medium 1 member 7 memory 3 mentality 1 mind 14 mouth 1

nail 1 nation 1 neck 17 nose 2

organ 5

pain 1 part 6 people 1 person 15 physiology 2 planning 1 Pope 1 power 3 president 2 pretty 1 principal 2 procession 1

quarters 1

rest 2 round 21 roundness 1 ruler 3

scalp 4 sense 3 senses 1 sensible 1 shape 4 shaped 1 shoulder 1 shoulders 12 skull 5 small 7 sore 2 square 1 statue 2

stomach 2 strong 1 superintendent 2 symmetry 1

tail 3 teeth 1 thick 2 think 9 thinking 6 thought 16 thoughts 4 tired 1 top 31 trunk 2

useful 2

whirl 1 wit 1 woman 1 woman's 2 work 1

71. STOVE

article 3

bake 1 baking 1 black 59 blacking 4 box 1 breakfast 1 bright 2 burn 12 burning 2

chair 1 chimney 1 coal 25 comfort 2 cook 24 cooking 34 cooks 1 cover 3

dark 1 dinner 1 dirt 1 dishes 1

fire 217 fireplace 3 flame 1 food 3 Franklin 1 fry 1 fuel 1 furnace 6 furniture 8 furnitureness 1

gas 7 German 1 good 2 grate 1

hard 2 hardware 1 heat 213 heating 1 heats 1 heater 2 heavy 2 home 1 hot 86 house 2 household 1

icebox 1 implement 1 instrument 2 iron 51 isinglass 1

kettle 4 kitchen 11

lamp 3 large 2 legs 2 lid 4 lifter 3 light 1 long 1

metal 2

oil 1 oven 1

painful 1 pipe 18 pipes 1 poker 5 polish 10

radiator 2 range 19 receptacle 1 red 1 room 2 round 1 rusty 1

shovel 1 sink 1 small 2 smoke 1 steel 3 structure 1

teakettle 1

using 1 utensil 2

warm 32 warmth 42 water 1 winter 2 wood 7

zinc 1

72. LONG

age 1 anxiety 1 arm 1 arms 1 avenue 2 away 1

barn 1 beach 1 bench 1 big 1 blackboard 1 board 2 boat 6 book 1 boulevard 1 bridge 1 broad 2 Brooklyn Bridge 1 broomstick 1 building 1

cable 1 chimney 1 coat 1 courage 1 craving 1

day 9 days 1 deep 1 depth 1 desirable 1 dimensions 1 distance 81 distant 3 dress 6 duration 1

elongated 1 endless 1 enough 1 eternity 2 extended 1 extension 1 extensive 1 extent 1

far 8 feet 1 fellow 1 fence 2 flagpole 1 foot 1 for 1

giant 2 girl 1 glass 2 grass 4 great 1

hair 2 hall 2 head 1 height 1 high 5 hill 1 hose 1 hours 1 house 1

Island 2

journey 8

labor 1 lane 3 lanky 2 large 7 lasting 1 lecture 1 legs 1 length 50 lengthy 6 level 1 life 4 line 5 linear 1 live 1 Lusitania 1

man 5 measure 7 medium 2 meter 1 mile 13 miles 1 Mississippi 1 much 1

name 1 narrow 15 night 2 nose 1

oblong 1

path 2 person 1 pin 1 pipe 1 plant 1 plenty 1 pole 20

railroad 4 railway 1 rails 1 reed 1 ribbon 3 ride 1 river 15 road 32 rod 1 room 1 rope 7 row 1 rug 1 rule 2 ruler 4

- 270 -

shape 1 sharp 1 shore 1 short 413 shovel 1 slender 1 slim 1 slow 1 small 1 snake 2 something 1 space 1 spacious 1 spire 1 square 1 stay 1 steamer 1 steeple 1 stick 8 sticks 1 story 2 straight 1 street 6 streets 1 strength 1 stretch 2 string 6 stupid 1 summer 1

table 3 tall 26 test 1 thin 2 thread 2 throw 1 time 15 tiresome 1 tower 1 track 3 train 2 tree 4 trip 1

vast 1 very 1

wait 1 waiting 2 walk 7 walking 1 walls 1 way 6 ways 1 weary 1 whale 1 while 1 wide 7 winter 1 wire 1 wishing 1 without 1 worm 1

yard 4 year 2

73. RELIGION

Abraham 1 aesthetics 1 aim 1 all 1 anything 1 association 1 atheism 2 atheism 4

Baptist 2 beauty 1 belief 39 beliefs 1 believe 2 believing 1 believer 1 belong 1 belonging 1 Bible 52 body 1 books 2 brain 3 Buddha 1

catechism 1 Catholic 56 ceremony 2 China 1 Christ 8 Christian 14 Christianity 7 Christlike 1 church 161 churches 4 churchman 1 civilize 1 clergyman 1 comfort 4 commandments 1 conduct 1 Congregational 1 conscience 2 conversion 1 Creator 2 creed 33 custom 1

deep 1 denomination 11 devotion 4 different 2 difficult 1 dislike 1 divine 1 doctrine 4 dogma 1 doubt 2 Druids 1 duties 1 duty 2

emotion 1 Episcopal 4 Episcopalian 1 eternity 1 ethics 2 everyday 1

fair 1 faith 47 fake 1 fanaticism 1 feeling 1 fine 1 foolish 2 free 1

gentle 1 German 1 God 31 godly 1 good 46 goodness 10 gospel 2 government 1 guide 3

happiness 3 harmony 1 health 1 heathen 3 heaven 8 Hebrew 1 helpful 2 hereafter 1 heresy 1 history 2 holiness 4 holy 10 honor 1 house 1 hypocrisy 1

idea 2 ideas 1 ignorance 1 indefinite 1 indiscreet 1 institutions 1 irreligion 1 irreligious 1

Jesus 3
Jew 3
Jews 1

- 271 -

Jewish 4

just 1

kind 2 knowledge 1

law 1 learning 1 life 4 living 1 Lord 1 Lutheran 1

man 1 men 1 mankind 1 many 1 mental 1 Methodism 1 Methodist 7 minister 15 modesty 1 Mohammed 2 morals 2 mystic 1

nationality 2 need 1 no 1 none 5 nothing 2 nun 1 nuns 1

obey 1 opinion 3 order 1 orthodox 1

paganism 1 peace 3 people 3 perfect 1 persecution 1 person 2 persuasion 3 piety 13 pious 13 poor 2 Pope 1 powerful 1 practice 2 pray 2 praying 2 prayer 21 prayers 5 prayer-book 2 preacher 2 preaching 2 Presbyterian 3 priest 28 profession 3 professor 1 Protestant 30 pulpit 1 pure 2 puzzle 1

question 1

race 1 rector 1 religious 2 reverence 3 right 2 righteousness 2

sacrament 1 sacred 4 sacredness 1 saintly 1 saints 1 salvation 2 scholastic 1 science 2 scripture 1 sect 3 sectarian 2 self 1 service 3 sheeney 1 society 1 solace 1 somewhat 1 soul 1 spirituality 1 stability 1 standby 1 study 1 superstition 1

tabernacle 1 table 1 teaching 1 temperament 1 temple 2 think 2 thinking 1 thought 12 thoughtful 1 training 1 true 1 trust 1 truth 6

uncertain 1 uncertainty 1 unknowable 1

virtuous 1 vow 1

want 1 wickedness 1 wide 1 woman 1 wonder 1 wonderful 1 work 1 worship 14 worshipping 1

Yankee 1

74. WHISKEY

abomination 1 alcohol 50 ale 1 amber 1 appetizer 1 apple 1 awful 1

bad 35 barley 1 barrel 2 bed 1 beer 46 beverage 9 biting 1 bitter 5 booze 10 Boston 1 bottle 29 brandy 24 breath 1 burn 1 burning 4

Carrie Nation 1 cider 3 closet 1 color 1 corn 1 curse 4

dangerous 1 dark 1 death 1 degradation 1 despised 1

destruction 1 devil 1 deviltry 1 Dewar's 1 disagreeable 1 discontent 1 disgust 1 distillery 1

distress 1 dope 1 dreadful 1 drink 232 drinks 1 drinking 17 drinkable 1 drug 1 drunk 31 drunkard 18 drunkards 3 drunkenness 26

evil 2

fast 1 fire 4 flask 1 fluid 4 food 1 full 1

gin 8 glass 3 good 15 grain 1

hard 1 headache 1 Hennessey's 1 hops 1 horror 1 hot 2 hotels 1 Hunter 1

indulge 1 indulgence 1 inebriety 1 insanity 1 intemperance 5 intoxicant 13 intoxicants 2 intoxicated 3 intoxicating 14 intoxication 14

jag 1

Kentucky 1 knock 1

law 1 liquid 12 liquids 1 liquor 70

malt 2 men 2 medicine 4 misery 1 money 1 moonshine 1

narcotic 3 nice 3 none 1

odor 1 old 1

pint 1 place 1 pleasant 1 poison 4 poor 1 poorhouse 1 powerful 1 prohibition 2 punch 1

rarely 1 red 2 ruin 1 ruination 1 rum 23 rye 9

saloon 15 saloons 1 Scotch 1 seasickness 1 sick 2 sickness 2 smell 2 smuggle 1 sorrow 1 sour 4 spirit 5 spirits 23 stimulant 88 stimulants 4 stimulating 1 stimulation 1 stomach 1 straight 2 strong 6 stupidity 1 suffering 1

taste 1 temperance 4 temptation 1 terrible 1 thirst 1 thirsty 1 tipsy 1 toddy 1 toper 1 trouble 2

unhealthy 1 unpleasantness 1

warm 1 water 9 wine 16 wrong 1

75. Child

adult 5 angel 8

babe 7 baby 193 bad 1 beautiful 8 beauty 5 being 8 bird 2 birth 2 blessing 2 body 2

born 1 boy 64 boys 3 burden 1

care 1 carriage 1 charm 1 childhood 1 childish 1 Christ 1 clothes 1 comfort 8 coming 1 companion 1 cradle 2 creep 1 crib 1 cries 1 cry 4 cross 1 cunning 1 cute 8

darling 1 daughter 2 dear 1 dearest 1 delight 1 disobedient 1 dog 1 doll 4 dress 4 dresses 1

Eleanor 1 Elizabeth 1 embryonic 1 expectation 1

family 2 fat 1 father 5 female 3 frolicsome 1 fun 2 fussy 1 future 1

girl 45 girls 2 glass 1 good 7 goose 1 Greta 1 growing 1 growth 1

habits 1 hair 1 happiness 2 happy 2 healthy 1 helpless 1 helplessness 1 home 6 hood 2 hospital 1 human 5 humanity 1

ill 1 immature 1 infancy 1 infant 122 injury 1 innocence 16 innocent 11 interesting 1

joy 1 juvenile 2

kid 4 kindergarten 1

labor 2 lady 2 large 2 like 1 little 11 lonely 1 loveable 1 love 8 loving 2 lovely 4

male 1 mammal 1 man 41 maternity 1 me 1 mite 1 mother 55 motherhood 1

naive 1 naughty 1 necessary 1 nephew 1 nice 1 night-dress 1 noise 1 nuisance 2

obedient 1 offspring 6

parent 6 parents 1 people 3 person 18 pet 1 play 14 playing 3 playful 3 pleasure 4 plump 1 precious 1 pretty 10 pupil 1 purity 1

rattle 1 religious 1

school 5 screaming 1 senses 1 simple 1 simplicity 1 sister 1 small 52 smile 1 son 2 spoiled 1 study 1 sweet 6 sweetness 2

table 1 tender 1 three 1 toys 1 trouble 1

weak 3 woman 18

young 30 youngster 2 youth 29 youthful 1

76. BITTER

acid 8 acrid 1 agreeable 1 ale 1 almond 4 almonds 3 aloe 4 aloes 6 altogether 1 alum 2 anger 3 apples 3 apple 1 apricot 1 astringent 1 bad 10 banana 1 beer 5 berry 1 biting 1 boneset 1 burdock 1

candy 1 cascara 1 chastisement 1 chickory 1 chocolate 1 cider 1 cold 6 cross 1 cup 1

deep 1 disagreeable 10 disappointment 1 dislike 2 distasteful 10 dregs 1 drink 2

enemy 2

feelings 1 flag 1 fruit 4

gall 42 good 2 grape 1 grapefruit 3 grass 1 grief 2 grudge 1

hatred 2 herb 2 herbs 5 hops 1 horrid 3 horseradish 1

icy 1 ill 1 irritating 1

lemon 8 lemons 1 lemonade 1 lessons 1 life 1 lines 1 liquor 1 love 1

magen 1 man 1 mandrake 1 medicine 37 Mirabar 1 morphine 1

nasty 3 nice 1 none 1 nux 1

offensive 1 olives 1 orange 3

peach 1 peel 1 pepper 9 persimmon 2 pickle 3 pickles 1 pleasant 1 plums 4 poison 1 puckering 1

quassia 1 quince 1 quinine 23

rank 1

sadness 1 salt 2 salts 2 sharp 3 sorrow 8 sound 1 sour 222 sourness 2 spice 1 strong 3 strychnia 1 strychnine 4 suffering 1 sweet 305 sweeter 1

tart 8 taste 66 tasteless 3 tasting 1 tea 1 tears 1 temper 1 thoroughwort 3 thought 1 tonic 1 tonics 2 trouble 1 turnip 1

ugly 3 unhealthy 1 unpalatable 1 unpleasant 19 unpleasantness 1 unsweetened 1 unwholesome 1

vegetables 1 vinegar 17

water 1 weather 1 wine 1 word 1 words 2 wormwood 2 wrong 1

77. HAMMER

action 2 annoyance 1 anvil 6 article 1 awl 1 axe 11

bang 3 beating 1 blacksmith 2 blow 6 board 2 bruiser 1 building 2 carpenter 13 carpentering 1 chisel 10 claps 1 claw 1 club 2 concussion 1 convenience 1

drive 17 drives 1 driving 5 door 1

easy 1 effort 1

finger 3 force 2

geology 1

handle 5 hard 53 hatchet 6 head 2 heavy 13 hit 21 horseshoe 1 hurt 1 hurts 1

implement 8 instrument 38 iron 45

J. 2

knife 1 knock 35 knocker 6 knocking 5

large 2 lost 1

mallet 3 mark 1 maul 1 metal 1

nail 185 nails 98 nailing 2 noise 36 nut 1 nuts 1

one 2

pain 1 picture 2 picture 1 plumber 1 pound 51 pounding 12 pounds 1

rap 1 repairs 1 revolver 1 road 1 rod 1 round 1

saw 9 scissors 1 shoemaker 1 shop 1 sledge 10 small 2 sound 9 spade 1 stay 1 steel 20 stone 1 strength 1 strike 28 striking 4 stroke 1

tack 3 tacks 11 Thor 1 thread 1 throw 6 throwing 1 thumb 1 thump 1 toe 1 tongs 29 tool 69 tools 3 turf 1

use 1 useful 5 utensil 1

weapon 3 weight 3 wood 6 work 8 working 2

78. THIRSTY

all 1 always 2 animal 1 appetite 3

bar 1 beer 4 beverage 1 bird 1 boy 1 brooks 1

cattle 1 child 2 cold 1 craving 4 cream 1 cup 2

desert 2 desire 4 desiring 1 dipper 1 disagreeable 1 discomfort 2 dog 2 drink 206 drinking 23 drought 8 dry 218 dryness 5 emotion 1 empty 1 exhausted 1

famished 1 fatigue 1 feeling 5 fluid 1 food 1 fountain 1

glass 1 good 1

hard 1 haste 1 heat 2 horse 1 hot 2 hunger 9 hungry 41

labor 1 lack 2 lawn 1 lemonade 7 liquid 1 longing 4

man 1 mouth 2

nauseated 1

oranges 1

pain 2 parched 3 parching 2 people 1 person 1

quench 12 quenched 4

refreshing 1

satiated 1 satisfied 3 sensation 1 soda 2 spring 3 stream 1 suffering 1

terrible 1 throat 1 tongue 1

uncomfortable 1 unpleasant 2

very 1 vichy 1

walk 2 want 9 wanting 2 warm 1 water 341 wench 1 wet 3 work 2

79. CITY

Albany 1

beautiful 1 big 9 Boston 5 bridges 1 Brooklyn 3 building 6 buildings 20 bulk 1 Burlington 1 business 1 busy 4 bustle 2

capital 6 cars 3 charming 1 Chicago 4 child 1 citizen 7 civilization 1 Cleveland 1 collection 2 community 5 complexity 1 confusion 1 congregation 1 corporation 2 country 74 Creal 1 Creal Springs 1 crowd 11 crowded 7 crowds 1

density 1 dirt 1

distance 1

earth 1 excitement 1

fine 1 fun 1

gaiety 1 good 1 government 1 governor 1 great 2 greatness 1

habitation 3 heat 1 hill 2 home 5 homes 1 hot 1 house 3 houses 52

immense 1 incorporated 1 incorporation 1 industry 2 inhabitant 1 inhabitants 12 inhabited 1

joy 1

land 2 large 62 largeness 1 life 2 live 7 loathing 1 location 2 lots 1

machinery 1 majority 1 Manhattan 1 manufacture 2 many 3 men 2 metropolis 6 mill 1 mountain 1 municipal 1 municipality 1

nation 1 New York 99 noise 12 noisy 6

park 1 pavement 1 people 48 place 37 pleasantness 1 populated 2 population 19 populous 1 Poughkeepsie 6

republic 2 residence 2 resting 1 rich 1

scene 1 sea 1 settlement 1 shopping 1 shops 1 sights 1 sin 1 size 1 slums 1 small 1 smoke 1 space 2 Springfield 1 state 26 stores 1 street 3 streets 11

tale 1 ten thousand 1 theatre 2 theatres 1 towers 2 town 258 towns 1 township 1 traffic 1 traveling 1 tumult 1 turmoil 2

village 44

wagons 1 welcome 1 world 1

80. SQUARE

accurate 1 acre 1 across 1 active 1 airy 1 angle 11 angles 6 angular 4 arithmetic 1 association 1

bed 1 best 1 big 1 block 71 board 4 book 4 box 36 brick 2 broad 5 building 2 business 1

carpenter 9 carpet 1 cars 1 center 2 Chatham 1 checkers 1 circle 22 circular 1 city 4 Common 1 Commons 1 compass 5 concert 1 Copley 1 corner 7 corners 18 cornered 2 correct 1 correctness 1 cover 1 crackers 1 crooked 3 crowd 1 cube 9 cubic 1 cubical 1 curse 1 curve 1

deal 1 dealing 1 decoration 1 desk 2 Dewey 1 dice 4 die 1 door 2 Düsseldorf 1

earth 1 ease 1 equal 6 even 19 evenness 1 exact 1

fair 3 field 4 figure 4 file 1 flat 4 floor 1 foot 2 form 1 four 10 frame 1 furlong 1

garden 5 geometry 10 Getty 1 goods 1 grass 1 green 3 grounds 1

hand 1 handkerchief 2 Harlem 1 Herald 2 heavy 1 honest 3 honesty 1 house 5 houses 3

inch 2 inches 1 instrument 1 iron 1

just 1 justice 2 junction 1 kindergarten 1 knob 1

land 2 large 5 Lawrence 1 length 2 level 10 lines 2 little 1 long 18 lot 1

Madison 12 man 5 mark 1 marks 1 masonry 1 mathematics 2 meal 1 measure 5 measurement 2 measurements 1 metal 1 mile 2 monument 1

New York 1

object 2 oblong 32 obtuse 1 open 1 oval 5

paper 5 parallel 1 parallelogram 1 park 14 pavements 1 people 2 perfect 2 picture 1 Pillow 2 place 4 plane 1 plot 1 proportion 1 public 2

quadrangle 1

rectangle 15 rectangular 3 rhomboid 1 right 5 Rittenhouse 1 road 1 room 5 round 250 rule 9 ruler 3

saddle 1 seat 1 shape 6 sharp 2 side 1 sides 6 sidewalk 1 size 1 sizing 1 small 6 smooth 1 solid 2 space 1 stand 2 steel 1 straight 7 street 9 streets 1 sugar 1 surface 1 surveyor 1

table 47 thoroughfare 1 times 3 tool 13 tree 1 trees 4 triangle 11 true 1

uneven 1 uniform 1 Union 4 upright 2

village 8

Walk 1 walks 1 wall 1 Washington 4 wide 2 window 1 wood 5

yard 2

81. BUTTER

bad 2 bill 2 biscuit 2 bread 206 breakfast 1 butter 1 butterine 1

cheese 41 churn 4 color 1 composition 1 cooking 1 cottolene 1 country 1 cup 1 cow 29 cows 11 cream 34

dairy 4 dairying 1 diet 2 dinner 2 dish 5 dripping 1

eat 34 eatable 12 eatables 2 eating 6 edible 1 egg 2 eggs 11 emollient 1 excellent 1

farm 1 farmer 1 fat 21 fatty 1 fish 1 flour 1 fly 7 food 63 fresh 3 fudge 1

goat 2 good 14 grease 76 greasy 6 grocer 1

healthful 1

indifference 1 ingredients 1

jam 3 jelly 2

kerosene 1 knife 7

lard 15 luxury 1

meal 1 meat 2 melt 1 melting 2 milk 101 molasses 1 mush 1

nourishment 1 nut 2

oil 9 oily 3 oleomargarine 5

peaches 1 plate 3 pleasant 1 plenty 1 pound 1 pure 1

rancid 2

salt 13 salty 3 salve 1 smear 1 smooth 1 soft 65 softness 2 sour 1 spoon 1 spread 3 square 1 strong 2 substance 1 sugar 4 supper 1 sweet 12

table 2 tallow 1 taste 2 tea 2 thin 1 tub 1

use 1

vegetable 3

yellow 80

82. DOCTOR

administer 1 aid 3 ailment 1 apparatus 1 attendant 2

bad 1 bag 1 beard 2 better 2 bill 3 bills 2 bottle 1 brains 1 brother 1 butcher 1

C. 1 C. 1 care 2 carriage 2 case 1 chief 1 clergyman 1 clever 1 college 1 convenient 1 cure 9

D. 1 D. 1 D. 1 death 1 dentist 6 disease 5 diseases 1 Divinity 1 doctress 1 dog 1 driving 1 Dr. 1 druggist 2

education 2

fakir 2 false 3 father 2 friend 3

- 280 -

G. 1 G. 1 gentleman 1 good 17 goodness 1 great 1 grip 2

healer 5 healing 2 health 18 help 3 helper 1 helpful 1 helpfulness 1 home 1 hospital 8

ill 5 illness 21 inquisitive 2 intelligent 2 interne 1 invalid 1

K. 1 K. 1 killer 1 kind 1

labor 1 laboratory 1 laborer 1 lamp 1 lawyer 36 learned 1 life 1

M. 1 McC. 1 McM. 1 magistrate 1 male 1 man 68 mean 1 medical 19 medicine 149 medicines 1 merchant 1 minister 7 mister 1 money 1 murder 1

N. 1 N. 1 necessity 2 need 1 needed 1 needful 1 nice 1 nurse 41 nurses 1

O. 1 office 1 old 1 one 1 operation 1

P. 1 pain 2 papa 1 patient 23 patients 1 people 1 person 3 pharmacist 1 physical 1 physician 213 pills 1 practitioner 2 priest 6 profession 9 professional 3

quack 1

relief 6 relieved 1 remedy 1

S. 1 satchel 3 science 2 scientist 1 sick 52 sickness 104 smart 3 student 1 suffering 1 supervisor 1 surgeon 5 surgical 1 syringe 1

tend 1 treatment 1 trouble 3 trust 1

useful 2 useless 1

W. 1 W. 1 W. 1 well 1 wise 1 woman 2 work 1

83. LOUD

angry 3 audible 1

band 1 bawl 1 bell 5 bells 2 birds 2 boisterous 38 boy 1 boys 2 bright 1

call 2 called 1 calliope 1 calm 1 cannon 12 check 1 child 1 children 1 city 1 clear 1 course 2 color 2 common 1 confusion 1 cornet 1

deaf 1 deafening 1 din 1 disagreeable 3 discontent 1 dislike 1 drum 3

ear 3 easy 12 explosion 4

fast 3 forte 1

game 1 gong 1 graphophone 1 gun 2 guns 1

hammer 2 hard 2 harsh 3 haughty 1 hear 6 heard 1 heavy 4 high 14 hog 1 holler 16 horn 4

impatient 1

knock 2

laugh 2 laughing 2 lofty 1 long 3 low 57

man 1 masculine 1 megaphone 1 mellow 1 mild 1 mouth 1 music 7

noise 205 noisy 112

objectionable 1 ocean 1 organ 1 owl 1

pain 1 painful 1 people 1 person 2 phonograph 1 piano 2 piercing 1 pistols 1 power 1

quiet 32 quietness 1

racket 1 real 1 report 1 rough 2 rude 2

S. 1 scream 9 sharp 2 shock 1 shout 6 shouting 1 shriek 1 shrill 9 shrinking 1 silent 3 sing 1 singer 1 singing 1 slow 4 smart 1 smooth 1 socks 1 soft 165 softly 1 song 2 sound 25 sounds 2 speak 3 speech 2 spoken 2 still 7 stone 1 strong 8 subway 1 sweet 1

talk 12 talking 1 talker 9 thunder 9 tie 1 tone 1 trolley 1

uncomfortable 1 unpleasant 5

voice 27 voices 1 vulgar 4

whisper 2 whistle 17 wide 1 wind 3

yell 3 yelling 2

84. THIEF

absence 1 abstractor 1 anger 1 arrest 1

bad 14 badness 1 bandit 1 bank 1 beggar 3 being 1 betrayer 1 boy 3 burglar 118 burglary 2

careful 2 catch 2 caught 4 caution 1 chief 1 clerk 1 clothing 1 court 4 crime 2 criminal 15 crook 3 cry 1 culprit 2 cute 1

dangerous 2 dark 4 deceit 1 detective 1 devil 1 dishonest 11 dishonesty 2 dishonor 1 dislike 1 distrustful 1 dirt 1 dog 1 dumb 1

enemy 1 evil 1

fear 2 felon 1

girl 1 glove 1 gold 2 good 1

harsh 1 honest 18 honesty 4 house 4 household 1

ignorant 1 injustice 1 interest 1 Irish 1

jail 11 jewelry 7 jewels 3 judge 1 jury 1 justice 2

killed 1 kleptomaniac 1

laugh 1 law 4 lawyer 1 liar 6 lock 1 loss 3 low 2

man 29 mask 1 McClure's 1 mean 4 meanness 1 men 1 mercenary 1 merchant 2 minister 2 mischief 1 misdemeanor 1 mistake 1 money 16 murder 5 murderer 3

necessity 1 neighbor 1 newspaper 1 night 16 none 1 noted 1

object 1

pencil 1 person 1 pickpocket 2 play 1 pocket 1 pocketbook 1 police 8 policeman 12 poor 1 prison 6 prisons 1 prisoner 1 punishment 2 purse 1

ran 1 rascal 4 reverses 1 revolver 1 rob 8 robber 126 robbery 10 rogue 19 roguish 1 run 1 running 2

scare 1 schemer 1 school 1 scoundrel 4 shot 1 silver 4 silverware 1 sin 1 Sing Sing 1 sinner 1 sly 1 snake 1 sneak 7 sneaking 3 sneaky 1 spoils 1 steal 212 stealing 69 steals 8 stole 9 stolen 9 stealer 2 stealth 1 stealthy 2

take 5 taking 3 time 1 tools 2 tramp 1 treasure 1 troublesome 1 trust 1

ugly 3 undesirable 1 unjust 1 unreliable 1

vagrant 1 valuables 2 vice 2 villain 5 virtue 1

want 1 watch 3 waywardness 1 wicked 4 wickedness 3 window 1 woman 1 wretched 1 wrong 3

85. LION

Africa 4 Androcles 1 anger 1 angry 2 animal 326 animals 3

bear 17 beast 67 beautiful 1 beauty 1 big 2 bird 1 bite 1 blood 1 boisterous 1 bold 2 Bostock's 1 brave 4 bravery 1 Bronx 1

cage 14 camel 1 cat 6 cave 1 Christian 1 circus 2 claws 2 cow 1 crouching 1 cruel 2 cub 5 cubs 2

danger 5 dangerous 6 death 1 den 13 desert 3 devours 1 disturber 1 dog 1

eat 1 eats 1 elephant 3 enraged 1

fear 3 ferocious 16 ferocity 1 fierce 36 fierceness 1 forest 6 fox 1 fright 1 frightened 1

giraffe 1 great 2 growl 1

hair 3 hearted 1 holler 1 horse 1 howl 1 huge 1 hungry 1 hunter 3 hunting 4 hyena 1

interested 1

jealous 1 jungle 5 jungles 1

king 16

L. 1 lamb 6 large 3 lioness 10 lionized 1 lookout 1

majestic 1 majesty 3 mane 13 menagerie 5 mice 1 mighty 1 monkey 1 mouse 27 mule 1

N. 1 noble 1 noise 1

panther 1 park 2 paw 1 picture 1 power 5 powerful 1 prey 1

rage 1 raging 1 revenge 1 roar 45 roars 3 roaring 6 Roosevelt 8 rough 1

savage 1 sea 1 shaggy 1 sharp 1 sheep 1 small 1 stealth 1 stealthy 1 story 1 strength 30 strong 15 Sultan 1

tame 4 tamer 1 tail 1 teeth 1 terrible 1 tiger 102 tigers 2

ugly 7

vicious 5

walks 1 wicked 2 wild 12 wildness 1 wilderness 2 wilds 1 wolf 10 woods 2 wool 1 wrath 1

yellow 1

zoo 5 zoology 1

86. JOY

action 1 amuse 1 amusement 3 anger 1 angry 1 anticipation 1 arrival 1 automobile 4

ball 1 bird 1 birth 1 birthday 1 bitterness 1 bless 1 blessing 1 bliss 10 boy 1 bright 1 brightness 1 buoyant 1

cheer 1 cheerful 2 cheerfulness 3 child 2 children 1 Christmas 2 comes 1 comfort 11 comfortable 1 company 1 complete 1 concert 1 contentment 1

dance 3 dancing 5 delight 6 delighted 2 delightful 2 despair 1 ecstasy 1 elated 2 emotion 1 engaged 1 enjoyment 2 excitement 3 expression 2 extreme 1 exuberance 1

fair 1 family 1 feel 1 feeling 5 felt 1 festivity 1 fine 2 food 1 forever 1 friends 1 fullness 1 fun 6

gaiety 1 gay 1 game 1 gift 1 girl 2 girls 1 glad 27 gladness 44 glee 3 godliness 1 good 7 grand 1 great 7 grief 18

hands 1 happiness 215 happy 71 harmony 1 health 1 heard 1 heart 3 heaven 2 holiday 1 home 6 hope 4

inexpressible 1

joking 1 jubilant 1

lady 1 laugh 7 laughing 4 laughter 15 leap 1 letter 1 life 3 light 2 like 1 line 2 lonely 1 lots 1 love 6 loving 2 lovely 1

man 1 marriage 2 meeting 2 merriment 1 merry 1 mirth 7 money 1 motherhood 1 much 2 music 5

news 1 nice 2 noise 1

outing 1

pain 1 passing 1 peace 23 picnic 1 picnics 1 pleasant 8 pleased 3 pleasure 121 pride 1

quality 1

rapture 4 rejoice 2 rejoicing 1 relief 2 ride 7 riding 2 rider 1

sad 1 sadness 13 sailing 2 Saturday 1 seldom 1 sensation 1 shouting 1 show 2 sing 1 singing 1 smile 2 smiling 1 song 3 sorrow 135 sorry 1 state 1 suffering 1 summer 1 sunlight 1 surprise 6 sweet 4

time 2 triumph 1 trouble 3

unalloyed 1 unattainable 1 unhappiness 2 unhappy 1

vacation 1

water 1 wedding 1 wetness 1 wish 1 wonderful 1 work 2 wrath 1

youth 1

87. BED

animal 1 asleep 1

baby 1 bedding 3 bedstead 4 blanket 4 blankets 3 boat 1 bowl 1 brass 3 bug 2

chair 11 clean 2 cleanliness 1 clothes 12 clothing 2 comfort 35 comforts 1 comfortable 12 cot 11 couch 26 counterpane 1 cover 4 covers 4 covering 1

desired 1 dormitory 1 down 1 dreamland 1

ease 1 easiness 1 easy 2

fatigue 1 feathers 3 flannels 1 floor 1 folding 2 frame 1 furniture 26

go 1 good 7

hammock 2 hard 5 head 1 home 2 house 2

iron 9

joy 1

large 2 lay 8 laziness 1 lie 21 lounge 6 low 2 lying 8

make 1 marriage 1 mattress 21

narrow 1 negro 1 night 11

object 1

pan 1 patient 3 peace 1 pillow 17 pillows 7 pleasure 1 post 3

quilts 1

recline 1 recuperation 1 refreshing 1 repose 9 respite 1 rest 132 resting 5 restful 1 robe 1 room 16

seat 1 sheet 6 sheets 7 shoes 1 sick 2 sickness 5 sleep 345 sleeping 41 sleepiness 3 sleepy 7 slumber 3 sofa 7 soft 31 spread 5 spring 1 springs 1 square 1 stove 1 structure 1

table 2 tick 1 time 1 tired 7 twilight 1

Vassar 1

want 1 warm 1 weariness 1 white 2 whiteness 1 wide 1 wood 4

88. HEAVY

air 1 animal 1 anvil 1 article 1 automobile 1 avoirdupois 1

baby 1 bad 1 bat 1 bed 2 big 3 body 1 books 3 boulders 1 box 1 boxes 1 boy 1 bread 1 brick 1 building 1 bullet 1 bundle 4 burden 12 burdensome 3 cake 1 cannon 1 carpet 1 carry 2 carrying 1 cement 1 chair 1 change 1 cloth 1 clothes 1 cloudy 1 coal 4 coarse 1 coat 1 comfort 1 cumbersome 1

dark 1 difficult 1 dirt 1 disappointment 1 discomfort 1 dope 1 drag 1 drill 1 drowsiness 1 drowsy 10 dull 3

effort 1 elephant 3

F. 1 fall 1 feel 1 firmness 1 full 1

gold 3 gorgeous 1 grief 1 grip 2

hammer 3 hard 38 head 2 heart 1 hearted 2 heft 1 help 1 horse 2 house 1

iron 70 irons 2

labor 1 laden 2 large 18 lead 60 lift 7 lifting 1 light 273 lightness 1 load 57 loadsome 1 loud 1

machine 1 man 4 marble 1 mountain 1 much 1 mud 1 muscle 1 myself 1

no 1

obliging 1 opposing 1 oppression 1 oppressive 1

package 1 pail 1 person 1 piano 1 ponderous 2 pound 1 pounds 1 pressure 2

quicksilver 1 quiet 2

rock 2 rough 1

safe 2 sand 1 satchel 1 scales 1 sharp 1 ship 1 short 1 sickness 1 sleep 3 sleeping 1 slothful 1 slumber 1 soft 5 soggy 1 solid 3 sound 1 steel 1 stone 17 stones 2 stout 2 stove 3 strain 1 strength 4 strong 3 study 1 suit 1

table 5 thick 3 things 1 thoughtful 1 tired 21 tiresome 2 ton 4 tough 1 trunk 3

uncomfortable 1 underwear 1

very 1

weak 1 weariness 3 weary 3 weather 1 weigh 1 weighing 1 weight 177 weighted 1 weighty 22 wood 4 work 2

89. TOBACCO

amber 1 anger 1

bad 10 bite 1 bitter 4 Bob 1 breath 1 brown 7

chew 28 chewing 13 cigar 19 cigars 17 cigarette 12 cigarettes 6 comfort 2 curse 1

death 1 decay 1 deviltry 1 dirty 6 disagreeable 3 disgust 1 disgusting 1 drug 3 Durham 1

elevate 1 enjoyed 1 enjoyment 1 execrable 1 exhilaration 1 evil 1

field 1 fields 1 filth 4 filthiness 1 filthy 1 food 1

garden 1 good 5 green 3 grower 1 growing 1

habit 12 habits 1 hard 1 herb 3 herbs 1 horrid 1 horrors 1

Indian 1 injurious 3 intoxicate 1

juice 7

leaf 17 leaves 2 light 1 liquor 1 lungs 1 luxury 2

man 3 men 1

narcotic 10 nasty 2 nausea 1 nicotine 18 none 1 not 1 nuisance 1

obnoxious 1 odor 3 odorous 1 opium 4

pipe 69 pipes 3 plant 38 plants 1 pleasant 3 pleasure 2 poison 6 poor 1 pouch 2 plug 1

refrain 1 ruin 1

scent 1 sensation 1 sin 1 smell 5 smoke 387 smoking 98 smoker 1 snuff 15 solace 1 spit 4 stalk 1 stars 1 stimulant 1 stimulants 1 strong 7 substance 1 suffocation 1 sugar 2 sweet 2

tasty 1 tobacco 1

unclean 1 unnecessary 2 unpleasant 2 unwholesome 1 use 2 used 1 useful 1 useless 2

vegetable 3 vice 1 Virginia 2 weed 44 weeds 1 whiff 1 whiskey 1 wickedness 1

yellow 1

90. BABY

animal 1

beautiful 5 beauty 2 beginning 1 being 3 bib 1 big 1 birth 1 blessing 1 blue 1 body 2 bonnet 1 born 2 bottle 6 boy 32 bread 1 buggy 1 bundle 1 cap 1 care 3 carriage 28 cart 2 child 239 children 3 childhood 1 chubby 1 clothes 4 comfort 3 cradle 22 creation 1 crib 1 crooning 1 cross 2 cries 3 cry 37 crying 29 cunning 3 cute 8 cuteness 1

darling 4 daughter 1 delicate 1 dirty 1 doll 1 dress 6

embryonic 1 eyes 1

fair 1 family 2 fat 5 father 1 feet 1 female 1 flesh 1 food 1 friend 1 future 1

girl 26 good 1 goodness 1 growth 1

happiness 1 happy 1 harmless 1 helpless 1 helplessness 4 home 4 human 3

infant 168 infinitesimal 1 innocence 10 innocent 4

joy 7 jump 1

kid 4

lamb 1 laugh 1 laughing 2 Lawrence 1 life 2 light 1 little 12 Lorenzo 1 love 9 loveliness 1 lovely 1

mama 2 man 4 mankind 1 Mary 1 milk 1 mother 41

name 1 nice 5 noise 6 noisy 1 nuisance 3 nurse 7

offspring 2

pacifier 1 paper 1 person 2 pink 2 play 1 pleasant 1 pleasure 3 population 1 powder 1 pretty 7

rattle 4 rocker 1 round 1 Ruth 2

sex 1 sick 1 sickness 1 simple 1 simplicity 1 sister 2 sleep 4 slight 1 small 42 smallest 1 smiling 1 soft 3 softness 2 squalls 2 squeal 1 squealing 1 stout 1 sunshine 1 sweet 23 sweetness 7 syrup 1

talk 1 talks 1 tiny 1 trouble 5 two 1

walking 1 weak 1 weakness 1 wee 1 white 1 wife 2 woman 5

yell 2 young 12 youngster 1 youth 4

91. MOON

astronomer 1 astronomy 1 atmosphere 1

ball 2 beam 2 beams 1 beautiful 7 beauty 6 body 7 bright 52 brightness 7 brilliant 1

calm 1 change 1 cheese 4 circle 1 circular 1 clear 3 clouds 2 cold 4 coldness 1 crescent 8 cute 1

dark 2 delicate 1 delightful 1 dim 1 distance 4 dreaming 1

earth 5 eclipse 3 equator 1 evening 6

fair 1 fire 2 firmament 1 full 10

girl 1 globe 1 glowing 1 grand 1 great 1 guard 1

half 3 heaven 2 heavens 3 high 4 illumination 1

lady 1 lake 1 large 9 light 231 love 3 loveliness 1 lovely 2 lunar 3

man 8 moonlight 3 mountain 1 mystery 1

necessary 1 new 3 night 66

object 1 ocean 1 one 1 orbit 1

pale 2 planet 23 planets 1 pleasant 1

quiet 1

reflection 1 rise 1 rises 1 rising 1 round 33

satellite 4 sea 2 see 1 seeing 1 sentimental 1 shine 26 shines 4 shining 12 shiny 12 silver 4 silvery 6 size 1 sky 73 solar 1 sound 1 splendid 1 spoon 2 spooning 1 star 32 stars 93 starlight 1 steamer 1 stone 1 struck 2 sun 120 sweet 1

turkey 1

valuable 1

wan 1 water 2 white 8 wish 1

yellow 11

92. SCISSORS

apart 1 article 4

barber 2 blade 1 blades 1 blunt 1

cloth 35 clothing 1 cord 1 crooked 1 crossed 2 cut 347 cutting 114 cutlery 1

dress 1 dressmaker 2 dressmaking 3 dull 6

edge 1

fate 1 firecrackers 1 flowers 1

garments 2 glistening 1 goods 5 grating 1 grind 7

handle 1 handy 1

implement 6 instrument 36 instruments 1

knife 66 knives 6

lever 1 linen 1 lost 1

machine 2 material 1 metal 1 millinery 1 mother 1

nails 1 necessity 1 needle 4 needles 4 nickle 1 nippers 1

paper 6 point 1 pointed 1

razor 1 ruching 1

Sarah 1 screw 1 severing 1 sew 2 swing 10 sharp 190 sharpness 6 sharpen 1 shears 40 shut 2 silver 1 skirt 1 spool 1 steel 23 string 1

tailor 2 thimble 3 thread 4 tongs 1 tool 10 tools 1 trousers 1

useful 1 usefulness 1 utensil 1

weapon 1 woman 1 work 2

93. QUIET

action 1 alone 2 always 1 asleep 1

baby 2 beautiful 1 beauty 1 bed 1 behave 2 boisterous 5 bore 1 boy 1 breeze 1 brook 1 butterfly 1

calm 20 cattle 1 child 6 children 1 church 4 color 1 comfort 2 comfortable 1 composed 1 contented 2 country 21 Creal 1 cricket 1 cross 3

dark 3 darkness 1 day 8 death 2 degree 1 demure 3 disposition 1 docile 1 dreary 1 dull 1 dumb 1

ease 8 easiness 1 easy 49 evening 5

family 1 feeling 1

genteel 1 gentle 3 gentleman 1 girl 2 good 7 green 1

happy 1 harmless 2 harsh 1 heaven 1 home 6 hour 1 house 3 hospital 2 humble 1

joy 1

landscape 1 laughing 1 library 1 life 2 like 1 loneliness 1 lonely 3 lonesome 2 looks 1 lovely l loud 48 low 1

man 1 melancholy 1 mind 1 Miss K. 1 moon 1 mountains 1 music 1 myself 1

nature 1 nice 2 night 38 noise 50 noiseless 16 noisiness 1 noisy 113 nook 1

park 1 peace 12 peaceable 2 peaceful 52 peacefulness 4 people 2 person 11 place 4 pleasant 4 pleasure 3

quick 1 quite 2

- 291 -

rabbits 1 refined 1 relief 1 repose 6 reserved 1 rest 68 resting 4 restful 19 restless 2 room 6 rough 1

sad 1 sea 1 serene 1 sheep 1 sickness 1 silence 18 silent 15 sleep 24 sleeping 3 sleepy 1 slow 3 slowness 1 slumber 1 slumbers 1 smart 1 smooth 1 sober 1 soft 10 softly 1 softness 1 solemn 3 solitude 2 soothing 3 sound 4 soundless 2 speechless 1 state 1 steady 2 still 136 stillness 16 study 2 stupid 1 subdued 1 summer 1 Sunday 1 sweet 2

talk 2 time 1 times 1 timid 1 tomb 1 tranquil 1 tree 1 twilight 1

village 1 violent 1 voice 1

walk 1 water 1 well 1 Wilton 1 wish 1 wood 1 woods 10

94. GREEN

apple 8

beautiful 2 bird 1 black 13 bloomy 1 blotter 2 blue 46 book 1 bright 5 brown 8 butterfly 1

cabbage 1 calm 1 carpet 1 cheese 1 cloth 3 color 200 colors 1 comfort 1 corn 1 country 1 covetous 1 cucumber 2 curtain 1

dark 8 Dartmouth 1 definite 1 dress 6

earth 2 envy 3 Erin 1 eyes 4

farmer 1 favorite 1 field 12 fields 10 flag 3 flower 4 flowers 2 foliage 2 food 1 foolishness 1 forest 1 fresh 3 fruit 1

gay 1 glasses 1 gold 1 grand 1 grapes 1 grass 284 gray 5 grew 1 grief 1 ground 1

hat 1 hill 1 horn 2 horrid 1 hue 1

Ireland 6
Irish 14

jealousy 1

landscape 1 laurel 1 lawn 5 leaf 8 leaves 13 light 4

meadow 1 meadows 1 mountain 2

name 1 nature 4

ocean 1 olive 1 orange 2

paint 3 paper 2 peaceful 1 peas 2 pink 11 plant 6 plants 1 pleasant 2 pleasing 1 pretty 4 purple 6 quiet 2

red 42 restful 6 ribbon 2 ripe 2

sea 2 shade 4 shamrock 2 shutters 1 sight 1 silk 1 sky 1 slow 1 small 1 soft 1 sour 2 spinach 1 spring 9 stain 1 summer 1

tea 1 tree 10 trees 29

unripe 1

vegetable 1 vegetables 1 verdant 3 verdure 1

warning 1 wearing 1 white 31 wood 1 woods 2

yellow 54 young 1

95. SALT

acrid 1 air 3 apple 1 apples 2 article 1

barre 1 barren 1 bath 1 beef 1 bitter 40 bowl 1 box 1 bread 2 brine 2 bromide 1 butter 7

celery 2 cellar 9 chemical 2 codfish 1 condiment 2 cook 1 cooking 2 cows 1 cream 1

deposit 1 digestible 1 dinner 3 dirt 1 disagreeable 1 dish 1 drink 1 dry 2

earth 5 eat 17 eatable 7 eating 8 eggs 2 epileptics 1

finish 1 fish 4 flavor 21 flavoring 3 food 46 France 1 fresh 11

glass 1 good 9

halite 1 ham 1 hard 4 horrid 1

ice-cream 1 ingredient 1

Kenilworth 1 kitchen 1

Lake 1 life 1 lot 1

mackerel 4 marsh 1 meat 18 meats 1 medicinal 1 melt 1 mine 2 mines 3 mineral 37 mustard 1

NaCl 1 necessary 5 necessity 3 needed 1 needful 1 nice 1

ocean 36

pantry 1 paper 1 pasture 1 pepper 142 petre 1 physic 1 pickles 1 pork 5 potassium 1 potato 2 potatoes 4 powder 1 preparation 1 preservation 2 preservatives 1 preserving 1

quotation 1

refreshing 1 relish 4 rock 7 rocks 1

saline 1 saltpetre 1 salty 3 sandwiches 1 Saratoga 1 saving 1 savor 10 savory 1 sea 18 season 12 seasoning 31 shake 2 shaker 4 sharp 8 sheep 1 smart 1 snapping 1 sodium 1 soup 2 sour 18 spice 5 spill 1 stickiness 1 sugar 88 sweet 27 Syracuse 1

table 14 tart 2 taste 87 tasting 1 tasteful 2 tasty 6 tasteless 1 temper 1 thirst 4 thirsty 2 trees 1

use 7 useful 2 uses 1 using 1

vegetable 5 vegetables 1 victuals 1 vinegar 1

water 34 wet 2 white 36

96. STREET

air 1 alley 18 asphalt 6 automobiles 1 avenue 63 avenues 1

better 1 bitter 1 block 12 boulevard 3 Bowery 1 boy 2 brick 1 broad 2 Broadway 6 Brooklyn 1 building 1 business 1 busy 4 byway 1

car 10 cars 8 carriage 1 city 82 Clarkson 1 clean 7 cleaner 1 colors 1 confusion 1 congestion 1 corner 2 country 1 crooked 2 cross 1 crowd 3 crowded 1

dark 1 Devon 1 direct 1 directions 1 dirt 4 dirty 5 distance 1 drive 1 driving 1 driveway 2 dry 1 dust 4 dusty 5 dwellings 1

earth 1 Eighty-sixth 1 Eleventh 1 Elm 1 even 1

fertile 1 Fifteenth 1 fine 1 flags 2 Forty-third 1

garden 1 going 1 gravel 1 gutter 2

hard 1 heat 1 Hester 1 highway 7 home 1 horses 2 hot 1 house 11 houses 21 hustle 1

land 3 lane 21 large 1 length 1 light 1 live 2 location 2 lonely 1 long 29

Main 5 Market 1 Maxfield 1 motion 1 mud 1 musician 1

name 2 narrow 21 New York 3 nice 1 noise 8 noisy 5 number 12 numbers 1

One-fifteenth 1 One-sixteenth 1 opening 1

passage 11 passageway 1 passway 2 path 12 pathway 2 pave 1 paved 13 pavement 25 paving 1 pebble 1 pecan 1 people 22 place 16 Pleasant 2 Pleasure 1 pretty 2

racket 1 residence 1 road 91 roads 4 roadway 2

see 1 shopping 1 short 3 sidewalk 26 sidewalks 2 Sixty-seventh 1 Sixty-third 2 smooth 2 space 1 square 4 stone 8 stones 8 straight 17 sun 1 sweep 1

tenements 1 terrace 1 thoroughfare 23 town 26 tracks 1 traffic 7 travel 8 tree 1 trees 1 trolley 2 turmoil 1

vehicles 1 village 9

wagon 3 wagons 2 walk 78 walking 23 walks 2 Wall 1 Washington 1 way 14 wet 1 white 1 wide 35 width 1 Woodhull 1

97. KING

Albert 1 all 1 Alphonso 3 antiquity 1 Arthur 1 authority 4

bad 1 boss 1

card 1 cards 1 chess 2 chief 1 command 3 commanding 1 commander 9 conqueror 2 country 13 court 1 courtier 1 crown 63 crowned 2

daughter 1 diamonds 1 dignity 1 dislike 1 dog 1 duke 1

Edward 30 emperor 11 empire 3 England 20 ermine 1

family 1 farce 1 first 1 fool 1 foreign 1 friend 1

garment 1 George 2 glory 1 good 1 govern 1 government 4 governor 6 great 2 greatness 1

Hamlet 1 happy 1 head 8 helmet 1 Henry 2 high 2 Holland 1 honorable 1 horrible 1

imperial 1 inheritance 1 Italy 1

John 1 judgement 1

Kaiser 2 king 1 kingdom 5

large 1 law 1 leader 2 lion 1 lord 1 Louis XVI. 1 loyal 1

majestic 1 majesty 8 male 2 man 43 master 3 mean 1 Midas 1 monarch 49 monarchy 4

nation 1 nobility 1 noble 3 nobleman 2 none 1

officer 1 old 1

palace 2 person 6 picture 1 pompous 2 Power 18 powerful 4 president 4 princess 1 Prussia 1

queen 354

regal 1 regent 1 reign 8 rich 1 Richard 1 royal 2 royalty 5 rule 10 rules 4 ruler 162 saxony 1 scepter 2 slave 1 somebody 1 sovereign 8 Spain 1 stories 1 subject 2 supreme 1

throne 21 title 1 town 1 tyrant 1

98. CHEESE

American 2

bacteria 1 bad 2 beer 2 biscuit 1 bitter 6 box 2 bread 56 brick 1 butter 136 buttermilk 2

cake 8 Camembert 2 casein 1 chalk 1 cheesecloth 1 churn 1 cloth 4 cold 1 color 4 corn 1 cow 9 cows 3 cracker 1 crackers 30 cream 30 creamery 1 crust 1 curd 9 curds 3 cut 2 cutter 1

dairy 4 delicatessen 2 derby 1 diet 2 digestible 1 digestion 1 dinner 2 dish 1 dislike 4 Dutch 1

eagle 1 eat 67 eating 29 eaten 1 eatable 19 eatables 3 edible 1 eggs 2

factory 1 fat 2 feast 1 fine 1 fondness 1 food 91 fresh 2 fromage de Brie 1

good 15 green 5 grocer 1 grocery 1

ham 1 hard 2 head 1 heap 1 hole 2 holes 2 holey 2 hoops 1 hunger 1 hungry 1

indigestion 1

jam 1

kind 1 knife 4

Limburger 13 lump 1 lunch 2

macaroni 1 maggot 1 maggots 2 meat 1 mice 25 microbes 1 mild 1 milk 106 milky 1 mixture 1 moon 2 mould 1 mouldy 1 mouse 13 mustard 2

nice 1 nourishment 1 nutrition 1

odor 9 odorous 1

pickles 1 pie 6 plain 1 plate 1 poor 1 poultry 1 price 1 product 2

rarebit 4 rat 8 rats 7 red 1 resentment 1 rich 1 Roquefort 4 rough 1 round 2

sage 1 salt 1 sandwich 8 sandwiches 2 sauce 1 scent 1 Switzer 2 sharp 3 skippers 1 smell 33 smells 1 soft 7 solid 2 sour 5 strengthening 1 strong 12 sugar 1 supper 5 sweet 2 Swiss 16 Switzerland 1

taste 8 tasty 1 thin 1

vegetable 5 vegetables 1

wafers 1 white 3 worms 1

yellow 32

99. BLOSSOM

apple 50 apples 4 art 1

beautiful 10 beauty 9 beginning 1 berries 1 bloom 28 blooming 7 blow 1 book 1 bright 4 bud 23 buds 3 bursting 1 bush 1 bushes 2 buttercups 1

cherries 5 cherry 4 clematis 1 clover 1 color 5 colors 1 country 1

dainty 1 daisy 2 delicate 1

eat 1

fair 2 falling 1 falls 1 field 3 flower 467 flowers 73 foliage 1 forth 2 fragrance 6 fragrant 4 frail 1 fruit 39

garden 2 gin 1 girl 1 green 1 grow 2 growth 2

handsome 1 happiness 1 hepatica 1

leaf 3 leaves 1 lilacs 2 lily 1

magnificent 1 May 2 mimosa 1

nice 1

odor 2 orange 2 orchard 2

pansies 1 pansy 1 peacefulness 1 peach 4 petal 1 petals 1 picking 1 pink 7 plant 13 pleasure 1 plum 1 pour 1 pretty 15

red 3 rose 17 roses 4

scent 1 seeds 1 shrubberies 1 small 1 smell 2 soft 1 spring 23 sprout 1 stem 1 summer 4 sun 1 sweet 15

T. 1 tree 40 trees 17

vine 1 violet 3

weeds 1 white 8

yellow 2 youth 1

100. AFRAID

accidents 1 action 1 alarm 2 always 2 anger 3 angry 2 animal 2 animals 2 anxiety 1 automobile 2 awful 1 backwardness 1 bad 2 bashful 2 battle 1 bears 1 blow 1 bold 2 boy 1 brave 18 bravery 1 brother 1 burglar 3 burglars 2

careful 1 cat 2 cheerfulness 1 child 8 children 1 cold 1 comfort 1 comforted 1 company 1 confidence 1 conscience 1 courage 11 courageous 5 cow 1 cows 1 coward 53 cowardice 5 cowardly 3 crowd 1 crying 1

danger 15 dangerous 2 dare 1 dark 114 darkness 16 death 2 deep 1 depressed 1 desire 1 dislike 1 do 1 dog 1 dogs 1 don't 1 doubt 1 dread 7 dreading 1 dreadful 1 dream 1

emotion 2

faith 2 fear 197 fearful 8 fearless 8 feeling 2 fierce 1 forward 1 fright 9 frighten 2 frightened 48 frightful 1 frog 1

gallant 1 ghost 4 ghosts 2 girl 1 go 4 goblins 1 God 1 guilty 1

happy 1 harm 2 heart 1 heroism 1 hide 1 home 1 hope 1 horse 1 hurt 1

insect 1

joy 1 joyful 1

licked 1 lightning 1 lion 3 loneliness 1 lonely 3 lonesome 5 loss 1

man 3 manner 1 memory 1 mild 1 Miss K. 1 mice 1 mouse 2

need 1 nerve 2 nerves 1 nervous 55 nervousness 4 never 3 night 12 no 3 nobody 1 noise 2 noisy 1 not 1 nothing 5

obsession 1 opposition 1

palpitation 1 patient 1 patients 1 plucky 1 police 1

quiet 1

rat 1 rats 1 retreat 1 riot 1 robbers 2 rocks 1 run 4 running 1

scare 1 scared 106 scary 1 scream 1 sensitive 1 shiver 1 shrinking 2 shudder 1 shy 2 sickness 1 sleep 1 soldier 1 somebody 1 sore 1 sorrow 2 sorry 1 spirit 1 spiritual 1 startled 1 startling 1 stay 1 stillness 1 strong 1 suddenness 1 suffering 1 sure 1

tempted 1 terrified 1 terror 9 thief 3 thought 1 threaten 1 thunder 1 timid 55 timidity 2 to-night 1 tremble 2 trouble 1 trust 1

unable 1 uncertain 1 uneasy 5 unhappiness 1 unknown 1 unprotected 1

woman 1 women 1 worried 1 worry 3

APPENDIX TO THE FREQUENCY TABLES

General Rules

1. Any word combination which is to be found in the frequency tables, but only in the reverse order from that in which it occurs in a test record under consideration, is to be classed as a normal reaction.

2. Any reaction word which is a synonym or an antonym of the corresponding stimulus word is to be classed as normal.

1. TABLE

Any food or meal.

Any room or apartment

Any article of table linen, china, silver, or furnishings.

Word designating any special variety of tables.

Any word pertaining to appetite.

2. DARK

Any source of illumination.

Any enclosure from which light is wholly or in a large measure excluded.

Word referring to physiological pigmentation of tissues exposed to view.

Any division of the diurnal cycle.

Any color or coloring material.

Anything which obscures light.

3. MUSIC

Any musical instrument.

Name of any composer or musician.

Special or general name of any musical composition.

Term designating rhythm, tempo, loudness, or pitch.

Name of any dance.

Term expressing subjective effect of music.

4. SICKNESS

Term designating any disease, symptom, injury, or physiological function.

Any cause of disease.

Any means or measure of treatment of disease.

Any anatomical organ or region.

Word denoting mode of termination, results, consequences, or indirect effects of disease.

Any term of prognostic import.

Common or proper name of any person.

5. MAN

Word denoting or implying age of a person.

Any of the well-known male sexual characteristics.

Occupation or profession more or less peculiarly masculine.

Word pertaining to familial relationships or domestic organization.

Word pertaining to sexual relationships; any word denoting the opposite sex.

The proper name of any male person.

Any article of male apparel.

6. DEEP

Any vessel or container.

Any natural or artificial body of water.

Any depression of surface.

Any object naturally situated or often artificially placed at a comparatively great distance below the surface.

Any act of progress from surface to depth.

7. SOFT

Any article of food.

Any fabric.

8. EATING

Any article of table linen, china, or silver.

Any organ of digestion; any function of nutrition.

Any article of food; any meal.

Any private or public eating place.

Word denoting taste.

9. MOUNTAIN

Name of any mountain, mountain range, or mountainous country.

Word pertaining to shape, geological composition, fauna, or flora of mountains or mountainous regions.

Any term of physical geography.

10. HOUSES

Any place of house location.

Any part of a house.

Any material used in the construction of a house.

Any part of the process of construction of a house.

Laborer or mechanic having to do with the construction of a house.

Any commercial term pertaining to ownership, taxes, mortgages, sale, renting, or occupancy of a house.

Any article of furniture.

11. BLACK

Any object or substance that is always or often black or dark in color.

Any color.

Word denoting limitation or obscuration of light.

Any word clearly related to the word Black used as a proper name.

12. MUTTON

Any article of food; any meal.

Any animal, or class or group of animals, whose meat is used for human consumption as food.

Any article of table linen, china, silver; any cooking utensil.

Word designating any person engaged in the preparation of meats for consumption.

Word denoting any process employed in the preparation of meats for consumption.

13. COMFORT

Any agreeable or disagreeable subjective state.

Any object, act, or condition that contributes to comfort or produces discomfort.

14. HAND

Any simple function of the hand; work requiring special manipulation.

Word denoting skill or any degree of skill.

Any part or any tissue of the body.

15. SHORT

Any word involving the concept of duration.

Common or proper name of any person.

Any word denoting shape, relative or absolute dimension, or distance.

Any object in which characteristically one dimension exceeds any other.

16. FRUIT

Any article of food; any meal.

Any process employed in the cultivation of fruits or in their preparation for consumption.

Word designating any person engaged in the cultivation of fruits or in their preparation for consumption.

Any article of table linen, china, or silver.

17. BUTTERFLY

Any bird, worm, or insect

Any flower.

Any color.

18. SMOOTH

Any object possessing a smooth surface as a characteristic feature.

Any fabric.

19. COMMAND

Word denoting any means of influence of one mind upon another intended to produce acquiescence.

Word denoting or implying acquiescence or lack of it.

Term applied to any commanding officer or to any person in authority.

20. CHAIR

Any article of furniture.

Any room or apartment

21. SWEET

Any substance having a sweet taste.

Common or proper name of a child' or woman.

22. WHISTLE

Any instrument or any animal producing a shrill musical sound.

33. WOMAN

Word denoting or implying age of a person.

Any of the well-known female sexual characteristics.

Occupation or profession more or less peculiarly feminine.

Word pertaining to familial relationships or domestic organization.

Word pertaining to sexual relationships; any word denoting the opposite sex.

Name of any female person.

Any article of female apparel.

24. COLD

Name of any location characterized by low temperature.

Any illness or symptom which may be caused by exposure to cold.

Any division of the annual cycle.

Any food that is always or often served cold.

Any means or measure of protection against cold.

Any state of the natural elements causing a sensation of cold.

Word denoting subjective characterization of or reaction to cold.

25. SLOW

Any means or manner of locomotion.

Any word involving the concept of rate of progress with reference either to time or to intensity of action.

Common or proper name of any person.

26. WISH

Word implying fulfillment of a wish either by achievement or through acquiescence.

Word implying non-fulfillment of a wish.

Word denoting any state of longing or anticipation.

Word denoting any state free from longing or anticipation.

Word denoting a prayer or request.

Word denoting a state of happiness.

27. RIVER

Any body of water.

Any part of a river.

Any plant or animal living in rivers.

Any term of physical geography.

Any vessel or contrivance for navigation.

28. WHITE

Any object or substance that is always or often white or very light in color.

Any color.

Any word clearly related to the word White used as a proper name.

29. BEAUTIFUL

Any word denoting aesthetic pleasure.

Name or any female person.

Any product of the fine arts or of decorative handicraft.

Any decorative plant or flower.

Any article of attire.

Natural scenery.

Any division of the diurnal cycle.

30. WINDOW

Any word pertaining to illumination.

Word pertaining to movements of air.

Any attachment to a window for the control of transmission of light or air.

Any building or apartment

31. ROUGH

Any object or substance which is characteristically rough to the touch.

Word denoting or implying irregularity of surface.

Any skin lesion which may impart to the skin the quality of roughness.

Any word implying carelessness, lack of consideration, or crudeness; any word used to designate action or conduct which may be characterized as careless, inconsiderate, or crude.

32. CITIZEN

Any word pertaining to political organization, or to factors either favorable or unfavorable to it.

Any term or proper name of political geography.

Common or proper name of any male person.

33. FOOT

Any means or manner of locomotion involving the use of the feet.

Any part or any tissue of the animal body.

Any article of foot-wear.

Any way constructed or used for walking.

Any unit of linear measure.

34. SPIDER

Word employed to designate subjective characterization of or reaction to an object of dislike.

Any insect.

Word pertaining to the characteristic habits of spiders, with reference either to location and construction of nest, or to manner of catching prey.

35. NEEDLE

Any material used in making clothes.

Any special sewing operation; any occupation in which sewing constitutes part of the work.

Any special kind of needles.

Any instrument which is used in connection with a needle in any operation, or of which a needle forms a part.

36. RED

Word which may be used to express subjective characterization of the red color.

Any object or substance which is always or often red in color.

Anything which is by convention or common usage connected with the red color.

Any organ, tissue, or lesion, exposed to view, which may have a red color imparted to it by the blood or by physiological pigment

Any color or coloring material.

Any word implying light through incandescence.

37. SLEEP

Word denoting somnolence or a state of lowered consciousness; anything which is a cause of somnolence or of lowered consciousness; anything which induces a desire to sleep.

Word denoting a state of active consciousness or a transition from lowered to more active consciousness.

Any division of the diurnal cycle.

Any word more or less commonly used to characterize sleep in any way.

Any article of bedding, bed-linen, or night-clothes.

Any article of furniture used for sitting or lying.

38. ANGER

Any affective state; any common demonstration of emotion.

Any common cause or provocation of anger.

Action or conduct caused by anger; word used to characterize such action or conduct.

39. CARPET

Any material of which carpets are made.

Any article of house furniture, hangings, or decorations.

Word denoting home, house, or any part of a house.

Word pertaining to the manufacture or care of carpets, or denoting a person engaged in the manufacture, sale, or care of carpets.

Any country especially noted for the manufacture of carpets or rugs.

Any color.

40. GIRL

Word denoting or implying age of a person.

Any of the well-known female sexual characteristics.

Occupation or profession more or less peculiarly feminine.

Word pertaining to familial relationships or domestic organization.

Word pertaining to sexual relationships; any word denoting the opposite sex.

Name of any female person.

Any part of a person's body.

Any article of female apparel.

41. HIGH

Any word denoting or implying skill, training, achievement, or position.

Any word denoting or implying valuation.

Any architectural structure.

Any object of which the vertical dimension characteristically exceeds any other.

Any act of progress from a lower to a higher level.

Name of any mountain or mountain range.

Anything characteristically situated at a high level.

Anything characteristically variable in height.

42. WORKING

Any occupation, profession, art, or labor.

Direct results or consequences of work.

Any place of employment.

Rest, recreation, inaction, or disinclination to work.

Word denoting energy, material, capital, equipment.

43. SOUR

Any substance or object which is always or often sour in taste.

Any word denoting a taste or flavor quality.

44. EARTH

Any substance which enters into the composition of soil.

Word pertaining to the utilization or cultivation of natural resources; any product of agriculture.

Any term of physical geography, geology, mineralogy, meteorology, or astronomy.

45. TROUBLE

Any affective state.

Any general cause of active emotional states.

Any common manifestation of emotion.

Word denoting or implying defeat.

Word denoting or implying caution or lack of it.

Any task.

46. SOLDIER

Word pertaining to military organization.

Word pertaining to any military operation.

Word pertaining to military discipline or to military decoration.

Any article of military or naval equipment or attire.

Common or proper name of any male person.

Name of any country.

Word pertaining to political organization.

47. CABBAGE

Any article of food; any meal.

Any article of table linen, china, silver; any cooking utensil.

Any process of cooking.

Word used to designate any person engaged in the cultivation of cabbages or in their preparation for consumption.

48. HARD

Any solid article of food.

Word denoting or implying impact.

Any task or labor.

Any substance which is hard or unyielding.

Any agency or process by which a substance is solidified or hardened.

Any article of furniture used for sitting or lying.

Any trait of disposition characterized by lack of readiness to yield or lack of consideration for others.

49. EAGLE

Any bird.

Any piece of currency.

Anything in connection with which the word eagle is used in a symbolic sense.

50. STOMACH

Any anatomical organ or region.

Any article of food; any meal.

Word pertaining to ingestion and assimilation of food.

Term denoting health or disease; any medicament.

51. STEM

Any object which has a stem.

Any part of a plant.

Any object which is long, slender, and more or less rigid.

52. LAMP

Any means or source of illumination.

Word denoting or implying illumination.

53. DREAM

Any product of imagination.

Any psychical phenomenon; any part of the psychical organ.

Word denoting or implying unreality or uselessness.

Word denoting or implying mystery or occultism.

Any division of the diurnal cycle.

Any article of bedding, bed-linen or night-clothes.

Any article of furniture used for sitting or lying.

Any narcotic substance.

54. YELLOW

Word which may be used to denote subjective characterization of the yellow color.

Any object or substance which is always or often yellow in color.

Any color or coloring material.

55. BREAD

Any article of food; any meal

Any article of table linen, china, or silver; any cooking utensil.

Any private or public eating place.

Word pertaining to ingestion and assimilation of food.

Any ceremony in connection with which bread is used.

56. JUSTICE

Any word implying crime or tendency to crime, legal trial, retribution or lack of it, or repentance.

Any officer of the law.

Word pertaining to judiciary organization.

Word denoting any kind of ethical relationship.

Any deity.

The name of any justice or judge.

Any function of a judicial authority.

Any word denoting or implying equality.

57. BOY

Word denoting or implying age of a person.

Word pertaining to familial relationships or domestic organization.

Word pertaining to sexual relationships; any word denoting the opposite sex.

Common or proper name of any male person.

Any part of a person's body.

Any article of male apparel.

Any common boys toy or game.

Word pertaining to educational organization.

58. LIGHT

Any source, apparatus, or means of illumination.

Any color or coloring material.

Word implying light through incandescence.

Any term of optics; any optical phenomenon.

Any object or substance which is characteristically light in weight.

59. HEALTH

Any emotion; any common manifestation of emotion.

Any disease or symptom.

Word pertaining to prevention or treatment of disease.

Word pertaining to any normal bodily function.

Word pertaining to the preservation of health.

Word denoting or implying a state of health.

Any athletic sport or form of exercise.

Any anatomical organ or region.

60. BIBLE

Name of any personage mentioned in the Bible.

Any religion or religious denomination.

Any name or attribute employed in reference to the Deity.

Any article or act of religious ritual.

Word denoting or implying belief, disbelief, or doubt.

Any term of theology.

61. MEMORY

Word pertaining to operations, faculties, endowment, training, or condition of the mind.

Word denoting any degree of accuracy.

Word denoting the cranium; any part of the psychical organ.

Word pertaining to the past.

Any word implying transiency.

Any subject of study involving the exercise of memory.

Any method or means for the reinforcement of memory.

Any of the senses.

Word denoting retention.

62. SHEEP

Any animal raised or hunted for clothing material, for food, or for its services as a beast of burden.

Any product manufactured from the skin or wool of sheep.

Any of the more or less distinctive characteristics of sheep.

Any food product derived from sheep.

63. BATH

Word denoting or implying an effect of bathing on the body.

Any body of water.

Any kind of bath; any part of bath, lavatory, or toilet equipment.

Any material of which a bathing equipment is largely made.

Word denoting a state of partial or complete undress.

Any beach or bathing resort.

Any aquatic feat of gymnastics.

64. COTTAGE

Word pertaining to landscape gardening.

Any place of cottage location.

Any part of a house; any color.

Any material used in the construction of a cottage.

Any laborer or mechanic having to do with the construction of a cottage.

Any part of the process of construction of a cottage.

Any commercial term pertaining to ownership, taxes, mortgages, sale, renting, or occupancy of a cottage.

Any article of furniture.

65. SWIFT

Any means or manner of locomotion.

Word denoting or implying motion or rate of motion.

Any animal or familiar object characterized by rapid locomotion.

Any word clearly related to the word Swift used as a proper name.

66. BLUE

Word which may be used to express subjective characterization of the blue color.

Any object or substance which is always or often blue in color.

Anything which is by convention or common usage connected with the blue color.

Any organ, tissue, or lesion, exposed to view, which may have a blue color imparted to it by the blood or by physiological pigment.

Any color or coloring material.

67. HUNGRY

Any animal.

Any article of food; any meal.

Word denoting taste or flavor.

Word denoting or implying privation or torture.

Any article of table linen, china, or silver.

Any private or public eating place.

Any organ of digestion; any function of nutrition.

Word designating any person engaged in the preparation or sale of foods.

68. PRIEST

Any religion or denomination.

Any article or act of religious ritual.

Any term of theology.

Word denoting or implying sanctity.

Word denoting or implying belief, disbelief, or doubt.

Word pertaining to church organization.

Proper name of any priest.

Any article of clerical attire.

Any profession more or less peculiarly masculine.

69. OCEAN

Any body of water.

Any plant or animal living in the ocean.

Any term of physical geography.

Any vessel or contrivance for navigation.

Word pertaining to navigation; any nautical term.

Common or proper name of any place bordering on the ocean.

Any aquatic feat of gymnastics.

70. HEAD

Any organization which has a person occupying the highest office.

Word denoting or implying the highest office of any organization.

Any intellectual faculty, quality, or operation.

Any part of the head.

Any pathological condition affecting the head.

71. STOVE

Any part of a stove.

Any kitchen utensil.

Any artificial heating apparatus; any fuel.

Any manner of cooking; any person engaged in cooking food.

Any article of household furniture.

72. LONG

Any word involving the concept of duration.

Word denoting shape, relative or absolute dimension, or distance.

Any object in which characteristically one dimension exceeds any other.

73. RELIGION

Any religion or denomination; the name of any race or nation.

Any term of theology.

Any branch of metaphysical philosophy.

74. WHISKEY

Any beverage; the name of any brand of whiskey.

Any material of which whiskey is made.

Word denoting taste or flavor.

Any occasion or ceremony commonly associated with the use of alcoholic beverages.

Word denoting a state of lowered consciousness.

Any physiological or pathological effect of alcohol; also any well known, indirect effect.

75. CHILD

Word denoting or implying age of a person.

Word pertaining to familial relationships or domestic organization.

Name of any person.

Any part of a person's body.

Any article of a child's apparel.

Any common child's toy or game.

Word pertaining to educational organization.

Any word descriptive of the natural physical or mental make-up of a child, or of the rate or degree of physical or mental development.

Word pertaining to any custom or ceremony connected with the birth or rearing of children.

Any term of obstetrics.

Any word clearly related to the word Child used as a proper name.

76. BITTER

Any substance having a bitter, sour, sweet, or salt taste, or a complex taste quality which may be characterized as strong.

Word denoting a taste or flavor quality.

Any organ of taste.

Any word in connection with which the word bitter may be used in the sense of poignant.

77. HAMMER

Any tool or weapon.

Any trade involving the use of a hammer.

78. THIRSTY

Any beverage.

Any animal.

Word denoting taste or taste quality.

Any part of the upper end of the digestive tract.

Any drinking place; any container of a beverage.

Any fruit; any dessert.

Any food ingredient commonly known to excite thirst.

79. CITY

Name of any division of political geography.

Any architectural structure.

Any part of a city.

Word pertaining to the political organization of a city.

80. SQUARE

The name of any city.

The name of any square in a city or town.

Any geometrical figure or part of one.

Any object that is always or often square in shape.

Any device used in the arts for measuring angles, arcs, or distances between points.

Any part of a carpenter's or draughtsman's square.

Any trade involving the use of the square.

81. BUTTER

Any article of food; any meal.

Any article of table linen, china, or silver; any cooking utensil.

Any process of cooking.

82. DOCTOR

The name of any physician.

Any medical speciality or practice.

Any medical or surgical procedure.

Any therapeutic remedy or method.

Any organization for the treatment of disease.

Name of any injury or disease.

83. LOUD

Any sound or sound quality.

Any part of the human vocal apparatus.

Any act of vocalization.

Any musical instrument.

Any apparatus for making sound signals.

Word denoting renown or commendation.

84. THIEF

Word denoting crime or wrongdoing.

Word denoting any circumstance propitious for theft.

Any common measure for the prevention or punishment of crime.

Any judicial, police, or penal authority.

Any readily portable article of value.

Word denoting renown.

85. LION

Word denoting or implying fear.

Any animal.

86. JOY

Word denoting a state, quality, faculty, or function of the mind.

Any common manifestation of emotion.

Any occasion, act, or means of recreation or of pleasurable excitement.

87. BED

Any article of bedding, bed linen, or night-clothes.

Any article of furniture.

Any living room, apartment, or building.

Any part of a room.

Any division of the diurnal cycle.

Any material of which beds are made.

Word pertaining to sleep or rest.

88. HEAVY

Word denoting or implying weight or lightness.

Any object or substance which characteristically possesses the quality of either great weight or marked lightness.

Any means of support or suspension.

Any fabric; any article of clothing or bedding.

Word denoting something to be carried or transferred.

Any painful emotion.

Word denoting a state of lowered consciousness.

89. TOBACCO

The name of any brand or variety of tobacco.

Term denoting any common quality of tobacco.

Any physiological or pathological effect of tobacco.

Any word which expresses subjective characterization of tobacco.

90. BABY

Word denoting or implying age or size of a person.

Word pertaining to familial relationships or domestic organization.

Name of any person.

Any part of a person's body.

Any article of a child's apparel.

Any common child's toy or game.

Word pertaining to any custom or ceremony connected with the birth or rearing of children.

Any term of obstetrics.

91. MOON

Any term of astronomy.

Word denoting or implying illumination or obscuration of light.

Any division of the diurnal cycle.

92. SCISSORS

Any operation or handicraft involving the use of scissors.

Any fabric; any article of clothing.

Any metal of which scissors are made.

Any tool for cutting, piercing, or sharpening.

Any operation of cutting, piercing, or sharpening.

93. QUIET

Any place where silence usually prevails or is enforced.

Word denoting or implying a state of lowered psychical activity or of psychical inhibition.

Word denoting heightened psychical activity.

Any word pertaining to the emotions.

94. GREEN

Word which may be used to express subjective characterization of the green color.

Any object or substance which is always or often green in color.

Anything which is by convention or common usage connected with the green color.

Any color or coloring material.

Any plant, collection of plants, or part of a plant.

Any word clearly related to the word Green used as a proper name.

95. SALT

Any article of food that is usually seasoned with salt; any seasoning; any relish.

Any article of table linen, china, or silver.

Any process of cooking.

Any term of chemistry.

96. STREET

Name of any street or city.

Any part of a street.

Any building.

Any manner or means of locomotion commonly employed in traveling through streets.

97. KING

Any name of the Deity.

The proper or common name of any ruler of a nation or of a smaller municipality.

Any nation or country.

Any title of nobility.

Any word clearly related to the word King used as a proper name.

98. CHEESE

Any article of food; any meal.

Word denoting any variety of cheese.

Word pertaining to taste, flavor, or odor.

Word pertaining to appetite.

Any article of table linen, china, or silver.

99. BLOSSOM

Any plant, collection of plants, or part of a plant.

Any term of botany.

Any division of the annual cycle.

100. AFRAID

Any affective state; any common demonstration of emotion.

Any common object of fear.

Word denoting or implying danger, courage; any means of defense or protection against danger.

www.ingramcontent.com/pod-product-compliance
Ingram Content Group UK Ltd.
Pitfield, Milton Keynes, MK11 3LW, UK
UKHW042146281224
453045UK00004B/184